Someone Said Parental Alienation

This book introduces readers to the concept of parental alienation (PA), a belief system that is used with increasing frequency in judicial child custody and parenting plan decisions.

PA is essentially a legal concept without validated psychological definition, assuming that children who resist contact with one divorced parent have in many cases been "brainwashed" or persuaded to do so by the machinations of the preferred parent. PA proponents assert that courts should transfer child custody to the avoided parent and prohibit contact between the child and the preferred parent. Unfortunately, the outcomes of such decisions, as reported by parents and their now-adult children, suggest that application of the PA concept is neither safe nor effective as a response to children's resistance to contact with a parent. Providing an overview of the concept of parental alienation, methods of identifying PA cases, and court-ordered treatments for children and parents, the book uses seven case-study chapters, each introduced with a brief recapitulation of the issues, and closed with a summary of events to offer suggestions about desirable family court changes.

This is the first book to tell a range of stories about the experiences of fathers, mothers, and children who have been separated and subjected to PA interventions after allegations have been made. It will be of interest to professionals practicing in psychology, psychiatry, social work, counselling, law, and the judiciary, and anyone involved in research and in legislative efforts relevant to family courts.

Jean Mercer has a doctorate in psychology from Brandeis University and is Professor Emerita of Psychology at Stockton University. Her work for decades has focused on potentially harmful psychological treatments for children and adolescents.

Someone Said Parental Alienation

About Divorcing Families Whose Children Avoided One Parent

Jean Mercer

Routledge
Taylor & Francis Group
LONDON AND NEW YORK

Designed cover image: Getty Images

First published 2025
by Routledge
4 Park Square, Milton Park, Abingdon, Oxon OX14 4RN

and by Routledge
605 Third Avenue, New York, NY 10158

Routledge is an imprint of the Taylor & Francis Group, an informa business

British Library Cataloguing-in-Publication Data
A catalogue record for this book is available from the British Library

ISBN: 978-1-032-59457-6 (hbk)
ISBN: 978-1-032-59458-3 (pbk)
ISBN: 978-1-003-45479-3 (ebk)

DOI: 10.4324/9781003454793

Typeset in Sabon
by Taylor & Francis Books

With much gratitude to all the interviewees whose openness made this book possible.

Contents

Foreword

David L. Corwin, MD, FAPSAC, DFAACAP, DFAPA
Professor and Director of Forensic Services, University of Utah Pediatrics Department

This is a very troubling book! It is also the first book to include personal accounts from young adults who attended intensive overnight parent reunification programs that are the focus of recent investigative journalism. "Parental Alienation" (PA) is a controversial topic that I have described as dangerous and oversimplified. As noted in this book, the usual foundational research on the PA concept has never been done. The base rates for behaviors included in checklists for identifying PA are unknown. PA's validity, reliability, safety for discriminating from other conditions including child maltreatment, poor parenting and other possible reasons why children may avoid contact with a parent are also unknown and unstudied. Despite its lack of scientific support and rejection by the major organizations overseeing mental and medical diagnoses, the American Psychiatric Association (DSM-5) and the World Health Organization's International Classification of Diseases (ICD-11), the PA concept and its potentially harmful recommended experimental treatments have spread around the world, as described in this book. PA and its proposed treatments are dangerous legal weapons that reflect poorly on the mental health professionals who promote them and the family courts who fall victim to PA misinformation. The primary beneficiaries of PA are the lawyers and mental health professionals who promote it. This book is a testament to the dangers of inadequately tested, unproven mental health concepts, and the unbridled hubris of those who promote them.

Recently, deaths, both suicides and child murders, associated with PA allegations in protracted child custody litigation appear to be increasing. These tragedies have given rise to new state laws described in this book. These new laws, named after murdered children, are modeled after Kayden's Law, part of the 2022 reauthorization of the Violence against Women's Act. Kayden was the 7 year old girl murdered by her father in Pennsylvania after a judge ordered unsupervised visitation with the father. In 2018, during a year-long custody dispute, Kayden's mother raised concerns about the father's violence. The father countered with a claim of PA, upon which the judge apparently placed more weight and ordered unsupervised visitation preceding Kayden's murder. Kayden's Law and its state progeny attempt to rein in the mental health professionals who mislead judges by claiming that PA is a proven and well accepted concept and who recommend inadequately researched treatments for PA. Among the more frequent outcomes of these mistakes are financial ruin, emotional pain and suffering, long-term separations of children from their preferred parent and, as described in this book, the creation of young people who no longer trust the legal system or therapists, and whose relationships with their less preferred parents are more seriously fractured. Civil lawsuits against PA-oriented therapists are beginning to appear. (However, there are also some parents, mostly fathers, who claim that their relationships with their previously "alienated" children benefited from the intensive multiday programs costing many thousand dollars. Two such examples are included in this book.)

As Dr. Mercer repeatedly notes, the 20+ cases whose accounts are included in this book are not a representative or random sample. It is unknown how representative they are. Family relationships are complex and multidetermined. When parents divorce, their relationships with each other and their children can become even more complex. There are so many contributing factors including the parents' and children's biological constitutions, child development, friends, extended family, new relationships including step-siblings and step-parents as well as the evolving cultural contexts, that constructing and implementing well designed and valid research on child–parent avoidance after divorce is a formidable task. Given these realities, it is unsurprising that limited research exists on this problem and no research adequately establishes the concept of PA and its recommended treatments. Nonetheless, the financial and legal incentives for making claims of PA have spawned a worldwide enterprise that presents PA as a proven and valid rather than as a legal weapon that works well for those with enough money to hire the lawyers and mental health professionals who promote it. PA aligns with power and money. It builds on the reality that there are some parents who, without good cause, seek to obstruct or sabotage their children's relationships with their other parent.

Observations like those included in this book are an essential step in the scientific process for building new knowledge. They help define the scope and complexity of a phenomenon but are only a beginning. They are also a potential alarm. In addition to these heart-wrenching personal accounts, Dr. Mercer describes the current scientific context and her thoughts for all parties involved in these cases. I thank her for her work in studying, listening, writing, and sharing these accounts from young adults and parents who have experienced PA claims firsthand. This book is an important step forward toward justice and improved care for these parents and children.

Preface

Sharon Jeu

The book you are about to read tells the stories of children, mothers, and fathers who were caught up in various ways in allegations of parental alienation—the idea that when children of divorce want to avoid one of their parents, the reason is likely to be that the other parent has "brainwashed" them. When such allegations are made, the consequences are potentially harmful for all concerned, and the narratives in this book give evidence of that potential.

The stories you are about to read were told in lengthy interviews by real people, but their identities have been disguised for fear of reprisals by litigation and otherwise. Details that might identify an interviewee have been omitted. But my own story is different—my name and all of the details of these past events have already been revealed in a major newspaper and elsewhere.

I would like you to read my story as an introduction to the anonymous stories in the book, to help you keep in mind that each of the anonymous stories, with its details removed, is in fact the story of a real person.

Here is my story:

"When I come in that door at night, I want the children there waiting for me." How I longed for that also. I remember running to meet my dad when he got home from work, thankful for his presence. But our children were afraid of their father. What child wants to greet a man who has repeatedly covered their mouth and nose, while they're gasping for air? What child wants to welcome a man who casually walks by them and smacks and pinches them? What child wants to cheerfully run towards a man who has picked them up by the neck, bruised them, bitten them, and intentionally endangered them with a car? The list could go on and on of things I'd rather not remember.

No matter how we tried to build connections, it grew worse. No matter the amount of attention and positive affirmations he received, he still created frightening chaos, seemingly so he would be the center of attention, and have ultimate control. He put the responsibility of his relationship with the children on me. It was up to me and the children to make good relationships with him, no matter how he acted. And now family court expected the same from us. The children were terrified, and their father kept them afraid. I asked him to please make it easy for the children. His reply, in an icy cold and threatening tone was, "If you don't come back to me and do exactly as I say, it will just get worse for them, do you hear me? It will just get worse for them." He repeated that statement three times in a row, like a machine gun volley.

I eventually asked for supervised visitation, which was granted. The psychologist supervising the visitation and working towards a better relationship between the children and their father kept hitting a brick wall. The children's father continued dangerous interactions, which kept the visitations largely supervised.

After years of minimal progress, the children's father asked for a change in psychologists. I was unaware of the court hearing, because my then-attorney neglected to notify me. The change was granted. With no psychological testing, and minimal interaction, the psychologist stated that the reason the children didn't want to go to visitation was due to parental alienation by me. He disregarded the children's cries for help, he disregarded the years of previous psychological reports, and the visitation history records. He told the children that if they wanted visitation to work, it would work. They came out of the session shaking and sobbing.

I was then court-ordered to take the children to the psychologist's office where they would be transferred into their father's custody and be sent to a reunification camp across the country. I was not to tell them that any of this was happening. I was ordered to take none of their personal belongings. I was ordered not to tell them that they would not be allowed to return home or to have any contact with me, for at least 90 days. I was just supposed to take them (ages 16, 13, 11, and 9) to a psychologist almost two hours away, on a school morning with no explanation. It didn't go down that way, but it did go down.

After the children were taken into their father's custody, I researched the reunification camp, and found that the psychologist running the program had his license revoked by the Board of Psychology for unprofessional conduct, gross negligence, violation of laws governing the practice of psychology and for dishonesty. I contacted the court in hopes that the children wouldn't be sent to that reunification program. The reunification camp responded that they weren't acting as a psychological program, but as an educational program. The court did not stop the order. The children were separated and sent to the reunification program by human transport agents. They were threatened that they and/or I would be jailed if they didn't comply with the program. They were not allowed to discuss the abuse, or any reason that they didn't want to be with their father. They had to pretend that everything was okay. They had to pretend that they were not being harmed. They had to live a lie, while being tortured. They still have great difficulty speaking of the experience, although it was nearly thirteen years ago.

I'm thankful that we were able to locate an ethical program, Child Justice, which helped save the children from this nightmare that was forced upon them by family court. During the hearing in which the children were returned to my custody, the judge stated that it was, "very, very troubling for me to hear, you know, how this was implemented, and I regret that. I just wish there was some way that we could turn back the clock and never have let those children experience something as traumatic as that." But there is no turning back the clock, there is no way for the children to have their childhood back. One of my sons noted, "I spent my whole childhood waiting for it to be over." The children couldn't wait until they were eighteen so they could be free from the torture. They didn't feel released until the youngest turned eighteen. At eighteen they each stopped all contact with their father. For them, the reunification program was the last nail in the coffin of an already dying relationship.

If the courts had understood, and focused on the root problem, maybe the children would have a relationship with their father today. If the courts had addressed the root problem, maybe their father wouldn't currently be going through a second divorce, triggered by domestic violence and a request for a protection order from abuse. However, it's not the court's responsibility to force a relationship. It is the court's responsibility to provide safety for children.

Family court has a very weighty and stressful responsibility in deciding the course of a child's life. Before I left the marriage, I sought help from the abuse shelter. The shelter noted the abuse, and offered us lodging; but they also stated that family courts tend to award visitation and custody to abusers. Their response to my questioning look was, "it seems that judges, lawyers, and others in the legal field go into those careers for power and money, or because they truly care about justice; and there are far too few of the latter." We've experienced both. I am incredibly thankful for the lawyers who worked to find truth and justice, rather than just brush us off, and dismiss us as a pathetic misfunctioning family that refused to get along. I've heard lawyers and judges speak very disparagingly about a parent who struggles to force their children into dealing with abuse.

I am encouraged by the recent laws that have been passed in some states, restricting reunification camps, and requiring domestic violence training for court personnel. But, I agreed to write this foreword because there are still children being abused and killed due to orders from family court. Many of these orders were made largely because someone spoke the words "parental alienation". Many of these orders were made because no one in power cared to make the effort to understand that one parent cannot force a child to have a positive relationship with another parent who is harming them.

I would like to spend time living now, rather than writing this emotional and mental rehash of the past. But, as I'm writing this preface, some parents are visiting the graves of their children who have been murdered, murdered although they pled with family court for safety. As I write this, some children are wondering why no one cares that they are being intentionally harmed. Some are trying to grasp why they have been ripped from safety and forced into an abusive situation by the very system that is set up to save them. Some children this moment are thinking of suicide as their only way out. Some children have lost all trust in our justice system.

I've heard it repeated many times by family lawyers and judges, "Family court is not for the faint of heart." And it's true, family court is not for the faint of heart, especially if you're a child who is court-ordered into visitation or custody with an abusive parent.

I'm extremely thankful to Professor Mercer for dedicating her time and effort on the issue of how courts handle allegations of parental alienation. And, to you lawyers and judges working in the stressful field of family court, thank you for caring to further your education on domestic violence. Thank you for caring whether a child lives or dies. Thank you for caring about the quality of a child's life.

1 An Introduction to Parental Alienation Concepts

Somebody said parental alienation. Why is this statement important enough to use as a book title? Most words that *someone says* have no magical effect—even "abracadabra" doesn't work in the real world. But when someone says "parental alienation", the results are often overwhelmingly powerful. Those words alone can start a process that separates children from a parent, labels one or both parents as child abusers, condemns children and parents to undergo experimental psychotherapies, and uses up family resources right down to the homes they live in. All these things can follow simply from the fact that someone has said "parental alienation". Saying "parental alienation" opens a gate that is difficult to close.

Defining the Terms

When people say "parental alienation", what are they talking about? This term (often abbreviated as just PA) refers to a situation that may arise during or following parental separation or divorce. In some divorce cases, *children align themselves strongly with one of the parents and avoid contact with the other parent; they may do this without having experienced serious abuse or even very deficient parenting from the avoided parent.* The children's avoidance is often referred to as the "resist/refuse dynamic" or by other terms such as "parent–child contact problem", but although the term parental alienation may properly be used to describe some of these cases referenced in these ways, it does not apply to all of them.

Parental alienation is a term that properly applies only to a rather narrow subset of child resistance or refusal of contact, and there are many non-parental alienation cases in which children avoid a parent for evident reasons of physical or emotional abuse, alcohol or drug problems, or seriously deficient parenting skills. These facts lead us to an

DOI: 10.4324/9781003454793-1

essential part of the definition of parental alienation: in addition to having the characteristics already described, parental alienation cases are cases in which *one parent—the preferred parent—is known to have persuaded or caused the children to dislike and avoid the other parent.* Children who avoid one parent under those circumstances are said to be *alienated* from that avoided parent.

Identifying parental alienation cases thus involves checking a number of boxes. There must be some sort of resistance to or avoidance of contact with a parent, there must be no obvious reason like neglect or abuse for this negative attitude on the children's part, and there must be some evidence that the preferred parent has manipulated or persuaded the children to take this view. The ways this evidence might be collected, when it exists, will be discussed in Chapters 2 and 3 of this book. Unfortunately, as will be discussed later, there is presently no well-established method that shows differences between children who have been alienated by a parent and those who avoid one of their parents for other reasons.

The "thing in itself"—parental alienation—is thus much discussed but ill-defined and only very roughly measurable. The topic of this book is not parental alienation in an exact sense, but what we may call *parental alienation cases.* Parental alienation cases are family situations where there is litigation because *somebody said parental alienation.* In these cases, it is alleged that parental alienation is present, but this may or may not be true. The allegation of parental alienation is the only criterion that must be met before a family's situation is classified as a parental alienation case.

Human beings do a lot of irrational or malicious things, especially under stressful emotional circumstances like divorce. Creating a parental alienation case by manipulating children's attitudes does not seem far out of the ordinary run of human peculiarities, and few would say that such behavior is impossible. However, no one has developed a reliable and valid method of identifying parental alienation, and as a result there is no trustworthy measure of the frequency of parental alienation cases. Although there are reliable records of the numbers of divorces involving children that occur in different countries in specific years, records are not kept about possible parental alienation cases, and cases involving children are considered confidential. Thus, we can only guess that the number of alleged or genuine parental alienation cases per country per year is probably greater than zero. How many of those cases actually involve parental alienation, as defined earlier, is impossible to know at this juncture.

Vocabulary Notes

Defining parental alienation is the first step in this discussion, but it would be a mistake to think that it's the last step. A range of other terms and definitions appear in any conversation about parental alienation. At the time of this writing, the term *parent child contact problem* (PCCP) is often used to describe a range of difficulties including situations where one parent has encouraged a child to avoid the other. Another common term is *resist or refuse dynamic* (abbreviated as RRD), a phrase that logically can describe all family situations where a child avoids one parent, but that is sometimes used to refer primarily to cases where a *preferred parent* has caused the child's avoidance (readers need to pay close attention in order to be sure they know how this term is being employed). Children who avoid a parent may also be said to be *estranged* from that parent, but estrangement is usually cited only in cases where the parent–child conflict is not thought to be caused by a preferred parent.

The set of tenets or concepts put forward by a small number of people thinking about parental alienation are sometimes referred to as *parental alienation theory*. However, there is no real theory of children's avoidance in existence, because a theory is a framework that brings together data, and remarkably few data on this topic are available. Rather than a theory, concepts associated with parental alienation amount to a belief system or ideology. *Alienationism* is a possible alternative term to describe the parental alienation belief system.

People who believe that child avoidance of a parent is often parental alienation (caused by the preferred parent) are sometimes referred to as *parental alienation proponents*—an ambiguous usage because it leaves unclear whether they think that parental alienation is a good thing, or that parental alienation concepts are suitable explanations of a child's avoidance. The term *parental alienation opponents* has been used for those who disagree about these explanations of avoidance, and this too is ambiguous, as anyone trying to prevent or cure parental alienation cases could be said to be an opponent of parental alienation. Less ambiguous terms are *alienationists* to describe proponents of alienationism, and *anti-alienationists* to describe critics of alienationist beliefs and assumptions. If this terminology sounds highly polarized, this is simply a reflection of the high degree of disagreement present.

Alienationists use the term *parental alienating behaviors* to describe the actions they believe preferred parents use to persuade children to avoid or reject the other parents. (Until these actions have been demonstrated to cause child avoidance, it might be preferable simply to call them parenting behaviors.) Anti-alienationists sometimes use the phrase *protective parent* to describe a child's preferred parent, whom alienationists consider to be an *alienator*.

Alienationists consider that specialized treatments called *reunification therapies* or *reunification programs* are needed to correct alienation and to cause children to feel positively about a parent they have been avoiding. Alienationists base their positions about treatment on the assumption that children whose alienation from one parent remains uncorrected will experience later adverse consequences, including social and emotional difficulties and related mental illness.

Alienationist authors frequently abbreviate terms they often use, saying "PA" for "parental alienation" and "PABs" for "parental alienating behaviors". This practice is tempting for its efficiency, but will be avoided in the present book because of its encouragement of reification—the tendency to think that the existence of a name, and especially of a shorthand version of a name, indicates that an entity exists, and exists in a particular, posited form.

Anti-alienationists, unsurprisingly, oppose many of the alienationist views, but do so in a skeptical rather than directly contradictory manner. Anti-alienationists do not propose that parental alienation cannot exist, but speculate that many parental alienation cases involve allegations used primarily to win litigation in divorce conflicts other than child custody. Anti-alienationists consider that little if any of the research published by alienationists meets scientific standards as put forward in psychology and medicine. Among other points, anti-alienationists have been severely critical of methods claimed to identify parental alienation and of studies of reunification therapies; anti-alienationists have noted that some alienationist claims, like the argument that it is harmful to leave parental alienation untreated, are without any foundation.

What Are the Basic Issues?

If there is an unknown, probably quite small, frequency of parental alienation cases, what is the point of discussing them at book length? And how can *someone saying parental alienation* have the devastating effects suggested at the beginning of this chapter?

There are three basic issues at work with respect to parental alienation. One is that parental alienation concepts are at the center of an ideology or belief system whose proponents have written and spoken at length in support of their ideas. *Alienationists* (as we may call them) are committed to the idea that parental alienation cases are common and are readily identified by examination of children's behavior and the behavior of the preferred parent (see Bernet, 2020; note that among parental alienation proponents, the preferred parent is often called the "alienating parent" and their behaviors are called "alienating behaviors", while the avoided parent is referred to as the "targeted parent").

A second idea to which alienationists are committed is that children are harmed by parental behavior that results in avoidance of the other parent, so that any parental alienation case should be seen as one in which children are being harmed. Some parental alienation proponents (Harman, Kruk, & Hines, 2018) have argued that child avoidance of one parent is evidence of experiences that are as harmful as any of the known adverse childhood experience (ACEs; Felitti et al., 1998). These arguments have not been supported by empirical studies, but alienationists have nevertheless concluded that parental alienation cases should not be regarded as situations where child custody or parenting plans need to be decided, but should be seen as *child protection* cases, where children should be removed from contact with parents who are thought to have caused the child's resistance to contact with the other parent.

The idea just described, that children in parental alienation cases are being harmed and should be separated from a parent who shows "alienating behaviors", leads to a third belief to which alienationists are committed. This is the idea that parental alienation arguments can and should play powerful roles in the family court. Parental alienation proponents hold that children in many child custody cases must be removed from the care of the preferred parent and placed in the care of the avoided parent. Preferred parents are to have no contact of any kind with their children for 90 days or more. Children may be sent to *reunification therapies* of more or less intensive forms, and both children and preferred parents must undergo continuing psychotherapy as approved by parental alienation proponents. (These treatments may be devastatingly expensive.)

A special issue in the family court is the position of parental alienation proponents about any allegation of child abuse by the avoided parent; it is not infrequently argued that such allegations are simply evidence that the preferred parent is continuing efforts to alienate the child from the other parent. In many cases, there are both allegations of abuse and *allegations of parental alienation*. Alienationists hold that allegations of alienation should be given special weight as evidence against allegations of abuse that might otherwise be taken seriously.

The concern about allegations of parental alienation is not so much about what parental alienation is or might be, but about the use of the concept for leverage in family courts. The idea of parental alienation can be, and is, used to establish draconian custody and parenting plans and to counter disclosures of abuse. It is a bargaining chip that can reduce child support or other claims on one parent. The demands it makes on the preferred parent can force that parent to give up all claim to contact with their child. The very vagueness of definition and identification of parental alienation cases makes it possible to use the parental alienation concept in cases where it is far from clear that alienation exists at all. When *someone says parental alienation*, courts have been known to give priority to that claim despite all evidence of other factors causing a child to reject one parent.

Some Well-Documented Cases Where Parental Alienation Was Alleged

So far, this description of parental alienation terms seems pretty cool and unemotional. But real cases are not like that at all—especially if they result in court orders for separation of children and their preferred parents. This book will recount the narratives of many real cases, and those cases will not include any identifying information, but we can start with one story that has already been told by a young adult who has written and spoken about her own experiences with a parental alienation-based family court decision. Arianna Riley (her real name) has presented her story at conferences and has written about it in an edited book (Barnett, Riley, & "Katherine", 2022). At the present writing in her mid-twenties, Arianna was in her teens when her parental alienation story began.

The Child's Experience

Arianna remembers a reasonably happy childhood with her parents and her younger sister. The parents separated in 2009 and, as Arianna recalls, difficulties arose very soon. Arianna's memories of that period include some physical abuse by her mother, and emotional abuse like being called a "slut". The two girls decided they would live with their father but continued to have regular contact with their mother for several years.

The mother then began a romantic relationship with a man the girls did not like, and when he moved into the house Arianna soon went to live with her father. Many angry scenes between the girls, the mother, and the boyfriend were to follow. Matters reached a crisis when Arianna's father filed a motion to stop paying child support, as the girls were living with him. This led to further angry reactions and a new custody hearing in which Arianna argued that she and her sister should not have to be with their mother because they did not feel safe there. Unfortunately, *someone said parental alienation*, and Arianna's father was alleged to have caused the girls to resist contact with their mother.

At the custody hearing, the judge's reaction was not at all what Arianna wanted or expected.

JUDGE: I am ordering you guys to be sent to Family Bridges reunification therapy [one of the intensive programs claiming to correct parental alienation].
ARIANNA: I'm not going, I refuse to go.
JUDGE: If you don't go, then they will send you to jail for 30 days.

Youth transport service workers, hired to take the girls to reunification therapy in another state, entered and told the girls that their father would go to jail if they did not cooperate. The transport workers put the girls in a van and drove to the airport, where Arianna begged people for help and finally announced that she had a bomb in her shoe, a strategy that eventually led to rental of a car by the transport workers and a 23-hour road trip to a hotel that was the therapy site. They were met there by their mother and her boyfriend.

The events of the therapy will be described later in this chapter and in other chapters. They included watching a series of videos and receiving instruction on how long eye contact should be maintained. The therapists, like the earlier transport workers, made frequent threats about what would happen if the girls did not cooperate; these threats were often about being sent to wilderness programs or residential treatment.

At age 17, after returning from the treatment program and experiencing further drama, Arianna sought and received emancipation. She went to live with her father, while the younger sister continued to live with the mother and moved to another state.

As we will see in later chapters, Arianna's experiences closely resemble those of other young people who have reported what happened when *somebody said parental alienation*. Although Arianna's efforts at the airport were unusually creative, her experiences can be considered as a model of parental alienation proceedings.

A Case of Parental Alienation Allegations: A Tragic End for the Mother

Catherine Youssef Kassenoff, a New York attorney and a mother alleged to have alienated her children from their father, committed assisted suicide in Switzerland following a recurrence of cancer and judgments depriving her of contact with her daughters. Her case became a subject of intense argument on the Internet and in print publications, with many contradictory statements about her health and behavior. As it happens, the present author spent some time in discussion with Ms. Kassenoff and her attorney about six months before she died, so some of the material here may be new to readers. Readers should note, however, that following Ms. Kassenoff's death, there have been so many different views of her story that it is not easy to know exactly what happened—except that *someone said parental alienation.*

The Kassenoff story began in 2019 with a daughter's disclosure of physical abuse by her father. Ms. Kassenoff supported the girl's disclosure, and this support was interpreted by the court as evidence of alienation by the mother. Not only were the girls placed in their father's care, but Ms. Kassenoff's contacts with them were to be only under supervision, an arrangement that had to be paid for by the mother, and according to her statement, cost $2500 a week at one point. Ms. Kassenoff was at various times evicted from her home, arrested on charges that were later dropped, and dismissed from her job with the New York governor's office. A report that she was "manipulating" her daughters (that is, alienating them from their father) was included in the case in spite of reasons to reject it.

Ms. Kassenoff continued to fight and did manage to get more contact, and unsupervised contact, with the girls. In late 2022 she was planning a lawsuit against a mental health professional who had evaluated the children as parental alienation cases. Sadly, however, within a few months she experienced a third occurrence of breast cancer, which she could hardly hope to survive, and this physical threat broke her resolve to go on fighting. In addition to her severe illness, Ms. Kassenoff heard in May 2023 that a judge had suspended all contact with the children. Ms. Kassenoff died from assisted suicide in late May of that year.

It will be some years before the Kassenoff daughters can tell their own stories, and their father has not made his narrative public.

Historical Background and Current Parental Alienation Concerns

The concept of parental alienation has a complex history, and for the purposes of this book it is necessary to simplify it and concentrate on major events. More detailed accounts, covering events in North America and in the United Kingdom and other parts of the world, are available (Doughty & Drew, 2022; Doughty & Rathus, 2022).

The idea of parental alienation was initially put forward by Richard Gardner, a psychiatrist who had worked with various childhood problems, in 1985. (Oddly, the alienationist author Bernet [2020] attributes the idea of parental alienation in part to Wilhelm Reich, a psychiatrist who in the 1950s died in prison after being convicted of fraud in the sale of medical devices.) Gardner stated that in a number of cases he had worked on, children of divorced couples who rejected one of their parents had been encouraged to do so by one of their parents; the "alienating" parent was usually the mother, who "targeted" the father out of spite, jealousy, and frustration, according to Gardner. Allegations of sexual or other abuse were seen as false and indicative of the mother's malicious manipulations. Gardner published a series of books on this topic and started his own publishing house, Creative Therapeutics. He died in 2003 without having ever produced systematic research to support his claims; nevertheless, his work is often referenced by alienationists, especially his lists of child and adult behaviors in what he considered to be parental alienation cases. Gardner's publications were the foundations of later and current efforts to identify parental alienation cases and to provide psychosocial treatment that could resolve such cases by creating a positive relationship between the child and the previously avoided parent.

Identifying Parental Alienation

A major thrust of Gardner's writing, and of later alienationist publications, was the possibility of identifying parental alienation on the basis of child and parent behavior. A protocol to identify parental alienation cases should discriminate between those cases and other cases in which children rejected a parent for different reasons. Gardner proposed 8 symptoms of parental alienation, such as statements that appeared borrowed from adults and a rejection of all members of a rejected parent's family. Amy Baker (2005) later proposed that 17 alienating behaviors, for example communicating to a child that the other parent is unsafe or unavailable, could be used to identify parental alienation cases; she claimed that there was empirical evidence for this supposition, although her data came only from the memories of a small sample of adults who recalled their mothers having done these things. Bernet (2020) described what he called the Five Factor Model to be used in identifying parental alienation; the five factors to be examined were 1) that a child rejects a parent without justification; 2) that the relationship between the child and the rejected parent used to be good; 3) that there is no substantiated evidence of abuse or severe parenting deficits; 4) that many of the 8 child behavior symptoms are present; and 5) that many of the 17 parental alienating behaviors described by Baker are present. (These factors will be discussed in detail in later chapters.)

A strong concern driving these efforts to define and identify parental alienation was the wish to have parental alienation, under some name, included in the *Diagnostic and Statistical Manual of Mental Health Disorders* (DSM) of the American Psychiatric Association, and in the *International Classification of Diseases* (ICD) of the World Health Organization. These inclusions would make parental alienation a diagnostic category, with the advantages that it could be argued in court to be a known mental health issue and that health insurance companies in the United States could be pressured to cover reunification therapies for parental alienation cases. Although attempts at inclusion of parental alienation in these publications were made in 2012 and again in 2022, as of this writing, parental alienation has not been made a diagnostic category. Although only the DSM committees know for sure, it seems likely that a lack of empirical research has handicapped the efforts of alienationists to include parental alienation in these publications. Publicly available discussion about addition of parental alienation to ICD suggested that the same issue was essential to the ICD decision.

Are children identified in family court as parental alienation cases actually identified through use of the Five Factor Model? This seems unlikely to be a universal method, in light of reports from parents and children about whom parental alienation has been alleged. Relevant anecdotes include cases in which children did not reject a parent, but asked for changes in parenting plans—for example, to spend every weekend with father and the school week with mother, rather than alternating weeks and having to shift school possessions from one house to the other frequently. Evidence that a good parent–child relationship once existed, and now has worsened severely, is difficult to establish objectively; a photographic record of people laughing at a birthday party is by no means conclusive, as few families photograph children crying or parents in a rage. With respect to abuse or neglect, a lack of substantiation by child protective services is not evidence that there has been no mistreatment, but simply shows that there was insufficient evidence to prove either abuse or neglect. As for the lists of child and adult behaviors, these are not meaningful except in context and in comparison to other behaviors; most of the listed behaviors occur occasionally in functional families, and their frequency is unknown, so it is impossible to know whether a child or a preferred parent show items from a list of parental alienating behaviors more often than most children and parents do. All these points suggest that the Five Factor Model of identifying parental alienation is probably not much in use.

Is parental alienation "in the child" or "in the relationship"? This question applies to many mental health issues that involve relationship problems. In studies of attachment disturbances, for instance, it has been said that "the client is the relationship", rather than the individual being the client. There has been little discussion of this issue with respect to parental alienation. On the one hand, alienationists argue that parental alienation is referred to in DSM under the rubric of parent-child relationship problems, suggesting that "the relationship is the client". On the other hand, some parental alienation proponents (Bernet, Gregory, Rohner, & Reay, 2020) have asserted that testing the child reveals whether parental alienation is present, suggesting that the child is the "client". This uncertainty as to where the problem (if any) lies has led to the use of the term *parental alienation case* in this book, to describe family situations in which parental alienation is alleged. That *somebody says parental alienation* is what makes a parental alienation case; no diagnosis is implied or needed.

Treatment

In anticipation of the efforts to include parental alienation in DSM and ICD, Gardner proposed that children in parental alienation cases were made mentally ill and needed treatment to save them from negative outcomes caused by their experiences with an alienating parent. Taking the same approach, Randy Rand, a California psychologist, suggested that children in parental alienation cases were much like children whom he had treated for difficulties after they had been abducted by a parent and then abruptly returned to the other parent. From about 2000 to the present, reunification therapies for children in parental alienation cases proliferated.

Confusingly, reunification therapies may come in a variety of forms (as will be discussed in Chapter 3). The common thread is that these are psychosocial treatments ordered by family courts with the intention of causing a child who has rejected a parent to accept and show affection for that parent. It is probably most common for a child to be sent to reunification therapy that is in the form of office treatment by a mental health professional. (However, as there are no statistics kept on this subject, it is not known how many children experience this, what form of treatments are used, or what the outcomes may be.) Less commonly, but much more dramatically, some children are court-ordered to intensive reunification therapies, often referred to as "camps" although most of them are not camps in any usual sense.

The intensive reunification therapies include the following: Family Bridges, Family Reflections Reunification Program, High Road to Family Reunification, Overcoming Barriers, Transitioning Families, and Turning Points For Families. There are other, less commonly-discussed programs, but Family Bridges and Turning Points are probably the most frequently ordered by family courts. Proponents of Family Bridges and Turning Points have provided descriptions of their methods (Warshak, 2010; Gottlieb, n.d.), but in both cases these descriptions are minimal and only people directly involved in the programs know all the details.

Overcoming Barriers and Family Reflections may be the only programs that involve a "camp" setting. As well as can be understood by outsiders, the other programs are not "camp"-like and resemble each other closely. They begin with a court order for attendance and an order for no contact between the child and the preferred parent, usually for 90 days but renewable. Children are to be transported to the treatment venue (often a hotel or apartment) without warning, and they may be taken there by youth transport service workers, a circumstance that will be discussed in a later chapter of this book. The rejected parent also goes to the treatment venue, as do several program therapists. Children's phones, IDs, and money are taken away. Children are threatened that if they do not comply, they will be placed in foster care or in residential or wilderness therapy, and their preferred parent may go to prison.

Children and parents watch videos that emphasize how easy it is to be persuaded to an attitude that is not really one's own. They participate in "family meetings" in which family members are called upon to compliment each other and prohibited from discussing any past events like allegations of child abuse or domestic violence. They play games, go out shopping and to dinner. In addition to these activities, Turning Points also requires that preferred parents send along items from the child's earlier life, like photos or videos, that can be used to demonstrate how the child's relationship with the rejected parent used to be happy and good. Children are told that if they cooperate, they may have to spend fewer days at the treatment venue, but the number of days there is usually four. Following the treatment days, the rejected parent and the child are to go on a vacation together, then to return to the parent's house for at least the 90 days of the initial order of no contact with the preferred parent.

While the child is at the treatment venue, on the vacation, or at the rejected parent's house, the preferred parent is given tasks to do, enforced by the court's order and subject to findings of contempt that could result in fines or even imprisonment for noncompliance. The preferred parent is to go to psychotherapy with a therapist who is approved by the reunification therapy program, to refrain from even accidental contact with the children, and, in most programs, to write a letter to the children. That letter is a point of difficulty for many of the preferred parents who are assigned to write one. The letter to the children is to apologize to the children, to acknowledge that the preferred parent made specific efforts to cause the children to avoid the other parent, and to assure the children that the family's difficulties are in no way their fault. This is a hard task for preferred parents who do not believe that they caused the parental alienation situation, and who are distressed at the idea of lying to their children. Possibly as a result of these issues for the preferred parents, parental alienation therapists and reunification therapy program staff not infrequently appear to have rejected letters and demanded that they be rewritten in more confessional, apologetic forms—sometimes 8 or 9 times. If parents argue with their therapists or resist writing what they consider to be an untruthful letter, they may be told that they will have no contact with the children until they cooperate, no matter how long it takes. Such parents may also be cautioned that their resistance to the treatment program places them in contempt of court, with all the associated possible consequences.

Are Reunification Therapies Psychotherapies, or Something Else?

Practitioners of reunification therapies aimed at treatment of parental alienation cases have maintained that their methods are not psychotherapy, but instead should be regarded as *psychoeducation*. Psychotherapies are treatments intended to help with mental health problems, both mild and serious, using non-physical methods such as discussion and practice of actions a client finds difficult. For example, mood problems or undue anxiety might be treated with psychotherapy. Psychoeducation, in contrast, involves instruction of a client or client's family on information about mental health. For example, clients with bipolar disorder might be given information about the predictability of their mood changes and about the kinds of treatment available to them; family members could receive the same instruction to help them navigate the difficulties created for others by one person's disorder.

Reunification therapies appear to be intended to correct negative attitudes and emotions a child has with respect to one parent. Alienationists argue that this is necessary because, they believe, untreated children will grow up to suffer mental health and social problems as a result of their compromised relationship with one parent. Reunification therapies are intended to prevent mental health problems and thus would appear to be categorizable as psychotherapies.

It is unclear whether any of the methods used in reunification therapies are also common among conventional psychotherapies in use today. Some aspects of the treatments do, however, resemble *unconventional* therapies both past and present; for example, the use of threats to force compliance, reported as part of reunification therapies, was also part of methods like Synanon, took place in some wilderness therapies, and is thought to remain an aspect of some "therapeutic schools".

The claim that reunification therapies are psychoeducation is accompanied by the idea that reunification therapy methods are well-tested, up-to-date *instructional* methods (Warshak, 2010). No doubt this is true, as repetition and practice are well-established methods of teaching. But some reunification programs also claim that they improve children's critical thinking, that better critical thinking enables children to resist undue persuasion, and that children with good critical thinking skills will conclude that the hitherto-rejected parent should be embraced. This interesting argument about the psychoeducational thrust of reunification therapies is unfortunately weakened by the fact that no test of critical thinking skills has ever formed part of the assessment of any reunification program. It is probable that children in reunification programs do remember the material in the videos they are shown (those interviewed for this book remembered what they had watched), but it has not been demonstrated that they generalize from that material to their own family situations as would be the case for effective psychoeducation.

It is reasonable to conclude that if reunification programs can be thought of as psychoeducational at all, they can certainly not be said to be effective psychoeducation. It would be more accurate to think of them as attempts at psychotherapies, although once again they have not been shown to be effective in that way.

What are the advantages to alienationists and reunification therapy practitioners of claiming to use psychoeducational rather than psychotherapeutic techniques? In the United States and many other countries, psychotherapists are required to be licensed, registered, or in some way regulated. Educators working outside schools do not have those requirements, so the mathematics tutor who works with a high school student and the ceramics teacher at the local arts center may or may not have any regulation of their qualifications or practices. Reunification programs may thus employ practitioners who are unlicensed, as no license is needed to practice psychoeducation. (Similarly, non-"camp" reunification programs held in hotel or apartment venues do not need the government approval or licensure that would be needed for a permanent facility.)

Context and Polarization

The development of parental alienation principles and practices occurred in a context of differences of opinion of an ideological intensity, with many strong objections to the parental alienation concept from the beginning. As the years have gone by, these differences have hardened and have resulted in polarized groups supporting one of two positions: 1) the alienationist position that parental alienation is readily identifiable and treatable, and failure to identify and treat it is harmful to children, or 2) the anti-alienationist position that parental alienation is vaguely described and its identification is often inaccurate, that the treatments offered are ineffective and may even be harmful to children, and that allegations of parental alienation serve primarily as weapons for one of the parents. (A small number of people hold a third position, that actual parental alienation does not exist at all, but this view is not common.)

Religious Issues

Although fathers are sometimes the target of parental alienation allegations (and some of their cases will be discussed later in this book), mothers are generally considered to be the group most often accused of persuading children to reject the other parent. Alienationism thus can be seen to include a patriarchal component, which argues that the father's position in the family hierarchy is paramount and both mother and children are obliged to honor the father. This idea of the supremacy of the father is a theme in the major world religions as well as elsewhere—although it is of course not the only theme in those belief systems. Some Evangelical Christians have expanded on the patriarchal theme by adding the element of permissible force by the father to guide women and children, with the general idea that some family members (especially children) must be forced to comply, for their own good.

As of this writing, there have been no studies of religious beliefs and practices as they may be related to parental alienation. However, as will be noted later in this chapter, one alienationist organization, Family Access–Fighting for Children's Rights, incorporates Bible study into its activities, suggesting the possibility that a patriarchal system is seen as a fruitful approach to parental alienation cases by this group.

Gender Differences

As polarized groups struggle to support their views, their focus is often on gender issues. Gardner, as mentioned earlier, made a point of blaming mothers for their roles in parental alienation cases and asserted that women's jealousy and vindictiveness caused them to "steal" their children's affection and attention from the fathers. Whether parental alienation cases are more commonly associated with the faults of mothers or of fathers has been a topic of ongoing research. However, it must be recognized that such work is highly challenging because of the difficulty of acquiring data.

Divorce, parenting plans, and other family court issues are highly confidential, and decisions on these topics are rarely published. If a case goes to an appeals court, it is more likely that the case material will be available to researchers, but the expense and other challenges of appeals mean that most parental conflicts do not reach the appeals level.

The absence of solid information about parental alienation cases does not give pause to polarized groups. If anything, it makes the conflict and mutual contradiction more intense, as there is little reliable information to moderate the disagreement or to make discussion nuanced. Instead, related beliefs and cultural movements strongly influence conclusions that would ideally be based on solid facts.

In the case of parental alienation, a major cultural movement that has influenced alienationist thinking has been the movement for "fathers' rights" (or, as it is sometimes said, "fathers' supremacy"). Beginning in the 1970s and 1980s (somewhat parallel to the beginnings of parental alienation concepts), this movement focuses on family law. Its concerns include the views that fathers are inequitably deprived of contact with their children but at the same time required to pay child support, and that fathers are falsely accused of abusive treatment of children and of domestic violence. Warren Farrell, a political scientist and author who is a fathers' rights advocate, has argued that greater attention to fathers' rights is supportive of the rights of children, who benefit from more involvement with their fathers. (Farrell has argued in court that a father who has remarried should have custody priority over a mother who has not remarried, as the children will benefit from being with "both parents".) Negative assessments of women have unfortunately been a part of the fathers' rights ideology.

The influence of the fathers' rights groups is seen in the intense discussion about men's and women's roles in parental alienation cases. From Gardner's day forward, discussion of parental alienation has included the idea that jealous and spiteful mothers cause alienation and make their children reject the fathers. More recently, it has included the idea that women in child custody suits are mistreated by misogynistic courts and denied custody when they should have it. The discussion has also involved the ideas that abusive fathers allege parental alienation in a tit-for-tat exchange allowing both sides to maintain or to drop their allegations, and that allegations of parental alienation can be used to moderate demands for child support.

As noted earlier, it is challenging to establish empirical data that support either position—that women are victims of these situations, or that men are victimized. When researchers investigate gender differences associated with parental alienation, methodological differences that appear small may cause larger differences in conclusions. Meier (2020) found that women were more likely to lose custody if they argued that their children's fathers had been abusive. Harman, an alienationist author, did not find this (Harman & Lorandos, 2021). Neither study has been replicated as of this writing and the reasons for their mutual contradiction are not clear—though it is far from unusual that similar empirical studies have somewhat different outcomes as a result either of chance or of differences in methodology. The whole issue of examining gender differences is more complex than it appears (Loh & Ren, 2023) and is far beyond what we can deal with in the present book. Unfortunately, it appears that the strong feelings about fathers' and mothers' roles in parental alienation and in family courts are just that—feelings—and as of this writing are not thoroughly substantiated by research. The narratives presented in this book include the stories of fathers who were alleged to have alienated children from the mothers, as well as the more common cases where the roles are reversed.

Adverse Childhood Experiences

Beginning with research in the 1990s, there has been much emphasis on the deleterious impacts on development of *adverse childhood experiences* (ACEs; Felitti et al., 1998). The original ACEs research looked at adults who as children had experienced a range of difficulties, including parental divorce and abuse or neglect. The investigators observed the adults for undesirable outcomes of mental and physical health. They found that larger numbers of ACEs in childhood correlated with larger numbers of mental and physical problems in adulthood. However, no specific ACE was a predictor of any specific adult problem. The ACE literature created both scientific and popular interest in examining adverse events in childhood. On the scientific side, there has been increasing interest in ways that adverse events interact with each other to cause adult problems; on the popular side, there are Internet "quizzes" that encourage adults to recall adverse childhood events.

The original ACEs studies did not include parental alienation, although the alienationists' concepts and terminology definitely existed at that time. However, in 2018 the parental alienation proponent Jennifer Harman published an article (Harman, Kruk, & Hines, 2018) equating parental alienation with ACEs and proposing, by analogy with ACEs, that parental alienation experiences could be expected to be followed by both physical and mental health problems in adulthood. Harman and her co-authors used this analogy to argue that when parental alienation cases are identified to the satisfaction of a family court, it is essential to separate the children from the preferred parent, who is presumed to have caused the rejection of the other parent. They asserted that parental alienation cases should be considered not as child *custody* cases, but as matters of child *protection*. It should be noted that this conclusion was reached entirely on the basis of analogy and not from any new empirical information. If the conclusion put forward by Harman and her colleagues were to be shown to be correct (which has not happened as of this writing), this would be the first time that a specific adverse childhood experience was found to have negative adult outcomes in and of itself.

The logical weaknesses of the Harman claim about ACEs have not prevented the use of this argument by alienationists in family court. This is perhaps unsurprising considering the oversimplification of psychological concepts that has been characteristic of legal thought, and the general tendency outside the field of child development to emphasize the impact of the social environment over any other factors guiding personality and emotional maturation.

Unconventional "Alternative" Therapies

Since the 1990s, both medicine and psychology have emphasized evidence-based methods—forms of treatment that have been shown to be safe and effective by rigorous testing. Unfortunately, these emphases have not prevented the use of untested treatments or treatments with weak supportive evidence. In medicine, these untested treatments are often called *complementary and alternative* medicine. Complementary methods are those that are used together with evidence-based treatments, while alternative methods (as the name suggests) are used instead of evidence-based treatments. In psychological treatment, it is rare to find the complementary use of untested treatments together with evidence-based treatments, but common to find untested treatments used instead of evidence-based therapies. It has been proposed that untested or weakly supported psychological treatments be called *alternative psychotherapies* (Mercer, 2014). This term would apply only to treatments not currently being subjected to investigation, because treatments in the process of being tested for safety and effectiveness are properly called *experimental treatments* (Kaminski & Claussen, 2017).

Alternative psychotherapies that have persisted over several decades include group treatments like Synanon, conversion therapy aimed at changes in sexual orientation and behavior, and "attachment therapies" that claim to make children obedient and grateful to their parents. Harms have been documented as possible outcomes of some of these alternative psychotherapies, with some of the "attachment therapies" particularly known as having caused child deaths. Efforts to regulate alternative psychotherapies for children have generally been unsuccessful; as adults, the clients often prefer to forget what they have been through or find that no one is interested in the problem. Uniquely, conversion therapy for children has been outlawed in a number of states, as a result of pressure from gay adults.

As will be discussed in a later chapter of this book, reunification programs have received weak support from less-than-rigorous testing. Nevertheless, they continue to be recommended by practitioners and ordered by family courts. Alienationists repeatedly claim a "scientific" background for their reunification therapy methods although this clearly does not exist. Reunification therapies share with many other alternative psychotherapies the belief that threats and force can create positive emotional change. The continued existence of other alternative psychotherapies may help maintain a positive view of reunification therapies, as the claims made about these alternative methods muddy the waters of any serious discussion of safety and effectiveness.

Organizations Associated with Positive or Negative Views of Parental Alienation

The groups with the most obvious involvements in parental alienation cases are family courts, lawyers, and mental health researchers and clinicians. These are the entities that make observable decisions about children and parents when *somebody says parental alienation*. But courts and professionals are not the only actors in parental alienation discussion and decision-making. Parents' organizations and hybrid parent–professional groups have considerable ability to publicize parental alienation cases and to influence public opinion in one direction or the other. (And, of course, judges, lawyers, and mental health professionals are themselves subject to the influence of public opinion.)

In the United States, and to a considerable extent internationally, two groups have exerted strong pressure toward an alienationist conceptual stance. One of these, the Parental Alienation Study Group (PASG; https://pasg.info) is an international organization that has hundreds of members, of whom a considerable number are parents who consider themselves to have been alienated from their children by the machinations of a former spouse (descriptions of the interests of PASG members are given on the PASG website). PASG holds an annual conference with presentations on clinical and legal issues associated with parental alienation. Its Facebook page has about 50,000 followers.

Expert witnesses testifying on whether parental alienation has caused a child to reject a parent may present PASG membership as a professional qualification, although PASG is according to its website an open membership organization that "does not certify that its members have any particular expertise". PASG has partnered with The Law Center (https://thelawcenter.net) to post videos stating the alienationist position. PASG also uses organizations like ResearchGate (www.researchgate.net) and Academia (www.academia.edu) to post both published and unpublished materials, which almost invariably support the alienationist view.

A second organization, also international in scope but based in the United States, is Family Access–Fighting For Children's Rights (https://www.familyaccessfightingforchildrensrights.org). This group is a non-profit organization that runs on donations and focuses on the handling of parental alienation cases, in which they include cases where grandparents do not have the desired contact with grandchildren (a position that is difficult to fit into most alienationist thinking). Family Access has created a YouTube channel, Families Divided TV (https://www.youtube.com/channel/uc0qet_h81bicf7B55uhxhkq). Family Access provides monthly webinars that allow attendees to post questions some days in advance. There is also an annual conference attended by concerned family members and alienationist professionals. Family Access is a Christian-oriented organization that includes Bible study among its activities.

Several organizations in the United States have opposed the argument that alienationism explains why children reject a divorced parent. One group dedicated to helping preferred parents who are alleged to have caused their children to avoid one parent is One Mom's Battle (OMB; www.onemomsbattle.com). This organization has hundreds of followers for its Facebook page. The group's founder, Tina Swithin, experienced a highly conflicted divorce and has written on ways to handle divorce conflict as well as offering instruction to divorce coaches. OMB's website concentrates on post-separation abuse as a divorce issue, including parental alienation allegations under this heading.

The Center for Judicial Excellence (CJE; http://centerforjudicialexcellence.org) based in California, is a parent–professional organization that has been particularly active in legal areas, including discussion of situations where parents have unsupervised access to children whom they may harm. Under the guidance of Kathleen Russell, CJE has been very much involved in cases where fathers have been given access to children over the mother's pleas, and have subsequently killed the children.

In addition to the organizations just described, which have parental alienation issues as their major focus, there are other organizations that have added to the parental alienation discussion. For example, both the American Professional Society on Abuse of Children (APSAC) and the Association of Family and Conciliation Courts (AFCC) have supported presentations on parental alienation and related topics—but the two groups have not generally been in agreement on their parental alienation positions. Investigative news organizations like Pro Publica have published stories about children forcibly removed from their preferred parent. A documentary film, *The Truth Behind the Experimental Therapy That Kids Say Starts with "Legal Kidnapping"*, discussed problems associated with parental alienation allegations as found by the investigative reporter Olivia Gentile; in contradiction, the film *We the Parents*, partly underwritten by the U.S. National Endowment for the Arts, argued for 50/50 child custody under almost all circumstances, including a child's objection to contact with a parent.

The views of judges, lawyers, mental health professionals, parents, and the general public may be more influenced by the groups discussed in this section than by professional publications on parental alienation.

Changing Laws

As will be noted in a later chapter, Brazil has enacted laws that criminalized the actions of parents who were alleged to have alienated children; these laws have changed back and forth and continue to be of concern to alienationists and to anti-alienationists. Parents' groups in the United States have taken a different approach to legal actions related to parental alienation cases. In 2023, when the U.S. Congress voted to reauthorize the Violence Against Women Act, the language of the act included a model law, Kayden's Law, named after a child who was killed by her abusive father after a court ordered the little girl to have contact with him. Kayden's Law prohibits courts from ordering reunification therapies for children alleged to be alienated from a parent. States may receive increased funding from the federal government if they pass laws that are similar to Kayden's Law in prohibiting courts from ordering reunification therapies which forbid contact between a child and the child's preferred parent. Despite strong opposition from alienationists, several states have enacted similar laws and others are considering them at the time of this writing. As these legal positions develop in the United States, Brazil, and other countries, family courts' positions on parental alienation cases will be changing—but the direction of change is unpredictable.

About This Book

As this chapter up to this point has shown, a lot has been written and said about parental alienation. But most of the discussion has focused on descriptions of reunification therapies and opinions of alienationist concepts—all at some distance from "lived experiences". There have been very few descriptions of the experiences either of young people or of their parents when *someone said parental alienation.* Arianna's story and that of one mother were told in some detail in a single book chapter (Barnett, Riley, & "Katherine", 2022). Catherine Kassenoff left letters and statements describing her experiences. A few articles have told brief anecdotes about people's experiences in parental alienation cases. Some videorecordings have shown us aspects of the events that transpire when *someone says parental alienation.*

Of course, there have been many books about parental alienation, written from the viewpoints of family lawyers and of some mental health professionals. There have been some books of advice for parents who feel their children avoid them because of parental alienation—a leading example is *Divorce Poison*, by the parental alienation proponent Richard Warshak. But there has been so little systematic research on parental alienation cases that few of these publications contain any serious description of events in these cases as they are experienced by the people most affected by them.

The plan of the present book is to focus on the stories told by parents and children who have been parts of parental alienation cases. These are the voices of families dealing with parental alienation allegations, as we can presently hear them. It would be a great mistake, though, to think that voices heard in this book are necessarily representative of all parental alienation cases. All we have here are the narratives of some parents whose children were said to have been persuaded to avoid a parent, and the stories of young adults who in the past were caught up in parental alienation allegations and in one way or another were subjected to treatments that were supposed to give them good relationships with both parents. None of these stories were told by people who are currently involved in parental alienation-related litigation; if they were still involved, it would be dangerous for them to tell, as this act would be interpreted as evidence of parental alienation. None of the stories were told by young people under the age of 18; to encourage minors to tell such stories would be seen as interference with child custody. And, regrettably, only two of the stories were told by parents who were happy about the experiences and treatments they received; in spite of efforts to find such interviewees, no more stepped forward, nor were any children found who would state their satisfaction with reunification therapies.

Methodology

Understanding and reporting the stories told by parents and by young adult children may not seem to be a form of science, and this approach is certainly very different from experimental studies that use careful measurement and can demonstrate causal relationships. But in the natural sciences, it has always been the case that a descriptive or "natural history" approach was the foundation of more complex investigations. Given that neither descriptive nor adequate experimental work on parental alienation cases has yet been done, these interviews can provide some initial foundational material and provide a basis for advanced investigations.

Scientific work today is beginning to include analysis of narratives in an approach sometimes called "storylistening" (Craig & Dillon, 2023; Dillon & Craig, 2021). Listening to narratives may seem at first glance to be an easy but potentially deceptive way to investigate a topic, but in fact requires special care in interviewing and interpreting interviews. Some authors discussing "storylistening" have even said that narratives may be "dismissed as too difficult to include in the provision of expert evidence" (Craig & Dillon, 2023, p. 134). Individual narratives can not only provide a foundation for work more easily recognizable as science, but can provide insights for interpreting that work when it takes place.

Research involving human participants—even relatively simple studies based on interviews—is carefully regulated because of potential dangers to participants. Interview studies do not have the obvious potential for harm that we would see in research on pharmaceuticals or surgical treatments, of course, but unless carefully conducted they can create threats to participants' quality of life. Before any study with human participants begins in the United States, it must be approved by an Institutional Review Board (IRB), a committee associated with a university or hospital who have the job of protecting human research participants. In looking at the plans for the interviews used in this book, the IRB had the job of deciding whether participation was mentally or legally either beneficial or endangering for interviewees.

The possible legal exposure of interviewees seemed to be the most serious issue. If a named interviewee stated that someone had broken a law (for example, by physical or sexual abuse), or that a therapist had committed malpractice, it would be possible for the accused person to begin litigation against the interviewee, the author, and even the publisher. Even if the litigation were unsuccessful, the cost of representation might be considerable. The solution to this problem was anonymity for the interviewees—not just a different name, but the removal of all identifying information like place of residence. In cases where interviewees had been sent to reunification programs, it seemed wise even to redact the name of the treatment program, as most of the programs have had so few clients that identification might be easy. The material as it is presented in later chapters of this book was read by the interviewees before publication and was either further edited or accepted by them as sufficiently anonymized. This decision was made on the advice of a First Amendment attorney specializing in this aspect of U.S. law.

References

Baker, A. (2005). The long-term effects of parental alienation syndrome: A qualitative research study. *American Journal of Family Therapy*, 33, 289–302. https://doi.org/10.1080/01926180590962129.

Barnett, A., Riley, A., & "Katherine". (2022). Experiences of parental alienation interventions. In J. Mercer & M. Drew (Eds.), *Challenging parental alienation* (pp. 63–86). Routledge.

Bernet, W. (2020). Introduction to parental alienation. In D. Lorandos & W. Bernet (Eds.), *Parental alienation—science and law* (pp. 5–43). Charles C. Thomas.

Bernet, W., Gregory, N., Rohner, R., & Reay, K. (2020). Measuring the difference between parental alienation and parental estrangement. *Journal of Forensic Sciences*, 65, 1225–1234.

Craig, C., & Dillon, S. (2023). "Storylistening" in the science policy ecosystem. *Science*, 379, 134–136.

Dillon, S., & Craig, C. (2021). *Storylistening: Narrative evidence and public reasoning*. Routledge.

Doughty, J., & Drew, M. (2022). History of the parental alienation belief system. In J. Mercer & M. Drew (Eds.), *Challenging parental alienation* (pp. 21–39). Routledge.

Doughty, J., & Rathus, Z. (2022). International expansion of the parental alienation belief system through the UK and Australian experiences. In J. Mercer & M. Drew (Eds.), *Challenging parental alienation* (pp. 40–62). Routledge.

Felitti, V., Anda, R., et al. (1998). Relationship of childhood abuse and household dysfunction to many of the leading causes of death in adults. The Adverse Childhood Experiences (ACE) Study. *American Journal of Preventive Medicine*, 14, 245–258.

Gardner, R. (1985). Recent trends in divorce litigation. *Academy Forum*, 29(2), 3–7.

Gottlieb, L. (n.d.) Sample four day treatment protocol. Unpublished paper.

Harman, J., Kruk, E., & Hines, D. (2018). Parental alienating behaviors: An unacknowledged form of family violence. *Psychological Bulletin*, 144, 1275–1299. https://doi.org/10.1037/bul0000175.

Harman, J., & Lorandos, D. (2021). Allegations of family violence in court: How parental alienation affects judicial outcomes. *Psychology, Public Policy, and Law*, 27, 187–208. https://10.1037/law0000301.

Kaminski, J., & Claussen, A. (2017). Evidence base update for psychosocial treatments for disruptive behaviors in children. *Journal of Clinical Child and Adolescent Psychology*, 46, 477–499. https://doi.org/10.1080/15374416.2017.1310044.

Loh, W., & Ren, D. (2023). Understated gender disparities due to outcome-dependent selection: Commentary on Mackelprang et al. (2023). *American Psychologist*, 78, 811–813. https://doi.org/10.1037/amp0001167.

Meier, J. (2020). U.S. child custody outcomes in cases involving parental alienation and abuse allegations. *Journal of Social Welfare and Family Law*, 42, 92–105. https://dpi.org/10.1080/09649069.2020.1701941.

Mercer, J. (2014). *Alternative psychotherapies*. Rowman & Littlefield.

Warshak, R. (2010). Family Bridges: Using insights from social science to reconnect parents and alienated children. *Family Court Review*, 48, 48–80. https://doi.org/10.1111/j.1744-1617.2009.01288.x.

2 When Parental Alienation Is Alleged

How Help or Harm Can Result

The first chapter of this book noted that problems arise primarily when parental alienation is alleged to occur, but is not actually present—when *somebody says parental alienation*, but that somebody does not provide any good evidence. It is possible that there are additional, or different, or (even) fewer problems when parental alienation is actually present, but it is difficult to know this because there is no established, valid, reliable method for identifying such cases. (Because parental alienation is not currently a diagnosis in either DSM or ICD, it makes no sense to talk about diagnosing such a disorder.)

The present chapter will discuss some of the crucial issues for identification of parental alienation in cases where children avoid one parent. The chapter will also consider methods by which researchers find out whether psychosocial treatments like reunification therapies are helpful, harmful, or without effect.

Identifying Parental Alienation: Are Methods Helpful, or Harmful?

If it is not possible to identify parental alienation accurately, claims that it has been identified may be harmful and may to lead to consequences that, if not directly harmful, are certainly not helpful. A mistaken identification may well lead to mistaken court orders and mistaken treatments.

Alienationists insist that they are able to accurately identify cases in which parental alienation is at work and to discriminate such cases from similar family situations in which children reject parents because of abuse or neglect. Some say they can do this by applying a Five Factor Model (Bernet, 2020; Freeman, 2020), as noted in Chapter 1 of this book, while others leave their methods unclear. Unfortunately, there has been no empirical work to support the claim that the Five Factor Model identifies the children who avoid a parent because the other parent has

DOI: 10.4324/9781003454793-2

persuaded them to do so, and discriminates those children from others who reject a parent for reasons like experiences of abuse or neglect.

The absence of evidence for the whole Five Factor Model is of overwhelming importance, but the individual five factors of this model are also lacking in both logic and evidence, as we will see.

Factor One: "The child actively avoids, resists, or refuses a relationship with a parent" (Freeman, 2020, p. 66)

This factor would appear to be an obvious and easily ascertainable one. However, in one case known to the present author, a child requested that instead of living with father and mother one week on, one week off, she stay at her mother's house during the school week and spend every weekend with her father. She gave practical reasons for this request, citing the awkwardness of moving all her school materials from one house to the other. Her father and an evaluator identified this situation as parental alienation. In another case, a girl asked for contact with her father, but he refused on the grounds that she might accuse him of sexual abuse; an evaluator argued that parental alienation was present. Alienationists have never shown that evaluators use consistent or systematic methods of identifying Factor One, whether they are or are not employing the Five Factor Model.

Factor Two: "Presence of a prior positive relationship between the child and the now rejected parent" (Freeman, 2020, p. 66)

Presumably, parental alienation could exist prior to a divorce; if one parent has interfered with a child's positive relationship with the other parent, it might have been impossible for such a good relationship ever to develop. However, the scenario usually assumed by alienationists is that all was well before the divorce or separation, and that subsequently the machinations of the preferred parent have led to the child's rejection of the other parent. Evidence for a prior good relationship is based on testimony of the parents and other knowledgeable people and on photographs and videos of interactions between the parent and the child. None of this evidence is objective. The stories told by the parents and their friends and relations are inherently biased and bound to be self-serving. Photographs and videos are heavily biased toward display of positive interactions, as few if any parents would record a parent spanking or scolding a child, the child crying or sulking, or any of the myriad angry or sad interactions that occur in every family. In rare cases, a psychotherapist who had worked with the family might be able to testify as to the child's prior relationship with the rejected parent. An objective measure might be the amount of time the avoided parent had spent with the child (for example, pick-up from daycare, coaching sports), but extensive contacts do not necessarily mean a positive relationship. In addition to the issue of subjectivity, it is notable that a parent who did very well with an infant or toddler might be less able to sustain a positive relationship with a sulky or depressed 12-year-old. Little evidence has been presented to show that clear evidence of prior relationship qualities is readily obtainable or necessarily relevant to the identification of parental alienation.

Factor Three: "Absence of abuse or neglect or seriously deficient parenting on the part of the now rejected parent" (Freeman, 2020, p. 67)

An important question about this factor is whether it is possible to demonstrate the absence of an event; unless there is some mutually exclusive event that is shown to occur, this is a logical impossibility. Some parental alienation authors alter this factor to focus on whether allegations of abuse (by the child or the preferred parent, against the rejected parent) are or are not substantiated. Substantiation of abuse or neglect allegations is a matter of investigation and conclusions by an official body concerned with child protection and legally empowered to make this decision. Abuse allegations are substantiated (or "founded") when such a body concludes that abuse has occurred, and unsubstantiated when the body does not conclude that abuse has occurred (which is not the same as an assurance that abuse has not occurred).

In families who are disputing child custody, about half of allegations of abuse are substantiated (Johnston et al., 2005). This does not mean either that half of the allegations were lies, or that the other half were necessarily correct. Unless the child sustains physical injury resulting from abuse or neglect, or unless unbiased observers report witnessing abuse or neglect, substantiation is in fact a probabilistic matter, with the investigating body having to make an "up or down" decision based on the information they have.

In cases where the abuse alleged is emotional abuse or non-penetrative sexual abuse, chances are that there is very little evidence to go on. Investigators may choose to give strong weight to the existing evidence because of concerns about long-term impacts on the child, as suggested by studies on adverse childhood experiences (ACEs; Felitti et al., 1998). However, in one study of girls who had been alleged to be abused, the outcomes studied were no different for girls in substantiated or in unsubstantiated cases (Kugler et al., 2019). Both groups for whom allegations were investigated had more unwanted outcomes (teen motherhood, HIV-risk behaviors, drug use) than was the case for girls without investigated allegations. Substantiation of abuse may not be an important factor in determining children's future development, but circumstances that produce allegations of abuse may be important to consider—the effects of allegations of abuse have not, however, been considered by alienationists.

Factor Three also references "seriously deficient parenting" by the rejected parent. This term is very much open to definition and is particularly vulnerable to cultural and gender bias. Certainly, the actions that could be called "seriously deficient parenting" are different for children of different ages. Suitable parenting for a three-year-old would be inappropriate when the same child is 13. In a general way, however, seriously deficient parenting can be considered as parenting in which children are not fed, given medical treatment, educated, disciplined in an age-appropriate way, and so on.

The Factor Three emphasis on parenting deficiencies ignores parent behaviors that are not abusive but are so distressing to children that the children wish to avoid contact with that parent. These distressing behaviors need not be associated with any specific form of abuse, and taken one at a time are perhaps trivial, but their cumulative effect is to make the child withdraw from the relationship with that parent. For example, the parent may repeatedly walk into the bedroom or bathroom without knocking when the child is undressed or using the toilet. The parent may "playfully" chase or tickle an adolescent and refuse to stop when begged. The parent may refuse permission for contact with friends or other age-appropriate activities. Children's attitudes may also be negatively affected if a parent drives recklessly or angrily, or if the parent is habitually late to pick them up or cancels or changes visits. None of these actions meets criteria for abuse or neglect, and if they occurred only once would probably not make a child reluctant to have contact with that parent. Adverse parenting practices have their impact because they happen frequently, and, especially, because the parent refuses to stop in spite of the child's entreaties and attempts to reason. Adverse parenting practices of this kind have received little study, and have had no attention from parental alienation proponents, but Milchman (2022) has suggested a method for identifying parental alienation cases that takes these practices into account.

Factor Four: "Use of multiple alienating behaviors (ABs) on the part of the preferred parent" (Freeman, 2020, p. 68)

Alienationists believe that, in the absence of Factor Three abusive or neglectful events, a child's rejection of one parent is probably due to the actions of the preferred parent in the form of *alienating behaviors*. The presence of parental alienating behaviors in the family of a child who rejects one parent is considered an indication that there is a parental alienation case going on.

Richard Gardner, the founder of alienationism, described alienating behaviors he had seen among his patients' families (Gardner, 1985, 2001). Later alienationist authors collected information about "alienating strategies" from adults who said they had been victims of such behaviors by one of their parents (Baker & Darnall, 2006), and from young adults who were asked if they remembered any of 20 possible alienating behaviors (Baker & Chambers, 2011). Some examples of alienating behaviors by preferred parents, as described by Baker and her co-authors, are badmouthing the rejected parent, telling the child the rejected parent is dangerous, limiting the child's contact with the other parent, and undermining the other parent's authority.

There are two major problems about the application of Factor Four in attempts to identify parental alienation cases. The first is that there has never been a systematic, empirical study of the occurrence of items on the behavior list as they actually occur either in conflicted, divorcing families in which a child rejects a parent, or in intact, well-functioning families. How frequently do any of the alienating behaviors occur in families of either category? What is the baseline—the lowest frequency seen—for any of the listed behaviors? Is there a significant difference between the frequency in families where parental alienation is alleged, and any other category of family? These questions have never been answered, and as a result alienationists can manage to argue that observation of any item from the behavior list indicates that the family is a parental alienation case. There is no research supporting this claim, or the claim that "alienating behaviors" by one parent cause a child to avoid the other parent.

The second important issue about Factor Four has to do with its application. Although Factor Four, as described in alienationist materials, involves observable alienating behaviors carried out by a preferred parent, parental alienation cases sometimes focus on the absence of preferred parental behaviors that are deemed desirable as ways to encourage a good relationship between a child and the rejected parent. A preferred parent who does not have the child give a birthday present or send a card to the rejected parent, who does not act as a "friendly parent" in this way, may be considered by a court to be causing the child to be alienated. There has been no standard set for parental behaviors that must not be omitted or for the frequency with which the desired behaviors must be performed. As a result, even in the absence of the listed alienating behaviors, a preferred parent may be considered to be causing alienation on the grounds of insufficient effort to encourage the child's relationship with the other parent.

Factor Five: "Exhibition of many of the eight behavioral manifestations of alienation by the child" (Freeman, 2020, p. 69)

As was the case for Factor Four, Factor Five's description of child behaviors is based on Gardner's earlier discussion of problems he saw in child patients who rejected a parent (Gardner, 1985). Baker and Darnall (2006) asked rejected parents whether they saw these behaviors in their children and they agreed that they did. (Baker and Darnall did not compare these responses to those of non-rejected parents, nor did they ask the rejected parents about other aspects of the children's behavior.) The behaviors included repeated denigration of the avoided parent, "frivolous or absurd" reasons given for the child's attitude, a lack of ambivalence (an entirely positive view of one parent, entirely negative of the other), a denial that one parent has influenced the child's opinion of the other, an absence of guilt for rejecting a parent, and "borrowed scenarios" that might have come from the preferred parent.

There is not enough space to discuss each of these "symptoms", but a few points may be made. First, there has never been systematic empirical research to show that these behaviors (however operationally defined) occur more often in parental alienation cases than in other kinds of families. Second, a number of the behaviors make perfect sense when considered in the context of a custody conflict and of the children's age (usually their teens).

It is not surprising that children repeat a "litany" of complaints and reasons for complaints when they are repeatedly urged to embrace their rejected parents and it is demanded that they explain their position. Such demands may go on for months or even years and may in themselves cause children to harden their stance. Whether the reasons children offer for their attitudes are said to be weak or frivolous depends to a considerable extent on what reasons would be accepted; if abuse, neglect, or serious parenting deficits are defined as the only reasons for a child to reject a parent, reports of adverse parenting practices or issues like objections to stepsiblings will be considered frivolous. Lack of ambivalence is characteristic of adolescent thinking about the complexities of human relationships. Adolescents, as they struggle for identity and autonomy, are offended by the idea that someone is influencing their thinking. Children are not likely to feel guilty about their rejection of a parent when they believe, rightly or wrongly, that the parent's own actions have brought about the rejection; in addition, their developing capacities for empathy remain oriented toward people like themselves, not adults. The idea of borrowed scenarios seems to be based on the idea that children learn from parents and not the other way around; however, if preferred parent and child say the same thing, this may be because the parent is repeating what the child said. Finally, spreading animosity to the rejected parent's extended family may be based on the likelihood of unwanted contact with, or at least reminders of, the rejected parent when with the extended family, not to speak of the pressure those family members may exert on the child to have contact with the rejected parent.

Factor Five is an effort to describe how characteristics of the child contribute to identification of parental alienation (although not to the development of avoidance). Alienationists (Freeman, 2020) have also claimed that psychological tests like the Parent Acceptance–Rejection Questionnaire and the Bricklin Perceptual Scales can identify parental alienation cases, but these claims have not been well-supported.

Omissions from the Five Factor Model

There are several possibly important points that are omitted from the Five Factor Model approach to identifying parental alienation. Characteristics of individual children would be expected to affect both the occurrence of parental alienation and the ways in which parental alienation might be identified. It is especially the case that child age, which affects so much behavior, could be at work in parental alienation cases. Children in parental alienation cases are most often from preteen ("tween") age to 18 (when, in the great majority of cases, the children are considered adults and are no longer ordered by family courts to receive reunification treatment). This age period is one of rapid and profound change in thinking, emotion, and physical characteristics. The time around puberty is one when we might well expect new concerns about modesty in front of parents and new concerns about parents' sexual relationships, among other things, which could precipitate avoidance of one parent. The teens are also at a time of developing autonomy and independence from parents, during which parental pressure for an affectionate relationship can backfire. Yet there has been no effort to connect normal developmental changes with "symptoms" of parental alienation, nor is the Five Factor Model adjustable to take age differences into account.

A second omission from the Five Factor Model has to do with characteristics of the rejected parent. Abusive or neglectful behaviors are given some consideration, but, as mentioned before, mild but repeated problematic parenting is not considered by alienationists as a cause of rejection. Are many avoided parents neurodivergent and unable to understand their children's viewpoint? Do many have religious or political positions of authoritarianism and feel committed to forcing the children to obey? Are the rejected parents impulsively violent and frightening to the children? Does previous domestic violence make a difference, even if it is no longer present? Are some rejected parents inappropriately passive and lacking in the parenting skills needed to negotiate their relationships with their maturing children? None of these questions have been answered. Instead, rejected parents are often presented as a uniform group of victims who have been harmed by preferred parents and by children.

Finally, there has been little attention paid to the roles of stepparents or stepsiblings in the parental alienation drama, although some authors have pointed out that remarriage can trigger or worsen children's avoidance of a parent (Warshak, 2000). What are characteristics of stepparents who seem to exacerbate a child's avoidance of a parent? What happens if there is a new baby? Is there an effect from having older stepsiblings—or from having younger ones? Like other questions on the nature of parental alienation cases, these remain unanswered.

Use of the Five Factor Model

Alienationist authors like Bernet (2020) and Freeman (2020) have emphasized the importance of the Five Factor Model as a method of identifying parental alienation and discriminating between alienated children and those who avoid a parent for completely different reasons. In over a hundred cases seen by the present author, however, the Five Factor Model has almost never been mentioned as the specific method of identification of parental alienation as a cause of a child's avoidance of one parent. As will be seen later in this book, the interview participants, whether parents or children, did not report knowing that the Five Factor Model had been used in their cases. Although the Five Factor Model is the only detailed method described by alienationists for identification of parent alienation cases, it does not seem to have been used or tested to any significant extent.

As mentioned earlier, Milchman (2022) has proposed a method for ruling out possible causes of children's avoidance of a parent, but this method has yet to be considered in published discussions of parental alienation. Similarly, Garber, Prescott, and Mulcahy (2022) have suggested exploring relationship "fit" for causes of child avoidance, but although their book was well received, this approach has not often been referenced when allegations of parental alienation have been made.

Treating Cases Where Parental Alienation Is Alleged: Help or Harm?

When family courts decide that a child's rejection of a parent is a parental alienation case, as suggested by one or more mental health professionals, a likely outcome is that the child will be ordered to *reunification therapy*, a form of psychological treatment intended to correct the child's avoidance of the parent, and eventually to create good relationships between the child and each of the divorced parents. It is not known how many children are sent to reunification therapies of various kinds.

Some, perhaps most, reunification therapies involve periodic office visits with a therapist. The rejected parent may or may not attend those visits. Little has been written about this form of treatment, and it seems doubtful that all therapists who do the office version of reunification therapy have the same approaches or use the same methods. Because so little is known about the office version of reunification treatment, it has not been possible to investigate its outcomes. Does this type of reunification therapy provide help, or cause harm, in parental alienation cases? This is not known. In fact, not much is known beyond the fact that the reunification therapists may write reports or testify in court, and that their testimony can affect judges' decisions about contact, custody, and parenting plans.

Less often, but more disturbingly, family courts order children to be sent to intensive reunification programs, sometimes referred to as "camps". These decisions include court orders for no contact between the child and the preferred parent, often beginning with a 90 day no-contact period, but renewable. In most cases, the child goes with or meets the rejected parent at a treatment venue and stays there for four days or so. Parent and child follow this with a "vacation" and then return to the rejected parent's house, where the child will live until the reunification therapy practitioner decides that a good parent–child relationship has been created, or until the child's 18th birthday, whichever comes first. Intensive reunification therapies have been described in some detail by their proponents, and reports on their outcomes have been published, but, regrettably, the outcome studies have not rigorously followed the rules agreed upon for this kind of investigation. Proponents of intensive reunification therapies claim that their methods successfully treat parental alienation and help children develop good relationships with at least the parent they had rejected, but this conclusion is questionable in light of the research methodology used. In addition, there have been minimal studies of harmful outcomes that might ensue after intensive reunification programs.

The present chapter will provide a general discussion of reunification therapies, concentrating on factors that most of the programs share. Details about specific reunification programs will be the focus of Chapter 3, which will describe treatment protocols and published investigations of the treatments' effectiveness.

How Would We Know That a Reunification Therapy Was Helpful?

In the 1990s, the *evidence-based medicine* movement began, followed by the interest of psychologists in *evidence-based therapies* (EBTs). EBTs are psychosocial treatments whose effectiveness has been supported by research that follows rigorous rules. Although there are many kinds of evidence, including anecdotes, the only kind of evidence that can be used to claim that a treatment is evidence-based is the kind that is obtained through rigorous empirical work. There are numerous relevant aspects of rigorous research, but a few are exceptionally important.

Rigorous research on psychosocial treatments must first of all involve some standard of comparison. Children receiving a treatment must be compared to a similar group of children who receive a different treatment, or no treatment. Studies comparing treated to untreated (or differently treated) children must define the outcome that is to be measured—the changes that the treatment is expected or hoped to make. Research that has these and some other characteristics is said to be at a high level of evidence, while other research designs like comparing child characteristics before and after treatment are at lower levels of evidence and do not permit the conclusion that the treatment is evidence-based. Treatments that are still in the process of being tested are properly referred to as *experimental treatments*; there are many such treatments, and there is no reason they should not be used—provided that they are transparently presented for what they are and no undue claims are made for their safety and effectiveness.

There are many evidence-based psychological treatments for children. A list of these, and further explanation of the EBT concept, can be found at effectivechildtherapy.org, a service of Division 53 of the American Psychological Association. A further list that includes treatments at both higher and lower levels of evidence can be found at cebc4cw.org.

None of the reunification therapies ordered in parental alienation cases are listed as evidence-based. None of them have been tested rigorously. Most of the efforts to argue that a reunification therapy was effective have been very weak in design and implementation. In two cases, the Family Bridges reunification program (Warshak, 2010, 2019) and the Turning Points for Families reunification program (Harman, Saunders & Afifi, 2023), the studies were at a low level of evidence, involving before-and-after comparisons of children going through the program. In addition to that problem, these studies did not measure the same things before and after treatment—that is, they had the "apples and oranges" difficulty. Showing that there were more "oranges" before a treatment and few "apples" afterward is not the same thing as showing that a treatment reduces the number of "apples" (in this case, of course, the "apples" are items showing that a child has been motivated to avoid one parent by the machinations of the other parent). In the studies of both these reunification programs, families were said to be parental alienation cases because a family court judge made this decision; the judge probably based the decision at least in part on opinions of evaluators, but judicial decisions generally do not state the evidence behind them. Thus, it is not possible to know either what the "before" situation was for a given child, and how it was measured, or what the "after" measurement should be. Also, as will be seen later in this book, some young adults describe their reunification experiences as being followed by a brief questionnaire answered while program staff were in the room. Neither the published material nor the young adults' descriptions suggest that the programs followed up to examine long-term outcomes, such as whether the children did indeed have adequate relationships with both parents following reunification programs. The various reunification programs are at the time of this writing best described as *experimental treatments*, and some do not even reach this level.

Can a Reunification Treatment Be Harmful?

It is a somewhat surprising idea that a "therapy" could be harmful rather than helpful. The very word therapy comes from a Greek word meaning healing or curing. Some practices called therapies do not do an effective job of healing or curing and are still called therapies, but it does not seem reasonable to call an actually harmful treatment by the name *therapy*. Given their name, reunification therapies would not be expected to be harmful—but it is possible that they do cause harm in one way or another.

Finding out whether a treatment is harmful is more complicated than it appears at first glance, but this issue has been given a good deal of attention in the last couple of decades (see Lilienfeld, 2007; Dimidjian & Hollon, 2010; Linden, 2013). First, it is necessary to think what the possible harms of a given treatment might be. Harms can be either direct or indirect. Direct harms mean actual physical or mental injuries resulting from the treatment, for example the increased anxiety and distress seen in people treated with Critical Incident Stress Debriefing (Lilienfeld, 2007) following exposure to serious traumas like acts of terrorism, earthquakes, or major fires. Indirect harms involve other forms of harmful impact, for instance loss of a family home as a result of an obligation to pay for an ineffective or unnecessary treatment, or lack of resources to pay for one child's sports activity when another child is court-ordered into a treatment. In the case of reunification therapies, direct harms could involve child depression, suicidality, or self-harm. Whether similar harms to a preferred parent could be counted as direct harms of a reunification therapy is a matter of opinion, but if such harms did occur, they would certainly have indirect effects on the child in the case, which could occur in addition to any other indirect harms. In cases where parental alienation is alleged, there have rarely but disturbingly been child deaths at the hands of the parent a child wanted to avoid, after a court has ordered the child to have contact with that parent.

How often would harms need to occur before a treatment was said to be harmful? This second issue is one that has not yet been clearly thought out. As a general rule, it seems reasonable to say that no psychotherapy should ever be harmful—yet it is possible that a treatment that is demonstrably both safe and effective for the great majority of children might not be so for, say, neuroatypical children.

As readers can see, there are problems of definition associated with questions about the potential harmfulness of psychological treatments. There are also some further issues about any investigation of a treatment's harmfulness. How would we go about answering the question—whether a reunification therapy, or any other treatment, is potentially harmful?

It is probably safe to assume that no psychological treatment for children that has been in extensive use is doing direct and obvious harm to many of the children. If this were the case, parents, practitioners, physicians, and others would have noticed and discouraged, even criminalized, the use of the treatment. If those adults did not speak up at the time, the children would later do so as they entered adulthood. The use of "conversion therapy" with the intention of altering children's sexual orientation is a good example here. Adults who had been negatively affected by "conversion therapy" began a movement that led to the partial banning of this treatment in many states, outlawing its use by psychologists but permitting clergypersons to continue the practice. People who objected to "conversion therapy" did not in fact have to show systematically that the treatment was harmful. They were able to pass legislation based on their personal experiences of distress. (This was made easier because there had never been published research claiming that "conversion therapy" successfully altered sexual orientation.)

Can reunification therapies be considered for potential harmfulness as "conversion therapy" was considered, or is there any more systematic way of accomplishing this task? Because, as was mentioned earlier, it is unlikely that every child will be harmed without anyone noticing the problem, a systematic investigation would have to involve very large numbers of children, even more than would be needed to test the benefits of the treatment. This is not going to happen. Although this book clearly is asking whether there are harms associated with reunification therapies, and although many would agree that too many children go through reunification therapies, there may not be enough children experiencing reunification programs to enable us to do a well-designed study of potential harmfulness. As a result, we are left with anecdotal evidence about harms caused by reunification programs, and this is almost our sole source of information right now. (It should be noted, though, that in a study of the reunification program Turning Points For Families, Harman et al. (2023) reported that none of the children either self-harmed or ran away while at the treatment venue; the children were also with an adult almost all the time, so this measure may not have been particularly valuable.)

The use of anecdotal information is looked down on in many circles, and to say "that's just anecdotal" is quite dismissive. However, when information is hard to get, or when researchers do not even know exactly what they might be looking for, anecdotes can be considered the first place to look and the first line of defense against harmful treatments (Dimidjian & Hollon, 2010).

There is nothing wrong with using anecdotes provided that the user does not draw unjustified conclusions from them, especially conclusions about cause and effect. An anecdote about the successful use of a reunification program cannot be used to demonstrate that all clients have had excellent results from the program, or that the program was the cause of an outcome; the anecdote is simply a demonstration that an event has happened on one occasion. Anecdotes are a starting point for research and have operated in that way for many studies of the natural world. For example, an ornithologist might report that a particular nuthatch ate certain seeds on a certain occasion, and that anecdote might lead to more and more complex work, first observational and later experimental, culminating in studies of nuthatch digestion. Clinical psychologists have often seen mood and behavior events in single clients and have used those anecdotal descriptions to build toward systematic research with large populations. But, useful as anecdotes may be in helping us build an understanding of a topic, they must be interpreted with care.

The present book's interview format employs what are essentially extended anecdotes to explore evidence of both harms and benefits of reunification therapies. What is important is for interviewees, the author, and readers to exercise great care in drawing conclusions from the interviews. If an anecdote shows that a child experienced great distress following a reunification program, it is wrong to suggest that we know the program was the *cause* of the distress; in the same way, if a family was left quite happy following a reunification therapy, an anecdote describing that situation is not good evidence that the program *caused* the happy outcome. Many other factors could be at work, causing either good or bad outcomes. In situations where some form of mental illness is present, it is important to remember that the mental health problem itself could cause a disturbing outcome following a treatment program and the therapy itself may have had little effect.

What Are Potential Harms of Reunification Therapies for Adults and for Children?

When no information about actual harms caused by treatments is available—perhaps because there are no such harms—it may still be a good idea to think about the potential for harm offered by the treatment. This approach has been used for some psychosocial treatments for children (Mercer, 2017), and although it cannot prove that a treatment is potentially harmful, it can suggest times when there should be close observation of treatment outcomes. For example, if aspects of a treatment would be considered abusive or otherwise inappropriate if they took place in other circumstances, it seems likely that those practices have the potential for doing harm; withholding food from children can be a part of abuse or neglect, so if food withholding is part of a psychotherapy (and it is part of some unconventional treatments, though not reunification therapies), surveillance of that treatment should be encouraged.

Although we usually talk about sending children to reunification programs for treatment when a family court decides that the case involves parental alienation, the fact is that reunification programs of all kinds can affect not only the child in question but all the siblings, the mother, the father, stepparents, grandparents, aunts, uncles, and even friends and neighbors. The effects on all these people can be positive, negative, mixed—or nonexistent. Our topic at this point is potential harm, so that will be the focus, and we can look at the possibilities separately for the child and the adults.

When there is discussion of the potential harmfulness of a psychotherapy for children, the focus is often on the treatment itself—the actual techniques used by therapists. Reunification therapies need to be considered differently, because they are not usually freestanding procedures. Most often, reunification programs are preceded by court experiences for adults or children or both, and by transportation to the treatment venue. The programs are followed by a change of custody that moves the child to the home of the avoided parent and cuts off all contact with the preferred parent, and that requires continued therapy with a practitioner approved by the reunification program. Children may later have supervised contacts with the preferred parent, or not, depending on the situation. If harms appear to have followed reunification therapy, it is not currently possible to use the available information to decide whether harm was done by the treatment program, by the no-contact order, by living with the avoided parent, or with any of multiple other possible causes. Nonetheless, we can explore some of the potential for harm from reunification programs, and in later chapters of this book it will be seen what interviewees think about their experiences.

What Are the Possible Harms for Children of Intensive Reunification Therapies?

As readers will see in later chapters of this book, intensive reunification therapies are often experienced by children as episodes where adults have complete control and children can make no decisions or exercise any preferences. Children's negative feelings about these experiences are likely to begin when they are taken without warning or preparation from a courtroom, school, or parent's house to an unfamiliar treatment venue. Preferred parents may know this is going to happen but have been ordered not to prepare the children for the experience. Children are likely to respond to these events with shock, anger, and even physical resistance, none of which they normally display or expect to see in others. They may show the consequences of these events in later emotional distress.

Transport workers. The children's experience of transportation to the treatment venue may involve encounters with youth transport service workers. Parents may have hired these people to move the children by car or plane to a distant location. Transport service workers may threaten children with wilderness programs or residential treatment centers or foster care if they do not cooperate; they may also tell children that the children's failure to cooperate can result in jail for the preferred parent. Transport service workers may display handcuffs and threaten to cuff resistant children, and may state that they will "take down" a child who tries to run away. Transport services are sometimes needed for children in non-parental alienation situations who should not be traveling alone, but they have received serious criticism as unregulated and been called "Kidnapping Incorporated" (Robbins, 2014). Although the transport service workers are said to provide food and care as children need them, they are also described by children as frightening, "mean", and threatening. Outside the alienationist milieu, a child who was seized and taken away by threatening strangers, even if later returned home without injury, would be expected to need supportive therapy and probably to be watched for symptoms of PTSD. The transport factor may be more important than the reunification program itself in creating distress in children.

No-contact orders. Children who are court-ordered into intensive reunification therapies are usually also ordered to have no contact with the preferred parent and to undergo the separation abruptly. Depending on the child's age and personality, and the child's relationship with each parent, this may be disturbing in itself. Most children in the industrialized world today will also find it startling and frightening to find that they cannot make their voices heard at all. That children have rights (as codified by the United Nations) and that they should participate in major decisions, are ideas that many children in parental alienation cases have heard repeatedly in the past, but with the court order it is made clear that their voices are not to be heard. These children may feel they have been kidnapped and imprisoned, and react as negatively as they would if their experiences had not occurred in a legal context. If the children had been abducted by criminals, there would be haste to recover them, and certainly they would be provided with therapeutic support to help them overcome the impact of the experience; in parental alienation cases, on the contrary, the court acts to maintain the separation, and the children are limited to therapists who agree with the alienationist approach. It would thus be unsurprising to find that children in parental alienation cases have both short- and long-term impacts that are equivalent to those of children who have been kidnapped—but no systematic research has yet investigated this.

School changes, home changes. Court orders for intensive reunification programs and prohibition of contact with the preferred parent lead of necessity to changes of residence. Except in the rare situation where parents have "nested" by leaving the children in place and having the parents alternate weeks in the home, parents have separate residences and have the children go back and forth according to an agreed-upon parenting plan. A child who has been refusing contact with one parent has in most cases been spending all their time in the preferred parent's home, but under the court order must move into the rejected parent's home following the reunification program.

Such a move demands a readjustment for the child in all cases, but extent of the readjustment, and its impact, depend on the specifics of the family situation. A child who has had their own room may have to share with a stepsibling, and the stepsibling may not be welcoming or pleased with the new arrangement. A child who has shared a bedroom and had a close relationship with a half-sibling may feel lonely and isolated as the only child in a house. Parents or stepparents who stress their own house rules may make readjustment even more difficult.

In public school systems in the United States, the decision about the school a child will attend is primarily based on the child's residence location. A child who is court-ordered to change residence may also be moving into a different school district, and, if the move is seen as permanent, may have to change to a new school, a transition requiring more readjustment. Both home and school changes demand attention from a child who is trying to make sense of the new situation.

Abusive parent or stepparent. In some cases where parental alienation is alleged, children argue that they have a very good reason for avoiding one parent—that the avoided parent has abused the child or the preferred parent and can be expected to abuse the child further. The abuse referenced by the child may be physical, sexual, emotional, or all of those. When child abuse is alleged, laws often insist that adults (especially those who work directly with children) are legally required to report the child's statements to the local child protective services agency.

Child protective services will make a decision about investigation of the child's claim, and if an investigation reveals evidence that abuse has occurred, the allegation will be considered "substantiated" or "founded". Insufficient evidence, or evidence to the contrary, leads to the conclusion that the allegation is "unsubstantiated" or "unfounded". It is quite difficult to produce evidence that a particular person did not abuse a child, unless it can be shown that the adult was elsewhere at the time, that another adult was seen with the child at the time, or similar circumstances. "Unsubstantiated" does not mean that there is evidence to show that an adult did not abuse a child, but simply means that there is not enough evidence that the abuse occurred. As a result of these complications, family courts may order a child into the custody of an adult who, according to the child, has been abusive to the child.

If the child is mistaken, though convinced that the abuse occurred, the result of the transfer is likely to be anxiety for the child, combined with a sense that no one in authority cares what happens to them and that no begging or pleading will be of help. If the child is not mistaken—if the abuse actually did occur—that anxiety may well be combined with new experiences of abuse, as the adult takes advantage of access to the child.

In fact, one study indicated that a significant proportion of cases where children had been placed with an alleged abuser were cases in which the child had to be removed because of repeated abuse (Silberg & Dallam, 2019). As was mentioned earlier, in rare cases placement with an abusive parent has ended in the death of the child or in murder-suicide.

A parent who is not abusive may nevertheless bring a child into a situation where there is abuse by a stepparent or stepsibling.

Serious self-harm by children. In some of the circumstances just described, children may miss out in school, with friends, in sports or arts involvement, as their responses to transitions distract them or discourage them. In other cases, children may experience depression or suicidality to the point where they harm themselves, by cutting, using drugs or alcohol, experimenting with hanging for sexual purposes, or intentionally killing themselves. Others may run away from the rejected parent's home, perhaps to try to go back to the preferred parent, perhaps to live on the streets. All forms of running away are dangerous to an extent, although the danger can range from exacerbating the parents' litigation to being trafficked or even killed while away from both parents.

Potential Harms to Preferred Parents

When decisions are made about children, the primary concern is usually the child's best interests. Children and adolescents are considered to be vulnerable to bad experiences, and the long-term ill effects of any decision are given due consideration—if they are known. However, it would be a mistake to think that only a given child in an alleged parental alienation case can be harmed by any decision. Decisions about one child can affect parents, grandparents, and siblings or half-siblings. These effects can loop back to influence the original child, who may be distressed about visible harms to others.

Possible harms to the preferred parent are evident in cases where parental alienation is alleged. Whether a child stays with the preferred parent and attends office reunification therapy, or whether the child is removed from the preferred parent's home, sent to an intensive reunification program, and placed with the rejected parent, there are potential harms, though they are likely to be at different levels.

The preferred parent in these cases experiences financial burdens that may necessitate selling their house or using up all of college funds or planned retirement funds. Few preferred parents can find legal advice given *pro bono*, and much of the financial outlay goes to needed counsel, as it is unusual for parents in these cases to be able to represent themselves effectively. The preferred parent may also be ordered to pay for therapy for the child and for themselves. Office treatment can cost USD100–200 per hour, and there may be no fixed end to the treatment of child or parent until the child reaches 18 years of age. The cost of intensive reunification programs is USD20,000 to 40,000 and these programs are to be followed by continuing treatment for both child and preferred parent. When a child has been placed with the rejected parent and the preferred parent is allowed only supervised visitation, the preferred parent must pay for supervision, with fees of about USD100 per hour. These costs may mean that the preferred parent cannot afford amenities of life like having a car, or may mean that they must work additional jobs.

Preferred parents, who are alleged to have caused parental alienation, experience high levels of anxiety and frustration. If they have not been ordered to stop all contact with their children, they are preoccupied by fear that this will happen. In cases where parental alienation is alleged, parents are often forbidden to talk to their children about the case, to describe what will happen in court, or to give the children any warnings about coming events; this prohibition distorts the parent–child relationship, especially if parent and child have a history of straightforward, open communication.

If preferred parents are under a no-contact order, they are fearful of what may be happening to their children, especially if the child's original resistance to contact with the other parent was based on experiences of abuse. Even accidental contact with a child may be interpreted as contempt of court and can in some cases lead to imprisonment. If there is supervised visitation, preferred parents may experience anxiety about the supervisor's notes and reports and whether any statements of parent or child were interpreted as contrary to court orders. In some cases, these experiences of fear and disturbance may go on for years, especially if a reunification therapy practitioner advises against increased or normalized contact.

A final point about potential harm to preferred parents has to do with the assertion made by some alienationist authors, to the effect that parental alienation is a form of family violence and abuse and is therefore a justification for separating parent and child (Harman, Kruk, & Hines, 2018). When preferred parents are said by courts to have alienated their children, a door is opened to the possible claim that the parents are guilty of child abuse. Such a claim has the potential to do serious damage to parents who are teachers, doctors, nurses, counselors, or in some other way work with children. Evidence of child abuse is a strong argument against hiring a person to work with children or letting them continue in that kind of job.

Potential Harms to Avoided Parents

It may seem that harms to rejected parents who allege parental alienation should be outside our consideration, as the rejected parents are presumably in a position to bring to an end the events that are distressing the children and the preferred parents. However, it is possible that in some cases rejected parents are themselves harmed by the situation they have walked into. It cannot be pleasant to live with children who have not been "cured" of parental alienation by the treatments given, but who continue to be resistant and rejecting and obviously long to be with the preferred parent. Rejected parents may respond to child resistance by becoming increasingly authoritarian, only to discover that the children are colder and more withdrawn as a result. Parents who have been rejected because of their poor parenting skills may be afraid to "give in" to children and may thus have no way to improve their parenting while in the midst of the parental alienation case.

Rejected parents may have entered into the alienationist argument at the behest of another person, without actually knowing what they were getting into. Lawyers may have recommended the alienationist approach as leverage for financial or other negotiations. A grandparent who wants more time with the children may have proposed that the son- or daughter-in-law has alienated the children and should not have contact with them, an argument that if successful would allow the grandparent more authority and more responsibility. A paramour or new spouse of the rejected parent may introduce the parental alienation concept as a way of fighting against the former marital connection or a step toward creating a new "family" without the child's preferred parent. In all these cases, the rejected parent may wish to get out of the situation but find it impossible to resist the pressure to keep on with the parental alienation allegation. (Or, of course, that parent may pursue the parental alienation argument with enthusiasm.)

Preferred parents may suffer from the idea that they have abused the children by any acts that can be argued to be alienating, but they are generally not accused of ordinary abusive acts, physical, sexual, or emotional. Rejected parents, on the other hand, may be plainly accused of child abuse and subjected to investigation; these accusations and investigations do not disappear even if they result in the decision that the allegations are unfounded. It is easy to imagine the anger and distress of a rejected parent accused of child abuse when he or she does not believe such abuse has happened. This is not the sort of problem that can readily be shared with friends or relatives, especially because attempts to confide can lead to public awareness of the situation.

Unfortunately, at the time of this writing very little is known about rejected parents who allege parental alienation, why they start their assertions, and why more of them do not decide to drop the assertions if it becomes evident that their children still reject them.

References

Baker, A., & Chambers, J. (2011). Adult recall of childhood exposure to parental conflict: Unpacking the black box of parental alienation. *Journal of Divorce and Remarriage*, 52, 55–76. https://doi.org/10.1080/10502556.2011.534396.

Baker, A., & Darnall, D. (2006). Behaviors and strategies employed in parental alienation: A survey of parental experiences. *Journal of Divorce and Remarriage*, 45, 97–124. https://doi.org/10.1300/J087v45n01_06.

Bernet, W. (2020). Introduction to parental alienation. In D. Lorandos & W. Bernet (Eds.), *Parental alienation—science and law* (pp. 5–43). Charles C. Thomas.

Dimidjian, S., & Hollon, S. (2010). How would we know if psychotherapy were harmful? *American Psychologist*, 65(1), 21–33. https://doi.org/10.1037/a0017299.

Felitti, V., Anda, R., et al. (1998). Relationship of childhood abuse and household dysfunction to many of the leading causes of death in adults. The Adverse Childhood Experiences (ACE) Study. *American Journal of Preventive Medicine*, 14, 245–258.

Freeman, B. (2020). The psychosocial assessment of contact refusal. In D. Lorandos & W. Bernet (Eds.), *Parental alienation—Science and law* (pp.44–81). Charles C. Thomas.

Garber, B., Prescott, D., & Mulcahy, C. (2022). *The family law professional's field guide to high-conflict litigation: Dynamics not diagnoses*. American Bar Association.

Gardner, R. (1985). Recent trends in divorce litigation. *Academy Forum*, 29(2), 3–7.

Gardner, R. (2001). *Therapeutic interventions for children with parental alienation syndrome*. Creative Therapeutics.

Harman, J., Kruk, E., & Hines, D. (2018). Parental alienating behaviors: An unacknowledged form of family violence. *Psychological Bulletin*, 144, 1275–1299. https://doi.org/10.1037/bul0000175.

Harman, J., Saunders, L., & Afifi, T. (2023). Evaluation of the Turning Points For Families (TPFF) program for severely alienated children. *Journal of Family Therapy*. https://doi.org/10.1111/1467-6427.

Johnston, J., Lee, S., Olesen, N., & Walters, M. (2005). Allegations and substantiations of abuse in custody-disputing families. *Family Court Review*, 43, 283–294. https://doi.org/10.1111/j.1744-1617.2005.00029.x.

Kugler, K., Guastaferro, K., Shenk, C., Beal, S., Zadzora, K., & Noll, J. (2019). The effect of substantiated and unsubstantiated investigations of child maltreatment and subsequent adolescent mental health. *Child Abuse & Neglect*, 87, 112–119. https://doi.org/10.1016/j.chiabu.2018.06.005.

Lilienfeld, S. (2007). Psychological treatments that cause harm. *Perspectives on Psychological Science*, 2, 53–70. https://doi.org/10.1111/j.1745-6916.2007.00029.x.

Linden, M. (2013). How to define, find, and classify side effects in psychotherapy from unwanted events to adverse treatment reactions. *Clinical Psychology and Psychotherapy*, 20, 286–296. https://doi.org/10.1002/cpp.1765.

Mercer, J. (2017). Evidence of potentially harmful psychological treatments for children and adolescents. *Child and Adolescent Social Work Journal*, 34, 107–125. https://doi.org/10.1007/s10560-016-0480-2.

Milchman, M. (2022). Distinguishing parental alienation from child abuse and adverse parenting. In J. Mercer & M. Drew (Eds.), *Challenging parental alienation* (pp. 107–137). Routledge. https://doi.org/978-1-003-09592-7.

Robbins, I. (2014). Kidnapping incorporated: The unregulated youth-transportation industry and the potential for abuse. *American Criminal Law Review*, 51, 563–600.

Silberg, J., & Dallam, S. (2019). Abusers gaining custody in family courts: A case series of overturned decisions. *Journal of Child Custody*, 16, 140–169.

Warshak, R. (2000). Remarriage as a trigger of parental alienation syndrome. *American Journal of Family Therapy*, 28, 229–241. https://doi.org/10.1080/019261800500081667.

Warshak, R. (2010). Family Bridges: Using insights from social science to reconnect parents and alienated children. *Family Court Review*, 48, 48–80. https://doi.org/10.1111/j.1744-1617.2009.01288.x.

Warshak, R. (2019). Reclaiming parent-child relationships: Outcomes of Family Bridges with alienated children. *Journal of Divorce and Remarriage*, 60, 645–667. https://doi.org/10.1080/10502556.2018.1529505.

3 Reunification Therapies

As noted in the previous chapter, there is no method that has been shown to identify children who avoid one parent because of the other parent's behavior, or to discriminate between children who avoid for that reason and those who avoid for a number of other possible reasons. Some alienationists, of course, claim that by using the Five Factor Model (or simply intuitively and as a result of "practice wisdom") they can identify alienated children. Family courts may or may not accept these identifications, as judges prefer—but they are frequently accepted.

When a child has been identified in family court as having been alienated by one parent from the other, on the basis of statements by custody evaluators, therapists, and others, it is common for the family court judge to order the child and the parents into some form of *reunification therapy*. The intent of the reunification program is to create or renew a positive relationship with the parent the child has been avoiding; it is sometimes mentioned that children should have positive relationships with both parents, but relationships with both parents are not the immediate concern of reunification therapies. The programs are intended to improve the connection between the rejecting child and rejected parent, but often suggest that the program is just a way to "jumpstart" the improvement, with a follow-up or aftercare program needed. Court orders may simply send the child and one or both parents to psychotherapy in a practitioner's office, or they may involve a series of requirements that include having the child and one parent attend an intensive multi-day treatment with plans for later work; the latter choice is far more common in North America than it is in the rest of the world.

Readers should note that the term "reunification" is also used outside the context of divorce. Originally, and to some extent still, reunification therapy is a term used to describe efforts to help children rejoin their biological families after the children have been placed in foster care because of neglect or abuse. That usage is, of course, not our topic here, but to avoid confusion it should be noted that this alternative meaning exists.

DOI: 10.4324/9781003454793-3

This chapter will focus on the details of a range of reunification therapies, to the extent that they are known.

Office-Based Reunification Treatments

Treatments in mental health practitioners' offices for children who avoid a parent have not been described in any detail and may be quite heterogeneous. It is rare to find so much as a published description of this form of therapy, though a few exist (see, for example, Smith, 2016).

It is common for office treatments (as well as some intensives) to be described as based on structural family therapy as proposed by Minuchin (1974) and later modified by other therapists working with families. Structural family therapy considers behavior of family members in terms of boundaries (family rules) and hierarchies (relationships between family members). These ideas are highly relevant to the problems that are inherent in a child's avoidance of one parent, and would be particularly so in cases where the other parent had acted (using "alienating behaviors") to cause the avoidance. Many, even most, families have unspoken rules prohibiting such behavior, and family hierarchies in which parents dominate children are generally present at least until the children reach adulthood, although they become tenuous when the children are adolescents.

In concept, family therapy requires the interaction of all family members. As a reunification treatment, though, family therapy focuses on the relationship between a child or children and one of their parents. This fraught combination is bound to be challenging to a therapist, and structural family therapy has long been noted as a cause of therapist burn-out (James & McKinnon, 1986). To bring in the other parent, in a family at loggerheads, and when allegations of bad behavior from either or both parents have occurred, is to increase enormously the difficulty of the therapeutic work.

Perhaps it is because of these difficulties in the therapeutic practice itself that there have been no publications reporting the safety and effectiveness of family therapy as reunification treatment. Whatever the successes of family therapy for other purposes, family therapy used in this way should still be classed as an experimental therapy, still under investigation (as the term is used by Kaminski & Claussen, 2017).

Intensive Reunification Programs

Intensive reunification programs are also programs intended to improve relationships between children and avoided parents and to increase the child's acceptance and positive behavior toward the parent, but they involve factors not seen in most office treatment. Court orders for these programs almost invariably include prohibition of contact between the child and the preferred parent for weeks or months (often for 90 days), and include the possibility that, at the recommendation of the therapist, the no-contact order may be continued repeatedly without limit until the child is 18 years old, or even longer if the avoided parent succeeds in arguing that the child is not competent. No-contact can mean exactly that, including prohibition of telephone calls, birthday cards, or Christmas presents; after a complete no-contact period, supervised phone calls may be allowed, and eventually there may be supervised visits, sometimes in a commercial facility that offers this service.

Intensive reunification programs are often referred to as "camps", although most of them do not share the "camp" ambience of outdoor activities with groups of children. Some intensive programs are in fact camp-like and include all family members, and presumably those are the ones that gave the name to the programs as a group. However, it is more frequently the case that the programs are in hotels or bed-and-breakfasts and members of only one family are present. Generally, the programs have no fixed venue or licensure, so it would not be legitimate for children or parents to sleep where the program is unless the place is a hotel or similar.

As will be seen in later chapters that describe children's experiences in the intensive programs, these experiences are later remembered as unpleasant; this is not characteristic of most memories of psychotherapy. It is possible that the unpleasant memories are not primarily based on the treatment itself (which appears to be innocuous and even banal, though frightening to children and annoying to adolescents), but on the initial experiences the children have with the program. It is common for parents to be forbidden to tell the children that they are going to a reunification program or what such a program might consist of. The children are, then, often shocked when they are approached without warning and taken in charge by two or more youth transport service workers, at a parent's house, in a courtroom, or as they are coming out of school. There has been extensive discussion of the role of the transporters in taking children to other programs, for example wilderness therapy, and some authors have concluded that there is no ethical way to use such services (Magnuson, Dobud, & Harper, 2022). Transporters have been described as threatening or using handcuffs or "taking down" (tackling) children who try to run, and also as making comments about the program they are taking the children to, predicting the difficulty the children are about to experience.

These experiences at the beginning of a program have the power to disturb children and mark the entire experience as frightening and unpleasant. They also establish the hierarchy in which children are subordinate and have little choice except to submit to authority—physically enforced if necessary. Whether these factors are or are not deliberately planned is not well understood outside the reunification programs, but it is possible that they are seen as a desirable way to begin the programs and cause behavioral and attitude change. Intensive reunification programs date from a period in the 1990s when forced emotional change was still considered an acceptable and practicable goal. For example, the addiction treatment program Synanon used threats and intimidation with the intention of changing adult behavior, and treatments for autistic children included the use of wearable packs that gave electric shocks. This was also a period in which physical restraint was argued by some to cause children to form emotional attachments to parents (see Welch, 1988). It is possible that the intensive reunification programs' history has led them to share some old attitudes about the roles of fear and intimidation in causing behavioral and emotional change.

Psychoeducation

Some intensive reunification programs have been described not as therapy but as psychoeducation by their proponents (see Warshak, 2010). The term psychoeducation is more usually used to indicate instruction about mental health issues, for example available treatments and usual course of a disorder, with the expectation that the instruction will help a client and the client's family handle the various difficulties caused by a mental health problem. Intensive reunification programs do not appear to do psychoeducation in that sense. Instead, they present children with instruction, often in the form of videos, that purports to explain in simple psychological terms why the children have negative attitudes toward their avoided parents. They employ terms like "brainwashing" which have never been psychological concepts, and present items of memory research to show how a preferred parent might have influenced a child's memories of the avoided parent.

Presenting the intensive program as educational rather than therapeutic has practical advantages for the programs' directors and staff. Educational programs that do not award degrees or credits toward degrees do not need to have licensed staff. Anyone can offer an educational program for a fee or for free, and non-degree programs are not regulated. One intensive reunification program is directed by a high school graduate.

When Both Parents Attend the Intensive Reunification Program

Some reunification programs are based on family therapy tenets and have both the preferred parent and the avoided parent attend the program. Court orders for specific programs determine the attendance of both parents. Children who have been through this type of program are usually expected to go with the avoided parent for a vacation following the program.

The Avoided Parent in the Intensive Reunification Program

Most intensive reunification programs have one parent, the avoided or rejected parent, attend the program together with the child. Ordinarily, only one of a child's parents is in favor of the reunification program. That parent may have been actively avoided by the child who resisted or refused contact, and those avoiding behaviors are the ones usually considered under the Five Factor Model. In some cases, however, the child has not refused contact but has asked for a change in the parenting plan or has proposed some other alteration from the parent's expectations. Whatever the situation, the avoided parent attends the program together with the child, participates in discussion and watching video material, plays games, and engages in activities as required by the program. Some programs also provide parenting guidance and counseling for the avoided parent, but how often this happens is not well described in published material. Following the program, the avoided parent takes the child on a vacation of some kind and then returns with the child to the parent's own home with no immediate plans for contact with the preferred parent.

The Preferred Parent in the Intensive Reunification Program

The position of the preferred parent in the intensive reunification program is a difficult one. Even if the family is attending a program where both parents will be present, the preferred parent is aware of the child's wish to avoid contact with the other parent and reluctance to go on the vacation that follows the treatment program; a preferred parent who fails to persuade the child to cooperate is regarded as encouraging the child's alienation from the avoided parent.

The preferred parent does not attend most intensive reunification programs. He or she knows the child is to be taken to the program but is prohibited from giving any warning or explanation beforehand. Court orders into most intensive reunification programs include orders for no contact between the child and the preferred parent, and children arriving at the program venue are relieved of their phones and any methods they may have of contacting the preferred parent.

Although the preferred parent does not attend most of the programs, he or she is required to participate in psychotherapy with a practitioner approved by the program. The goal of this therapy is to have the preferred parent acknowledge that they have caused the child's alienation from the avoided parent by performance of alienating behaviors or at least by failing to be a "friendly parent" who encourages the child's relationship with the other parent. Programs may also require the preferred parent to write a letter of apology to the child, stating that all the difficulties with the avoided parent are the fault of the preferred parent. Multiple efforts may be demanded before the apology is considered to be sufficient.

Preferred parents should not expect to have contact of any kind with the child soon after the intensive reunification program. Re-establishment of contact will depend on the child's behavior in the other parent's household and on the opinion of the program-approved therapist. It is possible that no contact will be permitted until the child "ages out" of the court orders, at 18 years of age. When contact is renewed, it will be gradual and under surveillance, and face-to-face visits will initially be under supervision. A preferred parent who alleges that the other parent is unsafe for the child to be with is likely to find re-establishment of contact delayed.

Preferred parents are usually ordered to pay much, if not all, of the cost of the intensive reunification program, which may amount to USD20,000 or more. One mother whose child had been ordered to a reunification program reported a demand for a nonrefundable preliminary payment of USD5,000. Preferred parents who have supervised visitation must pay for the supervision. Some preferred parents have reported having to sell their houses in order to pay these costs and cover legal representation. Others have given up claims to contact with their children because they could not pay as ordered.

What is the rationale for placing preferred parents in these difficult situations? The argument made by alienationists is that alienating behavior should be seen as a form of family violence and equivalent to child abuse, and that therefore cases where children avoid a non-abusive parent should be treated as a matter of child protection rather than of child custody (Harman, Kruk, & Hines, 2018). In child protection cases, the first step is almost invariably to separate the child from the abusive or neglectful caregiver, and alienationists argue that the avoidant, alienated child must therefore be removed from the care of the preferred parent. This argument is used to request judges to order separation and to treat the preferred parent as an abuser. (Legislation at the time of this writing is making it more difficult to use this rationale to order intensive reunification programs; this matter will be discussed in the concluding chapter of this book.)

About the Intensive Reunification Programs

Readers will see that in the later chapters of this book, which present the narratives of people who have been involved in intensive reunification programs, there is no mention of the names of programs attended by specific individuals. Program names are not mentioned because each program has a relatively small number of attendees, and the program names plus other information in the narrative could make it possible for program staff to identify an individual. Such identification could lead to litigation, for example for a complaint of defamation, against the interview participants, the author, and even the publisher of this book. Instead of linking individual narratives with specific program names, the plan here is to provide in this chapter information about a list of known intensive reunification programs which will give readers an idea about program practices, theories, and outcome information.

Some of these programs have been described in published literature and some have not. Of those that have been described, some have also been the subjects of some form of outcome study that examined the effects of the treatment program. Some other programs have neither been described in detail by their proponents nor had their effects studied. None of these treatments have been included in discussions of evidence-based treatments (for example, Hupp, Macphee & Pelham, 2018).

Reunification Programs That Have Been Described and Received Some Testing

Family Bridges

The Family Bridges program (sometimes referenced under the title Building Family Bridges) appears to be the oldest of the reunification programs used when a child avoids a parent. Family Bridges is said to have been developed in the 1990s by Randy Rand, a California psychologist who later lost his psychology license for unrelated reasons. Rand's original stated purpose was to provide treatment for children who had been internationally abducted by one parent, and were now returned to the care of the parent in the United States, whom they may not have remembered and who did not necessarily speak their accustomed language. Rand and other alienationists of the period, including Richard Gardner, considered their views on reunification to apply to the case of Elian Gonzales, a young Cuban boy who had been brought to Florida by boat, a trip in which his mother drowned; relatives in Florida attempted to keep Elian with them but he was returned to his father in Cuba after a dramatic seizure of the child by agents of the U.S. Immigration and Naturalization Service. Alienationists referred to this case as a model of the problems they wanted to address, apparently considering an analogy between a preferred parent and the Florida relatives who wanted to keep Elian in the United States.

According to published material (e.g., Warshak, 2010) and reports of individuals who have experienced the treatment, the protocol of Family Bridges is roughly as follows. A child custody trial, usually a part of a divorce proceeding, has included the statement that a child has been alienated from the avoided parent by the actions of the preferred parent—that is, *someone has said parental alienation*. Entry into the Family Bridges program is based on a court order for this specific treatment, which includes an order for no contact with the preferred parent, often for a period of 90 days (renewable). Children are not warned that they will be taken to the program, but are seized unexpectedly, sometimes by the avoided parent, but usually by youth transport service workers. They are transported by car or plane to a treatment venue that is often a thousand or more miles from their homes. Any money, identification, or cellphones the child is carrying are taken away. The treatment program takes place in a hotel or bed-and-breakfast place that has bedrooms for the child, parent, and others, but that is not a licensed residential treatment center, boarding school, or a recreational camp.

If the child has been taken to the treatment venue by transporters, the avoided parent joins them there. The stay for child and parent is about four days. During that time, child and parent spend a good deal of time watching video presentations, particularly a video called "Welcome back, Pluto", developed by the Family Bridges proponent Richard Warshak, which compares the changing discussion of whether Pluto is actually a planet in our solar system to the changing position of the avoided parent in the family system. Other videos include a presentation of the famous Milgram study of the early 1960s, which demonstrated how easily people can be made to carry out actions that they do not really want to do, when under social pressure. The videos and guided discussions in the Family Bridges program draw analogies between the child's position with respect to the avoided parent and a range of other situations in which social pressure and persuasion are used to change people's attitudes and behavior. The presentations communicate to the child that a person can be "brainwashed" or have their beliefs dramatically and involuntarily changed by others, and that "brainwashing" by the preferred parent is the source of the child's negative feelings about the avoided parent. In addition to watching videos and participating in discussions and presentations, the avoided parent and the child spend a great deal of time together, going out for meals and amusements. People who as children went through the Family Bridges program have reported that they felt threatened as they were told that if they did not cooperate they would be sent to a residential treatment center or to a wilderness program where they could not contact anyone they knew.

At the end of the four-day program, it appears that children are asked to complete a survey about the program. After that, parent and child are to go on a vacation together and then to return to the parent's home, with the no-contact order against the preferred parent still in force. "Aftercare" therapy with a therapist approved by the program takes place for some months. If progress is satisfactory, with the child becoming increasingly positive about the formerly avoided parent, contact with the preferred parent will be very gradually introduced, first phone calls, then supervised visitation, and so on. In some cases, however, contact is not resumed until the child "ages out" at 18.

A somewhat unusual position of Family Bridges proponents is the belief that a child's avoidance of one parent is caused by the other parent's alienating behaviors as they impact the child's capacity for critical thinking. That is, exposure to alienating behaviors, like a campaign of denigration against one parent, results, for example, in a child tending to use polarized or "black and white" thinking in which one parent is seen as entirely good and the other as entirely bad. The treatment program of videos, presentations, and discussions is seen as an educational effort that restores the child's critical thinking skills. Removing the child from contact with the preferred parent is also seen as preventing further damage to the child's thinking.

However, the emphasis on critical thinking does not take into account the typical development of critical thinking skills. It would be a mistake to assume that children in their early or middle teens (or younger children, for that matter) have achieved a high level of critical thinking ability even under ideal circumstances. University programs to foster critical thinking are considered necessary but not universally effective for many young people, and even older adults do not display high levels of critical thinking under all circumstances. Cognitive skills are well known to be negatively affected by stress like that experienced during divorce or any marital or custody conflict. Thus, without further evidence, it is unreasonable to argue that children who avoid a parent used to have better critical thinking ability, have lost it because of the alienating behavior of the preferred parent, and can regain it through Family Bridges. No research on Family Bridges has tested children's critical thinking skills at any point in the process; instead, there seems to have been the assumption that a child who is less avoidant of a parent must have altered because of improved critical thinking.

Richard Warshak, a proponent of Family Bridges, has reported that the treatment is an effective one (Warshak, 2010, 2019). The reported research does not meet high standards for studying the effectiveness of a psychotherapy or any other form of treatment, including instructional methods. Although we could hardly expect randomized controlled trials on this work, it would be possible to do clinical controlled trials in which a treated group would be compared to an untreated (or differently treated) control group. This has never been done; instead, conclusions are drawn from comparing pre- and post-treatment events. Unfortunately, the events "compared" are not the same before and after treatment.

Before treatment, the information is essentially that *somebody said parental alienation* and a judge ordered treatment on that basis. No information is reported to show on what grounds the identification of alienation was made, and a child's avoidance of a parent may result from a wide range of causes. After treatment, the information collected appears to be a survey purporting to show how well the child accepted the intervention, and the fact that the child (who has little choice in the matter) goes home with the previously avoided parent—two measures that were not used prior to the treatment program.

The published Family Bridges studies also fail to follow up the long-term effects on the children or the parents (either preferred or avoided), or whether the treated children end with good relationships with both parents, a goal often used to argue why a child needs treatment for avoidance of one parent. Like all too many studies of psychological treatments even today, the Family Bridges studies have not looked for evidence of harm that may have been caused by the treatment and not by the original family problem.

In spite of the various difficulties outlined here, Family Bridges has become the model for some other reunification programs, which have copied the circumstances and duration of Family Bridges and have used similar or identical video presentations.

Turning Points for Families

The program Turning Points for Families (TPFF), whose major proponent is the social worker Linda Gottlieb, closely resembles the practices of Family Bridges, although the reasoning and one or two features are different. Gottlieb is the primary force of TPFF, although she has a small number of subordinate practitioners who follow her methods. Information about TPFF is available on the Internet, both in the form of posted written materials (Gottlieb, 2024) and of YouTube features.

TPFF follows the four-day format of Family Bridges and has a similar price. The use of video presentations, even to the extent of using Warshak's "Welcome Back, Pluto" is the same. The requirement of a court order or court-approved commitment is similar. However, TPFF, according to Gottlieb, rarely has children brought to the treatment venue by youth transport service workers. They are usually transported by the avoided parent (raising questions about the extent of their avoidance) or by the preferred parent. A "therapeutic vacation" follows the program, and continuing therapy by a TPFF-approved therapist is required. Contact with the preferred parent is delayed, and when it occurs without approval, early contact is blamed for any failure of a child to accept living with the avoided parent. Given that early contact with the preferred parent does not occur, Gottlieb claims 100% success for the TPFF program.

When children are brought to the TPFF program, the preferred parent is asked to supply them with memorabilia of earlier life periods which can be used to demonstrate the positive nature of their prior relationships with the now-avoided parent. These may be photographs, videorecordings, or sound recordings, among other things. The point of the memorabilia is to counter any argument from the child that they have always hated the avoided parent, and to demonstrate that the present negative attitude developed only after the divorce and therefore can be argued to be the result of the machinations of the preferred parent, who has tried to alienate the child from the other parent. (This use of the memorabilia fails to take into account the facts that families generally record happy occasions and are unlikely to have records of times when a child was frightened by an adult or when family members were all angry with each other, and certainly does not provide evidence that any changing child attitudes were brought about by a specific adult's behavior.)

TPFF places a strong emphasis on a letter of apology to be written by the preferred parent and to be read to the child by the preferred parent at the treatment venue. The preferred parent may be required to write and rewrite this letter many times in order to achieve the approved level of blame-taking for the child's negative attitude, which is to be thought of not as the child's guilty responsibility but as that of the preferred parent.

Gottlieb's rationale for TPFF includes the argument that an affectionate attitude of a child toward a parent is due to a human instinct. These ideas, as expressed by Gottlieb, are very similar to those discussed in a similar context by the alienationist Richard Gardner (2001). Gottlieb has added to these views of instinct as a force in parent–child relationships the claim that foster children always long to be with their biological parents; other alienationists make the same claim despite the evidence to the contrary.

It is unclear what Gottlieb's claims about instinct might imply. Instinctive behaviors are unlearned behaviors that are shared by all members of a species of about the same age and of the same sex. Yet Gottlieb points to the avoidance of a parent by a child as counter-instinctual, suggesting that she believes that affection for a parent is not shared by all children and thus cannot be instinctive. If loving and wanting to be with a parent is instinctual yet not shared by all young humans, what is the implication? Although Gottlieb never states this in so many words, it seems to be suggested that a parent whose behavior causes a child to avoid the other parent has done such a profound injury to the child as to rob him or her of a basic human motivation. Gottlieb does not explain how the TPFF program could restore to the child an innate characteristic that has been destroyed.

As was the case for Family Bridges, an outcome study of TPFF has been published (Harman, Saunders, & Afifi, 2023), but it was quite weak in its design and implementation. The study used videorecordings made during the TPFF program to compare the relationships between children and avoided parents on the first day of the program, to those on the last day. Using no comparable untreated control group, the study was not able to indicate whether the reported improvement of the relationships was caused by the TPFF program itself, or whether any changes were simply due to adaptation to the treatment venue and lessened anxiety as the program became more familiar. The study reported that the program was safe, as no child ran away or self-harmed during the treatment period, but as the children were with adults most or all of the time they were in the program, this seems unsurprising. The study did not follow the children over time to see whether there were later indications of harm, or whether the children later demonstrated positive relationships with both parents.

Overcoming Barriers

Overcoming Barriers, an intensive reunification program, shares with Family Bridges and with Turning Points for Families the requirement that in most cases a court order is needed for entry into the program, and that court order is usually based on allegations of parental alienation, though this program stresses family conflict rather than parental alienation as the main concern. The reunification program is followed by a vacation and going home with the avoided parent, as is true of the other programs. Overcoming Barriers is different from the first two programs in that it is not only referred to as a "camp" but has many features that are shared with ordinary recreational camps for children or families. The program has an outdoor setting and facilitates outdoor and educational activities as well as serving as an intervention for families that have children who avoid one parent. Both the preferred and the avoided parent attend the program, as do the children, and several families participate in a large group. This format enables group discussions for parents, who may learn from each other. According to parents who have attended Overcoming Barriers, another feature of the program involves numerous counselor-interns who are constantly present and sleep in cabins with groups of mothers or of fathers as well as of children. At the time of this writing, Overcoming Barriers has apparently been on hiatus for several years.

Overcoming Barriers does not employ some of the more obviously potentially harmful methods that are characteristic of the previously discussed programs. An individual child is not the sole focus of attention for an avoided parent and two or more staff members, a situation in which bullying and threats may easily intrude, but instead children are in groups and near (although not necessarily interacting with) both parents. Children come to the venue with a parent rather than being brought by youth transport service workers, so unless a parent is abusive, a child attending Overcoming Barriers is not likely to experience some of the fear and distress associated with being brought to some other programs. Overcoming Barriers can legitimately claim that the intervention is a safe one on the basis of these facts, but no systematic study of possible harms has been done, although the one study (Saini, 2019) on the program did ask about possible harmful effects; a number of the respondents said some of their conflicts got worse.

Is Overcoming Barriers an effective treatment for a family when a child is avoiding one parent? One study (Saini, 2019) surveyed 40 parents who had been at Overcoming Barriers at some time during the previous ten years. About 25% of the respondents said that they had experienced benefits from the program. The study did not evaluate children's attitudes toward either parent and is primarily relevant to concerns about family conflict rather than to parental alienation issues, which is unsurprising because of the stated goals of the program. (However, some interviewees whose narratives appear later in this book attended Overcoming Barriers because parental alienation had been alleged.)

Family Reflections

The Family Reflections Reunification Program (Reay, 2015) combines some of the cognitive concerns featured in Family Bridges with the camp-like atmosphere of Overcoming Barriers. Children are usually court-ordered into the program and are initially prohibited from contact with the preferred parent, who is alleged to have used alienating behaviors to cause the child to avoid the other parent.

Children begin the Family Reflections program without either parent present and are provided with counseling and instruction intended to help correct the failures of critical thinking to which avoidance of a parent is ascribed. The avoided parent later joins the child at the camp-like venue. Meanwhile, the preferred parent is to be under treatment by a therapist approved by Family Reflections, in preparation for later restoration of contact with the child.

Potential harms of the Family Reflections program have not been studied. Reay (2015) published a report concluding that children benefited from the program and basing this conclusion on a range of child custody reports and statements by the avoided parents. This report cannot be considered an adequate way of studying harms or benefits of Family Reflections.

Untested Reunification Treatments

One Family at a Time

The program One Family at a Time, directed by the marriage and family therapist Lynn Steinberg, appears to have no material published in print journals but is described on an Internet site (https://lynnsteinberg.com). Notably, the site claims that parental alienation cannot be treated by traditional family therapy but requires specialized work. This claim, that conventional treatments cannot help a problem and may exacerbate it, is characteristic of fringe or unconventional psychological treatments for both children and adults.

The One Family at a Time website does not specifically discuss how parental alienation occurs nor how it can be identified, but stresses the bad outcomes to be expected in the absence of treatment. These include depression, "looking for love in the wrong places", anxiety, low self-esteem, and cognitive instability with breaks from reality in the form of delusions. One Family at a Time follows Turning Points for Families in its arguments that avoiding a parent is "anti-instinctual" and associates the event with delusional thinking. In one article posted on the website,

Steinberg accepts the view that parental alienation is an attachment disorder (Woodall, 2021) but does not explain how this claim fits the two quite different attachment disorder diagnoses in the *Diagnostic and Statistical Manual of Mental Disorders* (American Psychiatric Association, 2023).

The One Family at a Time website describes the program's four days of events and again generally follows Turning Points in its format. The One Family website does not mention how children are brought to the venue, but in at least one case it is known that youth transport service workers brought the children, who had been told they were going to visit their father at his home. Entry into the program must be court-ordered.

One Family at a Time employs family memorabilia to argue to children that their avoidance of a parent contradicts the record of previous good relationships. The program also uses discussions and activities to bring parent and child together, emphasizing that the child is to voice his or her "genuine feelings"—presumably not allegations of abuse or poor parenting, which would be considered to be scenarios provided by the preferred parent. A somewhat unusual feature is that members of the avoided parent's extended family are invited to take part on the third day. As is the case for most other reunification programs, children going through One Family at a Time go home with the avoided parent at the end of the program.

There have been no published reports of work studying the potential harms and benefits of One Family at a Time.

High Road to Reunification

The High Road reunification program closely resembles some other programs described in this chapter. Childress (2018) has noted the program's goal of "reestablishing an appropriate family hierarchy of the parent's role of providing executive leadership for the family and the child role of cooperation and dialogue" (p. 32), a goal that is not as plainly stated by other programs but would appear to be shared by most.

High Road involves a four-day treatment into which children are sent by court order and to which they may be taken by youth transport service workers. The avoided parent joins the child at the venue, where they watch videos like "Welcome Back, Pluto" and have related discussions and activities, go out for meals, and go shopping. Phones, IDs, and money are taken from the child, who is prohibited from contacting the preferred parent. The child later goes on a vacation with the rejected parent and goes home with that parent. The preferred parent is to be gradually introduced, but this step may be delayed. However, there are two unusual features associated with High Road—the program's theory of how avoidance of a parent develops, and the method of identification of parental alienation cases.

There are none of the usual professional publications about High Road to Reunification, but Craig Childress has discussed the nature of parental alienation at length in two self-published books (Childress, 2015, 2018). Childress, a psychologist originally based in California, attributes parental alienation to a suppression of attachment to one parent as a result of the alienating behaviors of the other parent. He has discussed this issue repeatedly in his blog. Childress posits that children begin with emotional attachments to both parents and those attachments motivate the children to seek proximity to the parents, and argues that a child who actively avoids a parent must be doing so because the brain system that naturally supports attachment has in some way been interfered with. High Road, according to Childress, is a method of restoring normal attachment to a parent when it has been suppressed. Childress has described High Road as a "catalytic intervention" that alters the child's thoughts and emotions about the avoided parent.

A proposed method of identifying parental alienation has been put forward by Childress and by his colleague Dorcy Pruter, a high school graduate who apparently runs the High Road program. Childress has presented in his books several scales intended to measure parents' and children's attitudes and behavior. These rating scales (see Childress, 2018) include, for example, rating the child's attitude on a continuum from openly hostile to warmly affectionate; the child's sociability on a continuum from withdrawn and sullen to easy, frequent smiling; and the parenting style on a continuum from lax and permissive to highly structured and firmly disciplined (this last scale does not include excessive discipline at one end of the continuum, it should be noted). These rating scales, while potentially useful, cannot help to identify parental alienation cases unless the scales have been used to collect information from large numbers of families; that information is needed to provide normative data that will allow scales to be employed in deciding whether a family is or is not quite similar to other families in similar circumstances. No such information has been collected, it would appear, and Childress has not published any normative material that would indicate the practical meaning of performance on any of the rating scales.

Childress has referenced Pruter's Custody Resolution Method (CRM), an analysis of material that yields a profile to be assessed by Childress (or, presumably, other practitioners). This method analyzes messages in emails, texts, court reports, and so on, and looks for specific types of statements. According to some sources, the materials are analyzed by staff trained to look for particular messages and are then organized into a report showing the contributions of each parent. Whether this method will shortly be replaced by artificial intelligence techniques is not presently known, nor is it known how staff are trained or how it is determined which messages are meaningful. In the absence of normative material on Childress' rating scales, it does not seem possible that the CRM could discriminate between children who avoid a parent because of abuse or poor parenting, and those who avoid a parent because of the other parent's alienating behaviors. In any case, there appears to have been none of the work that would demonstrate such discrimination, if it exists.

Childress (2015) states that High Road is 100% successful at resolving children's avoidance of one parent. Neither Childress nor Pruter has published any report of an outcome study of the High Road program. There has been no published report on the potential harmfulness of the program, although there has been at least one case of post-traumatic stress disorder following the High Road program.

Transitioning Families, Stable Paths, and Similar Experiential Programs

Some reunification programs, like Transitioning Families and Stable Paths, have minimal connections with the treatment methods mentioned so far. They are court-ordered following reports that a child avoids one parent and allegations that the other parent's behavior has caused this alienation, and they may include prohibitions of contact with the parent said to be alienating. However, rather than employing set treatment protocols that attempt to alter the child's attitude, these programs assume that pleasant shared experiences in beautiful natural settings will facilitate positive parent–child relationships even where earlier negative feelings have been strong (for example, see Isicoff, 2015). Grooming and working with horses together, or swimming with dolphins—these are the sort of pleasurable experiences with the natural world that are thought of as healing. In addition to these wholesome and enjoyable experiences, however, the experiential programs may consider it valuable to remove the child from the influence of the preferred parent, who is thought to have been causing the child to want to avoid the other parent.

Transitioning Families is unusual in that it is based on a specific theory of emotional change, polyvagal theory (PVT; Porges & Furman, 2011; Mercer, 2022). This much-criticized theory is associated with therapeutic methods that emphasize helping clients recognize their internal states and become both calm and interested, rather than numb or over-aroused. Bailey et al. (2020) have described working with clients using guided imagery of climbing a ladder to their goal and using sentence completions to help describe their emotional states. These therapists also use physical actions like grooming or caring for horses to create emotional change. They employ what they call "psychoeducation" to teach clients breathing techniques which they believe can provide a needed sense of safety.

There have been no published reports of attempts to test either the potential harms or the benefits of experiential programs using therapy animals or any other activities.

Discussion

Some reunification programs have failed to investigate either the benefits or the risks of their practices. Others have published reports on the outcomes of their programs but did not design or implement their studies to meet the usual standards for this kind of research. These conclusions about reunification programs are nothing new, having been stated repeatedly in critiques of reunification programs (Andreopoulos & Wexler, 2022; Avalle, et al., 2022; Mercer, 2019, 2022; Trane, Champion, & Hupp, 2022). Admittedly, it is very difficult for outcome studies on this topic to meet standards in the absence of an established measure of parental alienation, but the attempts that have been made are surprisingly weak.

A notable lack in the existing work on reunification programs is related to long-term effects of attendance at a reunification program. What are the outcomes for treated children, one, ten, or twenty years after their experience of a program? Is the adult frequency of depression or of social and affectional difficulties any different for treated children who were avoiding a parent, for untreated children who were avoiding a parent, or for children who were not avoiding a parent? Children leaving a program are required to go home with the parent they have avoided and have no choice about a continued relationship; what happens when they turn 18 and have a choice, or later in their lives?

It is also notable that only one attempt has been made to investigate possible short-term harms of any reunification program. Harman et al. (2023) looked at children's self-harming or running away while in the TPFF program; unsurprisingly, as the children were with an adult most of the time, no such events occurred. There have been no studies of harms like suicidality shown during the years between the program and the child's 18th birthday, a period during which children may be living with the parent they want to avoid and still prohibited from much contact with the preferred parent. If the avoided parent had been avoided because of abuse that was considered unsubstantiated on investigation, this period would be one in which further abuse was a distinct possibility, as was shown in a study of children who were given to the custody of an abusive parent and later had to be removed because the abuse continued (Silberg & Dallam, 2019).

Readers should take note that in the later chapters of this book, when narratives are presented about experiences with allegations of parental alienation, specific treatment programs will not be named. This is to help prevent identification of interviewees by program staff or family members.

References

American Psychiatric Association (2023). *Diagnostic and statistical manual of mental disorders*, Fifth Edition. Washington, D.C.: Author. https://dpi/org/10.1176/appi.books.9780890425787.

Andreopoulos, E., & Wexler, A. (2022). The "solution" to parental alienation: A critique of the Turning Points and Overcoming Barriers reunification programs. *Journal of Family Trauma, Child Custody, and Child Development*, 19 (3–4),417–437. https://doi.org/10.1080/26904586.2022.2049462.

Avalle, D., Smith, B., Wiedeman, K., & Garnica, C. (2022). How efficacious is Building Family Bridges? What the legal and mental health fields should know about Building Family Bridges and "parental alienation". *Journal of Family Trauma, Child Custody. & Child Development*, 19 (3–4),402–416. https://doi.org/10.1080/26904586.2022.2066595.

Bailey, R., Dana, D., Bailey, E., & Davis, F. (2020). The application of the polyvagal theory to high conflict co-parenting cases. *Family Court Review*, 58, 525–543. https://doi.org/10.1111/fcre.12485.

Childress, C. (2015). *An attachment-based model of parental alienation: Foundations*. Oaksong.

Childress, C. (2018). *An attachment-based model of parental alienation: Single case ABAB assessment and remedy*. Oaksong.

Gardner, R. (2001). *Therapeutic interventions for children with parental alienation syndrome*. Creative Therapeutics.

Gottlieb, L. (2024). *Turning Points for Families: A therapeutic vacation*. https://static1.squarespace.com/static/63894373c9be256a7b3b9df2/t/641b35db80fd0f78c3e437fb/1679504859831/TPFF-Treatment-Protocol-.pdf.

Harman, J., Kruk, E., & Hines, D. (2018). Parental alienating behaviors: An unacknowledged form of family violence. *Psychological Bulletin*, 144, 1275–1299. https://doi.org/10.1037/bul0000175.

Harman, J., Saunders, L., & Afifi, T. (2023). Evaluation of the Turning Points for Families (TPFF) program for severely alienated children. *Journal of Family Therapy*. https://doi.org/10.1111/1467-6427.

Hupp, S., Macphee, F., & Pelham, W. (2018). The science of psychotherapy with youth. In S. Hupp (Ed.), *Child and adolescent psychotherapy*. Cambridge University Press.

Isicoff, J. (2015). Reunification in parental alienation cases. *Family Lawyer Magazine*. https://familylawyermagazine.com/articles/reunification-in-parental-alienation-cases/.

James, K., & MacKinnon, L. (1986). Theory and practice of structural family therapy: Illustration and critique. *Australian and New Zealand Journal of Family Therapy*, 7(4), 223–233. https://doi.org/10.1002/j.1467-8438.1986.tb01184.x.

Kaminski, J., & Claussen, A. (2017). Evidence base update for psychosocial treatments for disruptive behaviors in children. *Journal of Clinical Child and Adolescent Psychology*, 46, 477–499. https://doi.org/10.1080/15374416.2017.1310044.

Magnuson, D., Dobud, W., & Harper, N. (2022). Can involuntary youth transport into outdoor behavioral healthcare treatment programs (wilderness therapy) ever be ethical? *Child & Adolescent Social Work Journal*, 41, 417–425. https://doi.org/10.1007/s10560-022-00864-2.

Mercer, J. (2019). Are intensive parental alienation treatments effective and safe for children and adolescents? *Journal of Child Custody*, 16, 67–113. https://doi.org/10.1080/15379418.2018.1557578.

Mercer, J. (2022). Reunification therapies for parental alienation: Tenets, empirical evidence, commonalities, and differences. *Journal of Family Trauma, Child Custody, and Child Development*, 19, 383–401. https://doi.org/10.1080/269045.2022.2080147.

Minuchin, S. (1974). *Families and family therapy*. Harvard University Press.

Porges, S., & Furman, S. (2011). The early development of the nervous system provides a neural platform for social behavior. *Infant & Child Development*, 20, 106–118. https://doi.org/10.1002/icd.688.

Reay, K. (2015). Family Reflections: A promising therapeutic program designed to treat severely alienated children and their family system. *American Journal of Family Therapy*, 43, 197–207. http://dx.dpoi.org/10.1080/01926187.2015.1007769.

Saini, M. (2019). Strengthening coparenting relationships to improve strained parent-child relationships: A follow-up study of parents' experiences of attending the Overcoming Barriers program. *Family Court Review*, 57, 217–230. https://doi.org/10.1111/fcre.12405.

Silberg, J., & Dallam, S. (2019). Abusers gaining custody in family courts: A case series of overturned decisions. *Journal of Child Custody*, 16, 140–169. https://doi.org/10.1080/15379418.2019.1613204.

Smith, L. (2016). Family-based therapy for parent-child reunification. *Journal of Clinical Psychology*, 72, 498–512.

Trane, S., Champion, K., & Hupp, S. (2022). Comparison of parental alienation treatments and evidence-based treatments for children and families. In J. Mercer & M. Drew (Eds.), *Challenging parental alienation* (pp. 138–158). Routledge.

Warshak, R. (2010). Family Bridges: Using insights from social science to reconnect parents and alienated children. *Family Court Review*, 48, 48–80. https://doi.org/10.1111/j.1744-1617.2009.01288.x.

Warshak, R. (2019). Reclaiming parent-child relationships: Outcomes of Family Bridges with alienated children. *Journal of Divorce and Remarriage*, 60, 645–667. https://doi.org/10.1080/10502556.2018.1529505.

Welch, M. (1988). *Holding time*. Simon & Schuster.

Woodall, K. (2021). Turning Points for Families: A therapeutic "vacation" with Linda J. Gottlieb, LMFT. LCSW-R. https://turningpointsforfamilies.com/wp-content/uploads/2023/03/woodall-Karen-on-TPFF.pdf.

4 Three Young Men Talk About Parental Alienation Allegations

Both boys and girls who resist contact with a parent may experience allegations of parental alienation and be ordered by a family court into some form of treatment. There has been no systematic investigation of the sex ratio in these cases, and it may well be that equal numbers of boys and girls have this experience, although in cases observed by the present author there have been more girls than boys affected. Nevertheless, there is no question that boys may be the focus of some parental alienation allegations.

This chapter looks at the experiences of three young men who before they turned 18 were alleged to have been alienated from one parent by the other. Each one had avoided a parent, but all felt that they had had good reason for doing so and that their resistance should not be attributed to the preferred parent's actions. One young man was able to avoid reunification therapy through the efforts of one parent, but the other two experienced intensive forms of treatment. Those who experienced intensive reunification therapies felt at the time of the Zoom interviews (a year or more after the treatment experience) that, far from reconciling them with their rejected parents, the treatments had had lasting ill effects on their relationships and their mental states. All of these individuals lived in the United States and were adjudicated by U.S. family courts. In one case, the mother alleged parental alienation against the father; in the others, the fathers claimed that the mothers had caused the sons to avoid them.

One or more of the boys had brothers with them during the reunification program, but information about that issue has been omitted in order to make identification of these interviewees more difficult. Similarly, this chapter will omit exact information about the reunification programs each boy experienced, but in each of the relevant cases, the program was drawn from the six treatment programs most often referenced as reunification therapies in parental alienation cases: Family Bridges, Turning Points for

DOI: 10.4324/9781003454793-4

Families, Family Reflections, High Road to Reunification, Overcoming Barriers, and Transitioning Families.

Quentin's Story

Quentin, who was 18 at the time of our interview, had not seen his mother for 7 years before she made allegations of parental alienation against Quentin's father. Those allegations resulted in a court order for Quentin to attend an intensive reunification therapy program. Quentin's father was instructed not to tell Quentin what was going to happen, and he complied with that order, so Quentin had no warning about the experience he was about to have.

The 17-year-old Quentin came home from summer camp and had been home for an hour when his father told him that he was about to go somewhere and that he must pack for a four-day trip. Quentin's father then drove the boy to the courthouse as he had been instructed to do. The judge told Quentin he was going to California and that he would be given an explanation when he got there. At this point, the youth transport service workers appeared and told Quentin that he could do the transfer "the easy way or the hard way" (their usual slogan).

Quentin complied and was driven by the transporters to a major city in his state, and from there they flew to California. Quentin now thinks that the town in California was Ontario and that they stayed in a Marriott hotel, though he is not sure about this and was not given any information at the time. At the hotel, he opened a door and saw his mother, whom he had not seen for the previous seven years, and his stepfather. (He cried and was distressed that he had not been able to say goodbye to his father.) Also present was a psychologist who remains a major figure in this particular reunification program in spite of having lost his license some time ago.

Quentin was furious at this treatment and banged on the table to emphasize his position, but this only made the psychologist and the stepfather grin. He also strongly resented what he described as being "called a liar face to face" when he gave his reasons for avoiding his mother. He now thinks that he did not realize at this point that the reunification program would culminate in at least 90 days without contact with his father, whom he missed very much—this information was withheld until the last day, as he remembers the situation.

On the second day of the reunification program, Quentin woke to realize that it was not "all a dream", as he put it, a phrase that suggests how bizarre this experience must have felt. That day was spent in watching videos (described by Quentin as "from the '90s") which carried the message that Quentin's father had lied to Quentin about the mother and had succeeded in manipulating the boy's thoughts so that he feared and hated the mother. One video featured a girl who told how she had been made to hate her mother but was reunited with her and happy about it. They also played "bonding" games, described by Quentin as "like kindergarten".

Quentin found it awkward trying to talk to his mother after such a long separation. He was told to practice calling his mother "Mom", which he refused to do (he called his stepmother "mama"). The program psychologist threatened that Quentin would be sent to wilderness camp if he did not comply and Quentin decided that continuing to refuse was not worth the risk. The program psychologist wanted Quentin to do a "one-on-one" session with the mother, but Quentin did not agree and there were no transporters there to force him to cooperate. Quentin described "constant arguments" during this and the later days of the program.

Quentin wanted to tell his own story about his avoidance of his mother, which occurred because of her abusive behavior when he was younger. The stepfather laughed when Quentin said this. Quentin was then sent out of the room while the adults talked; when he was called back, they acted as if nothing had happened. During the interview for this book, Quentin noted that his mother had both physically and sexually abused him from the time of the divorce when he was 4½ until he was about 7, when he told his stepmother and there was an investigation by child protective services.

On the third day of the program, Quentin, his mother, and his stepfather were to practice family meetings. Quentin remarked that he "hated that". Each person had an assigned role—some of these were timekeeper, note-taker, speaker, leader (a method often taught in cooperative learning programs). The first meeting was a discussion of the upcoming "family vacation" to follow the treatment program. There were 3 or 4 meetings.

On the fourth day, Quentin recalled that he had to "sign some sheets". The alternative to signing was a wilderness program. Quentin did not know what the "sheets" were and felt he had no choice. The program staff had found out the names of friends and other people Quentin might have contact with and created a list of those he could talk to, those he could not. His stepmother and stepsiblings were not on the approved contact list. At this point, as Quentin recalls, he learned that if he made prohibited contacts the 90-day no-contact period would start over. At the time, he now says, he thought it would be 90 days, but in fact it was a whole year until his 18th birthday and that was the day on which he was able to renew relationships with father, stepmother, stepsiblings, and friends.

Following the reunification program, Quentin was required to move to the town where his mother and stepfather lived and to change to a new school where he knew no one. Though Quentin did acknowledge that he managed to keep some secret connections with his old friends, the ensuing months were distressing and depressing for him. His emotions during this part of the interview seemed sadder than had been the case when he talked about the reunification treatment itself, when he had seemed primarily angry and frustrated. Quentin noted that he did not come out of his room at all during the first day and a half at his mother's house and that he felt his mother and the reunification therapists wanted to make him start "a whole new life". He missed his father and his dog.

The family meetings practiced in the reunification program were continued for some weeks, but Quentin yelled at his mother during meetings. He said he "hated those", that it was "pointless stuff", and that he did not feel the meetings were part of normal family functioning. Quentin finally refused to continue with the meetings. The progress of the therapeutic "aftercare" program was similar, with three meetings and Quentin walking out.

Quentin was depressed for several months but felt somewhat better when the judge said he could have his dog in October. However, he was in for a disturbing surprise, as he expected that when 90 days had passed he could see his father—but then was informed that it was 90 days, or "until the program worked", and as "working" would mean that he was no longer longing for his father or refusing to participate, the program had not yet worked. Quentin said that during this period he cried himself to sleep half the time or went to sleep angry. He realized that he would not be able to choose where to live until his 18th birthday, the following July. By January, however, Quentin decided that he should not "throw away" his junior year in high school and that he must use his time well. He got a job, made some friends, and waited for his birthday, all while feeling it was "terrible to have no one to talk to who knew him". He wrote a note to his father every night before bed.

At midnight on his 18th birthday, Quentin left his mother's house and made his way to his father's home in another town. He said that hugging his father was like a year's dream come true. Summing up his experiences, Quentin compared the reunification program to "alienation part 2" and an effort to make the child hate the preferred parent. He said the program tried to convey that "everything you think is not true", and that "they break you down until you cry". He also wished that the judge involved would have made an effort to know him, rather than calling him by the wrong name. As Quentin was out of the program for only a few months before our interview, it is not yet possible to know what long-term effects he may experience.

Jason's Story

Jason, now in his 20s, was in third grade when his parents divorced. He saw his father occasionally. The father was abusive, and Jason told a therapist about this, but no court actions resulted.

In 2015, Jason, now in 7th grade, was staying with his father. He felt sick but was afraid to tell his father he did not want to go to school. He went to school, then called his mother, who picked him up, took him to her house, then had to go back to work. Jason's father came to the house, screamed, and created a commotion over the idea that Jason was skipping school. The police were called.

Jason did not see his father for the next year. His mother told him that the father had mentioned parental alienation and accused her of putting ideas in Jason's head.

In 2016, the judge saw Jason in chambers and asked him what he wanted to do. Jason explained about the abuse but the judge did not believe him—instead, he said that the story was "too intelligent for an 8th grader". The judge ordered an intensive reunification therapy program. Jason's mother drove him there after being told that he would be forced to go.

Jason's father, his stepmother (as of this writing, now divorced from the father), and the stepmother's children were at the program. They stayed in a rented house.

Jason met the program manager, a social worker by training. She told Jason that his beliefs about past abuse were planted by his mother and were figments of imagination. In order to have contact with Jason, his mother would have to perform several steps, including writing a letter of apology. Meanwhile, Jason could have no contact with his mother or grandmother. The program manager also told Jason that his mother was "sociopathic" although she had not met or interviewed her.

In the course of the reunification treatment, Jason's father provided photos of events with the stepmother and her children. Looking at and talking about the photos was called a "family bonding experience". There was no material from Jason's mother. Everyone was in the room together including a stepsister and stepbrother. Jason does not remember much else that happened except that he watched the video "Welcome Back, Pluto" which emphasizes the restoration of a rejected family member to relationships.

Jason's concerns at the time of our interview seemed to be much more with the events of the ensuing years than with the reunification program itself. He did not see his mother for another 3½ years; her lawyer advised her not to write the letter of apology demanded by the program.

Jason's father was divorced again in 2018 and the former wife has a permanent restraining order against him.

Jason tried to run away when he learned his father was asking for full custody. His father tried to have him arrested as a runaway, but Jason sought and got a temporary "protection from abuse" order. This allowed Jason to go back to his father's house and get his clothes. His father claimed that Jason had stolen his car, even though there had been an arrangement made through the lawyer that Jason could drive it and Jason had already given the keys back to the police. Policemen were present at the house to go in and get Jason's clothes but his father resisted this and was arrested. Jason then went before a commissioner and got a protection order, following which the father dropped the custody suit.

Asked what his father had done that caused him to react so strongly to the custody suit, Jason listed a series of abuses. He recalled that his father often hit him or locked him outdoors. His father made him work with a small saw to cut down a tree and this took many hours, but when neighbors paid him for his work, Jason's father took the money away. Jason was also locked in his room for a week without much food. His father refused to take him to a doctor when his nose was broken—but, Jason says, he had gotten to a point where he did not care any more, even when he was pushed out of a moving car.

Jason also reported that following the intensive reunification program he was to continue working with a local therapist as "aftercare". This therapist was recommended by the intensive program as the only possible therapist in the state. Jason attended therapy twice a week and recalls being told by the therapist that his feelings were wrong. He was given books to read, including *Divorce Poison*, a book for popular audiences by Richard Warshak, a psychologist long involved in the reunification program Family Bridges. Jason's attendance at this therapist's office went on for 3½ years. He noted that the therapist did not interfere when Jason's father rushed into the office, screamed at Jason, and grabbed him.

Jason's father now has no contact with Jason, who has graduated from high school and has a college athletic scholarship. He is in contact with his mother and her long-term boyfriend whom he likes.

Although Jason seems to be doing well now, he recalls his experience, especially the therapies, as harmful. He says he feels as if he created a separate personality to deal with the treatments. He experiences flashbacks "as if the things are happening now", sweats, feels hot, and can't sleep. He experiences panic if going to a therapist's office even though he liked the therapist he had for some time. He has changed his last name to his mother's maiden name.

Martin's Story

Martin was 13 when his parents separated. His father moved to a house nearby, and Martin and the other children could simply walk back and forth between the homes. Martin's mother stayed at home and homeschooled the children (a decision that later became an issue as conflict increased).

It was agreed that Martin and the other children would be involved in developing a parenting plan that would guide the amount of time they spent with each parent, including one weekend day and one dinner. In a few months, there was an agreement to spend every Saturday with their father, all day, and having 16 vacation days together. But soon Martin's father decided he wanted a new parenting plan. Other family members were drawn into the conflict but some, like the father's stepmother, tried to stay neutral. To complicate matters, Martin's mother began to date.

In a year or so, conflicts over the parenting plan and other arrangements began to escalate. Martin's father wanted the children to go to school; he had been paying the mother to homeschool and he wanted to stop. He also wanted overnight visits, which had not been included in the initial parenting plan, although there were no sleeping arrangements at his house at the time. When the father was driving Martin somewhere, they got into a heated argument. Martin asked why he wanted to change the plan. The father responded by yelling and banging the dashboard. Martin also began to call his father by his first name, which provoked him. (Using a parent's first name is considered an indication of parental alienation by the concept's proponents.)

The father met Lisa and introduced her to the children. Not long before Christmas, at the father's house, there was a yelling argument that started when Martin wanted to change some plans that had been made, and Lisa was trying to defend Martin's father. The children were supposed to go to their father's house for Christmas Day but they told him they did not want to go because they did not want to see Lisa, who was beginning to accompany the father to children's events like sports and concerts.

About a year and a half after the separation, the children were on a camping trip with Dad. The weather was cold in their high desert camping area and a conflict began over a flat tire, culminating in Martin walking away, seeking a breather and to calm down before returning and helping out. Martin's father for some reason chose, a few hours later, to announce that Lisa would be moving in with him in a month. Feelings ran high and, as Martin recalls, he and his father had a physical struggle over pouring water later on the trip.

There was another argument after they made camp. The father left for a while, leaving the children (young teenagers) alone. When Dad returned, he told the children they were going home first thing in the morning, but Martin suggested walking to something he wanted to see in the morning. The father said, that if they went to see the thing suggested, he would just leave them there, in a remote campsite with very few people nearby. The children were scared of their father and slept locked in the car (though presumably the father could have unlocked the car if he had wanted to). They got into their father's iPad and sent messages to their mother.

The next morning, they agreed not to talk while the father drove. They went to the house of friends and spent the rest of their vacation period there. However, at the end of this period, the father wanted them to come overnight, but the children refused. Some time later, Martin started to talk about their situation with a friend who worked with the police.

During the next six months (now about two years after the separation), Martin's father stressed repeatedly that he wanted the children to stop homeschooling and go to school in "the real world". He also said they should be glad they had a large college fund—but they would have to do some things in order to get access to it. A family evaluation was done by a local psychologist who had specialized to some extent in cases where children avoided contact with one parent.

The conflict between Martin and his father continued to grow. The divorce was still not final. Asked for a time line for the divorce proceedings, the father responded that he would give this—but not in writing. He stated his concerns that the mother had post-traumatic stress disorder (PTSD).

Martin asked for permission to visit family in another country during the summer, but his father said there would be legal problems. The father offered instead a summer camp devoted to one of Martin's special interests, but Martin felt there were many obstacles to his attending. In a few months, Martin was sick with something that looked like measles. He had not been vaccinated and his father said he should be, and the vaccination was done, with the mother's encouragement, but the father later expressed concern with the possible side effects of vaccination.

A few years after the parents separated, Martin's father began to do family meetings with the children, as advised by some reunification therapists. These took 2–3 hours. The father's girlfriend, Lisa, moved into the house. Martin asked if he could do a full-day trip to pursue one of his interests, but his father said it would not be a "win-win", an idea Martin felt his father got from the popular book *Seven Habits of Highly Effective People* (Covey, 2013).

During the next several months, there was a lot of activity related to the children and the divorce. Martin and the other children were required to work when they visited the father's house. They got their own lawyer with help from adult friends. They met with the psychologist who had evaluated the family, once with the mother, once with the father—except that Martin says the father did not stay for the full session. The children met later with their lawyer and the evaluator and presented their own parenting plan. They were willing to continue seeing the father but wanted less conflict and tension. They thought their voices had been heard but later found that the point had been to discover whether the mother had disclosed to them some troubling information about the father. (Such a disclosure would have been considered an indication of parental alienation.)

Martin became less angry and more positive about his father over time. He now credits this change to advice from the lawyer and a training he took to help him handle the situation better. Some conflicts between them were successfully negotiated. However, another person entered the picture and was once present when Martin went to dinner at the father's house as well as being involved in some telephone conversations. This man, whom we can call John, was a "life coach" and claimed to have written parts of the popular book *Chicken Soup for the Soul*. He also said he ran a film company and had various other skills and accomplishments. John was present for the divorce trial and Martin's uncle also attended. Martin assumes that John was advising his father on various issues.

At a meeting with the children and father, Lisa mentioned parental alienation. Feelings ran high and escalated to the point where Martin called the police because the father kept telling the children details about the divorce, which the children's lawyer had told them they were not to know about. The father complained that the children had no respect for him. The father began to go to a nearby reunification therapist as ordered by the court, and the children also met with her.

In another month or two, there was conflict. Martin had skipped one visit and gone to see friends; his father called to threaten that the mother would go to jail if he did this. Subsequently, when the children went to the father's house with their bikes and other equipment, the father and Lisa wanted a family meeting. They called John, the life coach, for advice, and blocked the door when Martin tried to leave. The police were called again. Martin left and went to the home of some friends. The police came and took the children to their mother's house, and told them to stay there for the rest of the day, but the father was upset and did not want the children to comply with the police direction. The father still had the bikes and other equipment and would not return them.

It had been planned that the children would fly to see their step-grandmother in another state but the father objected; the father said they must agree to and sign a code of conduct before they could go. The children's lawyer went to court to get permission to go and the judge sided with them. The father had decided that he wanted the children to go to a reunification therapy program; he also wanted them to install some lights at his house, which they didn't know how to do. Martin happened to meet a girl who had been in a parental alienation case and became more aware of the pattern of allegations.

After their trip, the children gave their father a counterproposal to the code of conduct. They also took him out to dinner for his birthday. He still refused to return their bikes and equipment but was ordered to do so by the court. Meanwhile, the father was looking for a replacement for the reunification therapist, who had dropped the case. Martin believes this was likely due to threats of a lawsuit against the reunification therapist.

Two other professionals, one of whom had a parental alienation background, were brought in. The judge signed the new parenting plan, with the two new professionals as case managers. The plan was to step up contact with continuing reunification counseling.

Martin, now 17 years old, began to take notes in their sessions and send copies to everyone, as no records were being kept. In his interview, Martin reported that he did this after his father accused him of lying in the meetings and of undercutting him and Lisa when at their house and not in a meeting. The therapist did not prevent the father from punishing Martin for topics he brought up. Martin was forced to write a letter of apology for being rude and condescending in a meeting. Martin managed not to send the email to everyone he was told to contact, but he did have to write the apology.

Martin's father moved to a town in another part of their state and the children had to drive to see him, which made it difficult for them to have jobs or see friends. (Their father would pay them to clean his house.) A trip to Europe was planned for the father and children, but at the last minute, it was announced that Lisa was coming—though the beginning of the COVID pandemic made this trip impossible.

By April of 2020, there was considerable escalation. Martin's father started conversations about parental alienation and "brainwashing". He began recording all the discussion and trying to get Martin to say he loathed Lisa. John the life coach was involved in this, and the father sent an accidental text to Martin in which he discussed with John some details about dealing with their situation.

On a later occasion, the children went to the father's house and they started a family meeting right away. A sibling of Martin's walked out and called the family coordinator, who said they should leave. The children returned the next day, as the family coordinator advised them to show that they cared about the relationship with their father and were committed to working things out. The court, after that incident, cut the father's parenting time down.

Martin expected they would have a visit with their father on Father's Day, but they did not hear from him. Martin made a digital Father's Day card for his father, but the latter replied with a long email in which he said he did not want to see the children if they did not stop being "nasty". The court subsequently ordered no contact with the father. About a year later, the father sent a letter blaming the whole situation on John the life coach, repeating this twice in the ensuing year. Martin thinks his father may also have threatened to sue the case managers.

Martin is in therapy now and does not see his father at all.

Discussion

Are These Interviewees Typical of Young Men Who Have Experienced Parental Alienation Allegations?

As noted earlier, it would be wrong to assume that the interviewees discussed in this chapter are necessarily typical of the whole population of young men who have experienced allegations of parental alienation and related subsequent events. These interviewees cannot legitimately be thought of as known "average" responders to parental alienation allegations, as there is no systematic evidence about the range of responses displayed by young adults who as children and adolescents were exposed to parental alienation suggestions or decisions. These individuals' reports of their experiences may be "black swans" giving evidence of very rare occurrences, or they may offer "proof of concept" that others could have similar histories, or the reality may be somewhere in between.

The paucity of research on this topic is such that we do not even have clear evidence of the number of cases per year in which sons (or daughters) of divorcing parents experience parental alienation allegations. This situation makes it impossible to calculate even the probability of an individual's exposure to such allegations, much less to know what events result from the allegations.

Nonetheless, individual narratives, if considered cautiously, can provide a beginning for the study of a phenomenon—and that is all that this chapter and the rest of the book attempt to do.

Are the Actions of Mothers and of Fathers Typical of Families Experiencing Parental Alienation Allegations?

Historically, mothers and fathers have been assigned different roles in cases where parental alienation was alleged, but the assignments have changed over time. Gardner (1985) originally attributed parental alienation to the malicious claims of "scorned" mothers, who tried to punish ex-spouses by accusing them of abusive treatment of the children. An oft-quoted but poorly designed study on hundreds of divorce cases devotes an entire chapter to the claim that mothers performed many more alienating behaviors than fathers did, but fails to supply the data to support this view (Clawar & Rivlin, 1991). Later publications suggested that parental alienation allegations toward mothers were largely a method fathers used to gain legal and financial control, and that fathers were the ones who were working to separate mothers and children (Doughty & Drew, 2022). It appears that a (possibly small) majority of cases where parental alienation is alleged involve situations in which a father is arguing that his former wife, the children's mother, has caused the children to avoid him. However, there are certainly more than a few cases in which a mother alleges that children's avoidance of contact with her is caused by the machinations of the children's father.

In the three interviews reported in this chapter, two of the young men said their fathers alleged that the mothers caused the children to avoid contact with the fathers. The third case involved an interviewee who as a boy preferred to be with his father and whose mother alleged parental alienation against the father. These proportions may or may not reflect what happens in the larger population.

How Was Parental Alienation Identified in These Cases?

Because parental alienation is not an agreed-upon diagnostic category and is not listed in the *Diagnostic and Statistical Manual of Mental Disorders* of the American Psychiatric Association, such a condition cannot be said to be diagnosed, but some ways to identify it have been suggested. Most commonly, authors propose the use of the Five Factor Model (Bernet, 2020) to assign cases to the parental alienation category. This model, as noted in an earlier chapter, employs the following criteria: a child must avoid contact with one parent; the child must at some earlier time have had a good relationship with the parent; there must be no substantiated evidence of abuse or neglect by the avoided parent; the child must show some behaviors from a list associated with parental alienation, such as denigration of the rejected parent; and the preferred parent must show some sort of a list of alienating behaviors, like interference with parent–child contact.

Even after they reach adulthood, children in parental alienation cases may have no idea how they were identified as showing parental alienation, except for the simple fact that they wanted to avoid one parent. The young men interviewed for this chapter did not report any awareness of having been assessed in terms of the Five Factor Model, though they often knew many details of the judicial proceedings. Their ignorance may have had to do with their concentration on issues that were important to them as teenagers, such as permission to talk to friends or to use phones; it may also have come about in part because parents were prohibited from giving them information about planned future events. Even parents who were prepared to give their children the information they had, might have been without access to assessment information or found it too confusing or opaque to pass along.

The young men interviewees reported on their own attitudes and behavior and showed that they had met some of the criteria of the Five Factor Model. They acknowledged their desires to avoid contact with one parent, or at least, in Martin's case, to negotiate that contact.

The Five Factor Model notes that children in parental alienation cases not only avoid or denigrate one parent but, importantly, do not feel guilty about these behaviors. Certainly, none of the three interviewees appeared to feel guilt or remorse about their attitudes—nor does it seem reasonable to expect them to have such emotions. They reported distressing behaviors by a parent and their efforts to avoid being distressed by that parent's actions. Guilt or remorse would seem expectable only if there were the mindset that children must always obey and gratify parents no matter what the parents do, as long as the parents' actions are short of substantiable abuse or neglect. However reasonable the children's lack of remorse may be, there is no question that their attitude would easily be observed and interpreted as evidence of parental alienation.

The Five Factor Model limits identification of parental alienation cases to those where abuse or neglect are unsubstantiated. (Many allegations of abuse or neglect are not substantiated in spite of careful investigation; this outcome may mean that there was no abuse or neglect, or may simply mean that because of the passage of time or other factors it is not possible to know what occurred.) This chapter's interviewees did not necessarily know whether there had been investigations of abuse allegations by child protection authorities, or whether the allegations had been substantiated. In Quentin's case, he was quite young when he disclosed abuse to his stepmother and he did not report any details, but the fact that he did not see his mother for many years suggests that there was some substance to the allegations and that the Five Factor Model would not ordinarily have identified this as a parental alienation case. Jason reported ongoing physical and emotional abuse such as failure to seek needed medical care, but did not say that these events were reported or investigated. Martin also reported some physical conflict and a number of threats, but these do not seem to have been reported, so it is impossible to know whether there would have been substantiation of abuse of neglect in this case.

Only one detail given by an interviewee seems to suggest a further effort to identify parental alienation according to the Five Factor Model. This point is seen in Martin's interview, where he notes that there was concern about whether Martin's mother had told the children something troubling about their father. If she told the children this even though it had not happened, she would clearly be guilty of denigrating the father, a parental alienating behavior used to identify the family situation as involving parental alienation. If she communicated such an event and did so truthfully, the mother would still be considered to be parentalizing children, confiding to the children about the marriage, and badmouthing the other parent—all actions that would help identify the case as a parental alienation matter. (In fact, Martin only heard about this after he turned 18 and read the court transcripts.) As evaluators are not therapists, the effort to find out what the mother had told the children is likely to involve identification of parental alienation, not supportive treatment; if a therapist were to ask such questions, the goal could well be to support the children as they try to process this distressing information.

Adverse Experiences: Other Reasons for Children's Resistance to Contact with a Parent

The Five Factor Model for identification of parental alienation leaves open the possibility that a child's avoidance of one parent may not be a matter of parental alienation. If there is substantiated abuse or neglect, or if the preferred parent cannot be argued to have manipulated the children's attitudes, or if the children show none of the behaviors said to be "symptoms" of parental alienation, the avoidance should not be attributed to parental alienation, according to proponents of alienationism (Bernet, 2020; Freeman, 2020). Alienationist authors thus have implied that there may be non-parental alienation reasons for avoidance of a parent, but they have not proposed any such factors other than a history of abuse or neglect. Abuse and neglect have been described as "justified" reasons for avoidance, and other reasons reported by children appear to be regarded as unjustified—even assuming that the children are permitted to speak of their reasons.

Attention to reasons for avoidance, as shown in the interviews with Quentin, Jason, and Martin, suggests that children may have repeated adverse experiences with a parent, and that these may culminate in avoidance even though none of the experiences rise to the level of abuse. Just as a marriage may founder because of mild but repeated disturbing behaviors by one partner, a child's attitude toward a parent can become increasingly negative because of the parent's frightening, hostile, or unresponsive behavior, especially if the parent refuses to comply with the child's requests to stop.

In Quentin's case, the adverse experiences reported were all at the level of abuse. Quentin was quite young at the time of his original experiences with his mother and may not remember any events except the abuse that he disclosed at age 7 or 8. Jason, on the other hand, reported a range of adverse experiences with his father. Some of these, like refusing medical care for a broken nose, were at the level of abuse or neglect, but other events were not at that level. Jason reported that his father not only hit him and locked him outdoors but required that he do unnecessarily difficult tasks and took away money he had earned. Jason noted that he responded very badly to his father's suit for full custody because of the lengthy catalog of distressing behaviors and his fear of being at his father's mercy.

Martin presented a rather different history than the other two interviewees. He did not, in fact, refuse contact with his father, but stated his distress with the conflict and tension occurring during their visits. Martin tried to negotiate with his father and proposed an alternative parenting plan. He wanted to avoid the family meetings in which he was yelled at and not allowed to take a break from the discussion and allow tempers to cool. The father was not abusive or neglectful in any ordinary sense, but caused distress by a number of efforts apparently intended to "win" in the conflict with Martin. These efforts included threats with respect to money, to schooling, and to permission for Martin to do things he had proposed. They also involved a lengthy proposed code of conduct to which Martin was supposed to agree, and which appears to have been based on parental alienation concepts. Martin's father's behavior seems to have fallen into the realm of coercive control rather than abuse, but was nevertheless a reason for Martin's increasingly negative attitude.

Stepparents and Other Social Influences

Discussions of parental alienation often focus on the relationships between an avoidant child and each of the parents, as if there were no other relationships and no social context within which these relationships function.

This focus is not a reasonable one, as can be seen when we consider post-divorce dynamics and behavior for both parents.

Divorcing spouses may have been involved in extramarital affairs, and these may have been instrumental in causing the divorce and lasting ill feeling. Such affairs may or may not be maintained for long after the divorce and may or may not lead to remarriage, but the dynamics of these relationships are likely to affect parent–child relationships. Ongoing romantic relationships influence the amount of time available for parent–child contacts. They may limit the time during which the parent and the child are alone, as either the parent or the romantic partner may wish to combine the relationships in a marriage-like manner. The other parent, whether or not in a similar relationship, may be concerned (or even furiously angry) about the effect of the romantic partner on the child and on parenting. These issues can be exacerbated by remarriage, or the adults may be able to settle into some calmer mode of interacting. In all these cases, the parent's evident sexual activity can feel embarrassing, even humiliating, to a teenager who is just beginning to deal with their own sexual impulses.

In Quentin's case, the father had remarried and the stepmother played an important role in Quentin's life. He called her "mama" and had regarded her as his mother for years, and she was the person to whom he disclosed the abuse by his biological mother. She took a protective role when parental alienation was alleged by the biological mother. The biological mother also had remarried and brought her husband along to the intensive reunification therapy, where generally one might expect only the concerned biological parent to be present. Jason's father, too, had remarried (although the marriage did not last), and brought the new wife and her children to the intensive reunification therapy. Martin's father had a girlfriend who was not completely welcomed by the children.

Although it would seem excessive to demand that a divorcing parent remain celibate for years, there nevertheless seems to be no question that new partners change the parent–child dynamics and do not always do so in a positive way. The existence of new partnerships is a factor that needs to be considered as reasons for avoiding a parent are analyzed; it is a mistake to assume that only the original parent–child dyads are influencing child attitudes or that new relationships cannot "justify" a child's negative attitudes.

New romantic partners provide an obvious explanation for some parent–child conflicts, but other relationships may also be factors in avoidance of a parent. Grandparents and other people closely related to one of the parents may be eager to attack the other parent and may find parental alienation allegations a convenient method of doing this;

grandparents may be concerned that they will be excluded from contact with children because of their conflicts with one of the parents (in Martin's case, however, the grandparent loyalties did not follow the pattern one might expect). Martin's case provides additional examples of social influences from outside the family, including self-help books. Martin named the father's "life coach" as an influence. According to Martin, the father himself later admitted that the "life coach" had been influential.

Effects of Reunification Therapy

Intensive reunification therapies were employed in two of the cases described in this chapter and threatened in the third; the third case actually used some of the techniques proposed for "aftercare" of families who had been through reunification programs. Is it possible that the reunification programs themselves caused increasingly negative attitudes and increased avoidance of a parent by their child?

The reunification programs, as described by Quentin and Jason, used increased levels of coercive control with the intention of changing the children's attitudes in a positive direction. If, as was suggested above, experiences of coercive control are factors in causing avoidance of a parent, this strategy would seem unlikely to be an effective one—on the contrary, it would seem more likely that controlling approaches would exacerbate negative feelings. Reunification programs prohibit children from talking about the negative events in the past that are their reasons for avoiding a parent and that most children want to explain and to receive apologies for. Reunification programs tell children that they have been brainwashed and that their explanations are simply borrowed from their preferred parents, messages that are at distinct odds with adolescents' sense of autonomy and personal dignity. In short, reunification programs repeat the parental mistakes that may have caused avoidance, and in doing so are possible causes of increased avoidance of the parent who has forced the child to participate.

Quentin disliked the "family meeting" protocol taught during the intensive program and used as part of "aftercare" (this was even used by Martin's father, although that family did not attend a reunification program). The interviewees felt that family meetings were artificial and not part of any normal family interactions. Again, they experienced "family meetings" as controlling methods and resented them rather than feeling more positively about the parent who had sought this kind of treatment.

An aspect of reunification therapy that was quite distressing to the children was the withholding of information. They were sent to reunification programs without information about what would happen. Even when told about the 90-day no-contact provision, they did not understand that there would be no contact with the other parent, siblings, or even friends until the program "worked"—that is, until the children themselves took pleasure in their relationship with the hitherto rejected parent and stopped wanting the preferred parent. The withholding of information created further resentment and anxiety rather than helping create an improved relationship.

Both the reunification programs and the "aftercare" events used isolation of children as a strategy to create a positive relationship with an avoided parent. Not only was the child prevented from contact with the preferred parent, but they were isolated from siblings, grandparents, and friends, all of whom are important figures in adolescent personality development. The resulting loneliness and sense of social restriction potentially influenced increased negative feelings toward the avoided parent and any other adults seen as instrumental in this situation.

In the absence of any strong evidence that reunification programs are effective forms of treatment, these examples of distress caused by the programs suggest strongly that children exposed to these treatments may feel an increasing desire to avoid the parent who has brought them to the programs. Indeed, none of the interviewees for this chapter, now young men, has a good relationship with the parent who wanted the program.

What Is the Timeline and What Does it Mean?

Attempts to identify parental alienation cases include the criterion that the children once had good relationships with both parents, but that at some time following the divorce, the children began to prefer one parent and to avoid the other. This timeline is taken to suggest that changes toward preference and avoidance must have occurred because of the influence of the preferred parent.

There are several problems with this assumption. The first is that it is difficult to ascertain what a parent–child relationship was like in years gone by, if the first real indications of avoidance did not occur until the teen years. Some reunification programs require parents (especially preferred parents) to submit photographs and recordings of happy occasions in the past—birthday parties, trips to the beach, celebrations of sports or other successes—and these are used to argue that good relationships existed in the past. However, such records clearly indicate only that there were some happy times and cannot present an over-all picture of a parent–child relationship, as few parents photograph or record children's tears and distress or show themselves screaming at or striking a child. In addition, children's needs for qualities of relationships with their parents change as they mature, and the parent who was comforting and nurturing for the 5-year-old and behaves in the same ways to a teenager can be experienced by the older child as controlling and suffocating, as what was once positive becomes negative; if the earlier positive relationship does not change with time, it may press a child toward avoidance.

A common misunderstanding about children's development is that changes occur only because of things adults do. In this view, parents and teachers are seen as the sole or at least primary shapers of a child's developmental outcome, though outcomes may also be attributed to experiences like poverty, war, or disease. Such a perspective ignores the role of biologically determined maturation as children move toward adulthood.

The teenage years, especially, are a period of movement toward increased autonomy and independence, lessening of intense affection for parents, and increasing involvement with peers and potential romantic partners. All of these maturational changes draw teenagers away from childish relationships with parents and sensitize them to controlling or disapproving parental attitudes. Adolescent idealism is another factor that makes teens intolerant of negative behavior by a parent. As a result, teens may be strongly predisposed to avoid a parent who does not meet their standards of adult behavior or who appears to reject the child's newly developed attitudes and abilities. Strong parent avoidance or preference may grow without any action on the part of the preferred parent.

References

Bernet, W. (2020). Introduction to parental alienation. In D. Lorandos & W. Bernet (Eds.), *Parental alienation—science and law* (pp. 5–43). Charles C. Thomas.

Clawar, S., & Rivlin, B. (1991). *Children held hostage*. American Bar Association.

Covey, S. (2013). *The seven habits of highly effective people*. Simon & Schuster.

Doughty, J., & Drew, M. (2022). History of the parental alienation belief system. In J. Mercer & M. Drew (Eds.), *Challenging parental alienation* (pp. 21–39). Routledge.

Freeman, B. (2020). The psychosocial assessment of contact refusal. In D. Lorandos & W. Bernet (Eds.), *Parental alienation—Science and law* (pp.44–81). Charles C. Thomas.

Gardner, R. (1985). Recent trends in divorce litigation. *Academy Forum*, 29(2), 3–7.

5 Young Women Talk About Allegations of Parental Alienation

Readers may wonder why this book gives separate chapters to young men and young women who as boys and girls have experienced allegations of parental alienation. It's easy to assume that kids are kids and have similar experiences, but in fact boys and girls have dissimilar experiences with adolescence itself. Gender differences during adolescence cannot be ignored—and, as we will see, those differences themselves can affect children's behavior and relationships with their parents. Some characteristics particular to girls should be kept in mind when reading the narratives of the four girls interviewed for this chapter.

Physical Changes and Parent–Child Relationships: Sex Differences

A very noticeable difference between boys and girls involves their paths to physical maturity, puberty, and their full adult height. Girls are on a faster track to reproductive maturity than boys are. On the average, girls experience puberty two years earlier than boys do. They develop breasts and begin to menstruate, and very soon have achieved their adult height, while boys of the same age may still be prepubescent children who are inches short of their adult height.

Girls' early maturation means that they can appear to be older than they are, especially if they use make-up and clothing to achieve that effect. Adults may find that girls' appearance creates confusion about what can be expected of girls and how they should be treated. Whether divorced or not, parents may become anxious about the social "messages" girls seem to be sending about their sexuality and about the responses of older boys and men to a girl who seems sexually inviting. Parental anxiety about pubescent girls may be expressed in increased efforts at discipline and exercise of authority, which result in heightened resistance and rebelliousness by the girls. Parents of boys, on the other

DOI: 10.4324/9781003454793-5

hand, may want to keep their children under strong control, but are less concerned about how others see and respond to them.

Along with puberty, girls develop sensitivity about their bodies and often find menstrual hygiene awkward and difficult to talk about, especially to their fathers. Although boys soon find that masturbation and "wet dreams" are embarrassing, these phenomena are easier to hide than menstruation is. Boys do not generally need practical adult help in dealing with pubertal events, but girls often do, especially as menstrual hygiene supplies need to be bought. Girls are likely to depend on their mothers, older sisters, or aunts for help of this kind.

Mood, Emotion, and Parent–Child Relationships

Children may experience depression, and girls after puberty are increasingly likely to be depressed. As is the case for older people, adolescents experience loneliness, a sense of worthlessness, and self-blame as aspects of depression. However, irritability is the most frequent symptom of depression in children and adolescents (Fava et al., 2010). Irritable children (or family members of any age) are likely to experience critical or angry responses from family and friends, especially if irritable reactions are not recognized as part of depression but are "read" as self-centeredness or even as symptomatic of narcissism (Yong et al., 2022). Displays of irritability may get children punished by being sent to their rooms or scolded for thinking themselves important enough to complain about trivia. These negative responses worsen depression and irritability in a vicious circle which girls are more likely to experience because of their increased tendency to depression after puberty.

The connections between adolescent depression and better or worse parent–child relationships are complex and far from completely understood. Depression impacts parent–child relationships, but parent–child relationships simultaneously affect depression, and these outcomes may work differently for boys and for girls. Highly supportive relationships with fathers are thought to help protect both boys and girls from depression, but it may also be that the same-sex parent has a greater importance (Brouillard et al., 2018).

Allegations of Parental Alienation: Narratives of Four Girls

Four young women were interviewed about their experiences with allegations of parental alienation that occurred during their adolescent years. As was the case for the young men whose stories were told in the previous chapter, real names are not used here, and other identifying material is altered or omitted. Three of the young women live in the United States and one is in Canada. One is an only child and the others have brothers, sisters, or both, but as it happens, the interviewee is the eldest in every case. All experienced one of the usual reunification therapies, that is, Family Bridges, Transitioning Families, Overcoming Barriers, Family Reflections, Turning Points for Families, or High Road to Reunification. All of the young women made contact with the author either in the course of their own legal proceedings or out of a wish to help educate the public about the nature of reunification therapies. All participated in the interviews by Zoom, and in some cases answered further questions by email or by telephone.

Melanie's Story

Melanie's divorce story began when she was 8 years old. While she was going for a walk with her father, it happened that a phone fell out of her jacket pocket. It had been put there accidentally, and contained the number of her mother's boyfriend—up to that point, not known to the father. Melanie recalled in the interview that the mother had previously taken the children with her to visit this boyfriend but had made them wait in the car for long periods.

After the parents separated, Melanie and her brother had a week on/week off schedule with mother and father. Melanie felt that her mother concentrated on getting remarried and on "making Dad look terrible". The children did not like their mother's house or the school they were attending, and their father was trying to arrange for them to go to a better school.

In the interview, Melanie recalled that her mother told the children that their father and all his family were "awful". The mother also dug her fingernails into their arms for punishment, and this led to a referral to a therapist. The children found themselves uncomfortable with this therapist but went to her for a year.

After Melanie's mother remarried, she wrote a letter saying that the children could live wherever they wanted to. However, not long afterward, Melanie, who was now in high school, was called to the school guidance counselor's office. She was told that there was a court order that her mother would pick her up after school, and that her mother was suing for custody of Melanie and her brother.

In court, the judge would not let Melanie or her brother speak, but listened to the testimony of the first therapist they had gone to, whom they had not seen for years. The children were told that there would be 90 days of no contact with their father; alternatively, they could go to foster care or a juvenile facility, and their father to jail.

Melanie and her brother started to see a third counselor who was in the same practice as the first two they had seen. This therapist told the children they were to get on a plane and go to a western state to have reunification therapy. The mother, stepfather, and therapist all went along.

For three days, they all sat in the lawyer's office that was the treatment venue. The earlier threats of "consequences" were reiterated. There were nine people present: two lawyers, two reunification therapy staff members, the mother, stepfather, and therapist, and Melanie and her brother. The court order was read out but the children were not allowed to read it.

They did "worksheets" in which they circled words that were traits of particular people. They learned to have family meetings, which they would be doing once a week; in these meetings, they had to say something positive about each person. The treatment focused strongly on watching videos. These included "Welcome Back, Pluto", a presentation with the message that someone who has left a family may happily be brought back in; a video on the obedience study by Stanley Milgram, which emphasizes that people may be persuaded to act against their own intentions; "The Wave", which describes how Hitler persuaded Germans to do horrible things; and "The Butterfly Man", a film concerned with the sense of acceptance (and related in their discussion to Melanie's mother's feeling that she was not accepted by the children). Melanie also recalled a video that involved children lying about child sexual abuse. There were discussions between videos, and the children were reminded of "consequences" when they argued with their mother.

The program director said that Melanie's phone should be taken away for a month, but Melanie argued with him and pointed out that she and her brother had done everything they were told to do. The director relented but said Melanie could not use the Internet. Melanie said she just wanted things to be normal, but the director replied that "this is the new normal".

The children were in their mother's custody, but according to Melanie they "put on an act" so they could go back to their father. Melanie described herself at this time as "scared to death". She kept a hidden journal and wrote in it at school. She was told that her phone was scanned. When her boyfriend kissed her at a football game, her mother immediately called her and asked why, so Melanie knew someone was watching her. She was afraid she would be watched on the security cameras at school.

After about six months, the court no-contact order was vacated and the children were back with their father. Melanie does not know exactly what happened. Her father had her journal and it was not put into evidence but Melanie thinks it might have been used for leverage. According to Melanie, the therapists and reunification therapy staff did not want depositions taken from the children.

Melanie's mother is blocked from the now-adult children's phones. She apologized to the children for everything but refused to unseal the case; she also sued the children for attorney's fees.

Amy's Story

Amy's parents divorced when she was 7 or 8. Subsequently, Amy alternated spending weeks with father and with mother, and this 50/50 plan worked smoothly enough. By the time Amy was 14 or 15, however, she was tired of hauling her school and sports equipment back and forth from one house to the other. Amy says she wanted some choice, some flexibility, and a "home base". She proposed to spend school weeks with her mother and to go to her father for weekends. This was not well received by Amy's father.

Amy's father's reactions, and Amy's preferences, made more sense when Amy explained the background. Amy's father remarried soon after the divorce, and Amy found her stepmother abrupt, strict, and critical. (The stepmother had not wanted to have children.) Amy felt safer and more secure with her mother. Her father did not do a lot of care for the children; the stepmother made lunches and drove to school. The mother and father did not talk to each other well and were always abrupt and cold at transfers. (Amy said she did not know whether the marriage had been similar.)

Amy's father had strict house rules. For example, clothing he bought for the children was to remain at his house and to be marked D for "Dad". Amy says she wanted more stability and that was why she asked for a changed parenting plan, but the strict attitudes at her father's house may have been a factor in her feelings of discomfort.

Amy was at her mother's house during a Christmas break when she could not sleep because of a sense of stress. She told her mother what she was thinking—that she would like to have a different schedule. The mother said they could think about what to propose.

Amy's father was not pleased by Amy's proposal that she spend school weeks at her mother's house, which she presented to him a couple of weeks later, when again she could not sleep. He interpreted this as meaning that the children wanted no contact with him, which was, Amy says, not at all the case. He got lawyers to work very quickly, although parental alienation was not mentioned for a long time afterward. Amy feels that her father simply made assumptions about what was happening and did not ask for explanations or clarifications.

After Amy made her statement, her father sought character witnesses, who said he was a good father and they did not see the problem. One witness was Amy's brother's martial arts teacher at a school the father also attended. The other, however, was an afterschool teacher in the school system, who Amy had thought was her mother's friend. Amy spoke of "corruption" when talking about these character witnesses.

The conflicts Amy was experiencing went on unchanged. She reported that she once heard her stepmother yelling at the father that he must make Amy treat her with respect. Amy also described a vague memory that there had been a threat of contempt of court against the mother. Amy and her brother ran away several times over the next years, but always told where they were going. Amy thought there had been a contempt threat when the mother did not send the children back to the father's house when they came to her. A police escort took them at least once. (Amy's stepmother had been a police officer, and Amy wondered whether the escorts were friends of hers.)

Amy was feeling greatly stressed. Her insomnia was worse and she was very anxious. She was planning to go to a friend's cabin but got palpitations and chest pains. Her mother took the 15-year-old Amy to the emergency room but the problem was diagnosed as anxiety. The chest pains stopped but for the next two years Amy continued to have palpitations and insomnia. When one symptom would stop, another would start.

Amy's mother had remarried and her stepdad was now also involved in the parenting discussion. Amy had many talks with her mother and felt compelled to tell her everything; she experienced palpitations and a feeling of guilt. Amy's stepfather became a leader of "battle strategies" and talked about what the father's lawyers were doing. The mother also had a lawyer by this time. They had to sell the house to get lawyer's fees and move into a rental house, which meant that they had to get rid of their cats, a devastating event for Amy's brother.

Amy started dating her high school boyfriend in secret, because her mother and stepfather had forbidden her to date until she was 17. When the dating was revealed, Amy's mother seems to have been uncertain what to do. She took away Amy's phone as punishment, then gave it back; she "grounded" Amy, then ungrounded her.

Amy and her brother had phone calls with their father and a meeting at a restaurant. There were therapy sessions too, in which Amy felt she was looked on as "some dumb kid". She walked out of the final session. She decided the therapy was not working, but recognized that there was still some time to go before the custody trial.

Amy had previously felt that school was a "nice, neutral" place, but now began to feel uncomfortable about school too. She felt her father was too involved in the school and wanted to change to a different school for grade 10, where there would be a special program she wanted. Her father and stepmother preferred another school that was farther from the mother's house. Although there was no fight about this, Amy felt her father did not hear what she was saying.

Soon after this, the custody trial took place. Amy's mother and stepfather were told not to give information to the children. Her mother testified first. Some weeks later, her stepfather made an excuse to get the children into the car and took them to the courthouse. In the courtroom, the judge announced that he was giving full custody to Amy's father and that the children were to go to intensive reunification therapy. The judge also stated that Amy's mother had no control any more.

The children were put into separate cars and driven to the airport. As they approached airport security, the stepfather came and said the mother was appealing the decision. There was a four or five hour standoff outside security, with parents on phones to their lawyers (but as Amy now says, no one asked the kids how they were doing.) The appeal was successful for one week.

Amy's mother and stepfather took Amy and her brother home and now felt they could explain more. They described what they knew of the reunification program and tried to prepare the children. By this time, the father was speaking of parental alienation as an explanation of Amy's request. For Amy's mother to talk about the reunification program was to be taken as evidence of parental alienation. Amy did not understand what the program would involve and thought it would be herself and a therapist "hounding her for hours"—in fact, she later felt that the program was not as bad as she expected. Although it was very unpleasant, the program was a bit more tolerable than Amy's expectation that she would be alone with a therapist who would berate her for a whole day.

Amy's mother's appeal pause was only good for a week, and at the end of that time the stepfather was told to bring the children to the police station. The children were told they could not talk to their mother or stepfather. Their phones and credit cards were taken. Amy was allowed to call her work and say she would be away for two weeks, and to text her boyfriend. The children were then driven in separate cars to separate airports. They met in a major city from which they drove to see their grandfather and also went on a "family vacation" to a well-known resort, reversing the usual reunification therapy plan in which the "vacation" follows the treatment.

At another resort, Amy, her brother, and their father and stepmother met with the three therapists who would do the reunification program. A primary rule for the program was that there should be a moratorium on discussion of the past. For five days, they sat on a couch "as a family" and watched videos presented by the therapists. According to Amy, the content of the videos showed mothers as alienators—she wonders now if there was a matching set for fathers. They played a word association game in which they had to say something positive about the parent. The children were told of the bad outcomes to be expected if they did not come to terms with their father. They would become addicts and their lives would fall apart. (This was significant to Amy, who had always been afraid of doing drugs, even prescription medication.) In the evenings, they sometimes went to play miniature golf. There was no individual therapy. Amy was trying just to get through the program and not to confront anyone.

On the last day, the children were asked in a family meeting if they wanted to say anything, although the moratorium on speaking of the past was still on. Amy brought up an incident in which her father had pushed her. In the interview, she said her father "looked like 'you don't remember that right.'" Soon, the therapist turned to Amy and said, "You are uncooperative. We will kick you out. You will be on [your brother's] no-contact list." (Amy cried while telling this, for the first time in the interview.)

Amy felt that the separation from her brother was "the worst thing that happened". She could not even say goodbye to him privately.

Amy was taken to a separate room and told that she could choose either to go to her aunt, thousands of miles away, or to her grandmother in her home town. She chose the grandmother, and, once near home, she managed to find a *pro bono* lawyer and to get in touch with her mother. The lawyer asked Amy about personal effects of her experiences on her, for example weight loss. In court, the lawyer put forward the argument that Amy was now 17½ and the judge agreed that she could go back to her mother's house. Amy's brother remained with the father and was to have no contact with Amy or her mother.

Asked about the long-term effects of these events, Amy felt that her relationship with her mother had been ruined. There continued to be complexities surrounding the father's custody of Amy's brother. Once or twice a year, Amy and her mother would "lie in wait" for the brother on his route home from school. Her mother and stepfather were angry that the brother did not run away. Amy felt that her mother resented Amy's having left her brother behind in the father's custody. She also felt that it was not possible to talk to her mother normally. The stepfather's conduct was also problematic; he told Amy he had met secretly with the brother and told him that Amy and their mother had been killed in a car accident. Subsequently he told the boy that this was not true, but that it might happen so the boy should run away and be with them while he could. Amy felt that neither her mother nor her father acted to protect the children against the stepparents' behavior.

Amy continued to live with her mother and stepfather until her early 20s, but disliked the stepfather's controlling nature. She eventually moved out and has not seen them for about five years. She is back in contact with her brother and sees him often. Amy is now seeing a new therapist who encourages her to have compassion but to "demand accountability".

Polly's Story

Polly was only two years old when her parents divorced. She spent Thursdays and alternate weekends with her father, and there were occasional disagreements about this schedule. Polly spent most of her time with her mother, who had a full-time job; there were baby-sitters and sometimes people who lived in, in order to help with Polly's care. Polly's mother drove her to the private school she attended for primary school.

When Polly was about 12, her mother had a man—possibly an old college friend—staying at the house. Polly said he watched "inappropriate" TV and did not take care of his own hygiene. Polly talked to her mother about this man and her mother understood the issues; Polly also mentioned the man to her father.

By the time Polly was 14 and in 7th grade, there was increased conflict with her mother, who continued to have full custody. Polly asked to spend more time with her father. Some decisions that were not what Polly wanted were made about a new school for her to attend. The court advised her to have meetings with her parents about this. The parents would check in with their attorneys from time to time, and the attorneys advised meeting to discuss conflicts. Initially Polly felt that she did have a voice in these meetings, but as conflict increased and communication lessened, she no longer felt that way.

Polly's parents were in conflict on several points and each wanted to win. The school decision was one problem, as Polly's father wanted her to go to the school he had attended. The mother wanted Polly to go to a Roman Catholic school. Although Polly's mother was not herself a practicing Catholic, she had had Polly baptized at age 14 (her father did not know about this). However, Polly did not attend church or go to confirmation classes as might have been expected.

Polly attended the Catholic school for one year, as her mother wanted, but then said she wanted to change schools. In the interview, Polly said that at this time her mother became more "hostile" (though Polly was not sure this was the right word). Polly continued to want more time with her father.

Polly's mother decided unilaterally to take Polly to a counselor, although this decision was supposed to be made jointly by the parents. She also went to the counselor and told her side of the story before Polly ever saw the counselor. The court disqualified that counselor, and 8 or 9 others were tried before Polly found one she liked (all the others were disqualified for interference). The preferred counselor testified in court about Polly's conflicts with her mother and noted that the mother had several times "badmouthed" the father, saying that he was "evil" and Polly should not trust him.

Polly, now 15 years old, stopped going home with her mother. In the interview, she described the situation as "horrible" and said she could not focus on school. She felt calm only when with her father. There were altercations at the school when Polly's mother arrived to pick her up and Polly refused. She described her mother as "manic", yelling and calling Polly a liar. The mother also sometimes arrived so late that Polly would have called her father to come pick her up. Eventually, Polly's mother stopped coming to pick her up.

Polly's parents went back to court when the mother filed a motion for a new order. Polly was allowed to testify, but the court said that she needed to have a relationship with her mother. A court-ordered report said that Polly's father was alienating her from her mother.

Polly knew that the counselor had already decided and recommended one intensive reunification therapy. The court refused that one, and a different reunification program was suggested but was not considered by the court. The court ordered that Polly continue to see her mother, and she spent spring break of that year at her mother's house.

There was no court order for Polly to attend the newly suggested reunification program, a highly unusual situation. Most reunification programs require a court order for attendance, but in this case the mother decided on her own to have Polly go there. A friend of the mother helped out by making plane and hotel reservations. The friend was planning to meet them, go to a resort, and have a vacation together after the reunification therapy.

Two youth transport service workers came to the house and pushed Polly against the door. She was screaming to the neighbors and was told not to speak, with the threat of handcuffs. The transporters told Polly that her mother had hired them and they were to take her to the reunification program. Polly argued that this was contrary to the custody order and demanded to see their documents, but she was shown only a blank piece of paper with the judge's signature at the top. Hoping to let people know what was happening, Polly asked the transporters to turn off her phone. She knew her grandmother was expecting her to call and thought the grandmother might figure out that something was wrong if the phone was off.

The transporters said it was time to leave. They took Polly's phone and keys but missed her Apple watch that she could use to call. They drove to the airport and returned their rental car, then started to go through security. The transporters warned Polly not to make a scene, and she did not, although security asked questions because the transporters were not Polly's parents and she had visibly been crying and had a puffy face. Nevertheless, they were allowed through security. The woman transporter subsequently stood outside the cubicle as Polly used the toilet.

After the plane landed in a major city in another state, Polly and the transporters were allowed to get off first. They were met by airport police and by a phone contact with Polly's father. Polly's mother's friend was also on the way. Polly was not sure how her father knew where to go, but thought that since she had an account with the airline he might have been able to use that for information. Also, the grandmother had been upset when the phone was off and had called the father. The police let Polly talk to her father on the phone but were shown documents indicating that the transporters had custody. The police walked Polly to the exit and were sympathetic but said they could do nothing—Polly had to go with the transporters.

Polly and the transporters went to the rental car and drove to a hotel. The transporters talked about the situation and tried to de-escalate and to rationalize what was happening. They said they do transporting all the time, but focused on mental illness as the reason young people needed to be transported. They said they did not usually go to reunification program places and told a pathetic story of a suicidal girl. Polly responded that she was not "bad" or acting out. She asked the transporters, "what would you do if you were kidnapped?". They responded, "you should be ashamed".

At the hotel, Polly went into the bathroom and called her father with the Apple watch the transporters had missed. Later, she went to sleep, with both transporters in the room all night.

In the morning, they had breakfast and checked out. When they got to the rental car, Polly's father was there with the local police. Polly's mother arrived with the program director, who was angry and told Polly to be quiet.

Polly told the police that taking her to the program was against the court order. She asked, "what if they drugged me?". She was distraught and wearing tear-stained clothes, but the police said the problem was outside their jurisdiction. They added that it was in Polly's best interests to go with her mother and the program director. Polly's mother yelled and the program director told the father to stay away.

The transporters pushed Polly into the car and the woman pinned her down and yelled at her. They drove for a couple of miles and then parked by a culvert. Again, the transporters told Polly she should be ashamed. They said "you're such a manipulator" and spent an hour trying to make Polly apologize. They were waiting until the program director called with instructions. Next, they drove to a shopping mall where Polly's mother and the program director were waiting. They went in to have lunch and the program director told the transporters to pat Polly down; this time they found the Apple watch she had concealed.

Polly was then driven to the bed-and-breakfast where the program was to take place. The program director introduced herself, acted "cheery and happy", and told Polly "we're so glad you're here". She told Polly to tell them if she thought she might harm herself or others. A therapist was also present. Polly was told about the program and informed that she would be "graded" every day and that what happened one day would help determine what happened the next day in the 3-to-5-day program. The program director asked the transporters to stay while she described the program, then dismissed them when she began to show videos. Later there was dinner and the program director stayed all night in case Polly was "bad".

On the second day of the program, there were more videos and a focus on terms like cooperation, communication, alienation, and distrust. Some of the videos were about cognitive errors of the sort that might be created by "brainwashing" and about problems caused by unthinking obedience; there was also a slide show created by a psychologist proponent of the reunification program. Polly listed the titles of the videos as "Butterfly Circus". "The Wave", "Darren Brown: Mind Control", "Animal Heaven", and "The Invisible Gorilla".

The program director said Polly had been "brainwashed" and must have a moratorium on talking about the past. Polly disagreed with this and stated that it was her mother who had caused her to be unhappy. The program director said not to say that, but to embark on a new relationship. Polly and her mother were supposed to talk about how they were feeling and to compliment each other.

There were separate bedrooms for Polly and her mother. Polly described camera cubes in the kitchen but did not think there were any in bedrooms, bath, or living room. However, the program director told stories about kids being caught on camera doing inappropriate things.

Polly and her mother practiced their roles and made lists of things each would do. They were to make eye contact, address each other directly, use the right tone, compliment each other, and be sincere. The program director asked about pets, especially the horse that Polly had had since she was two years old. Polly had always felt that her horse was her "safe place" and did not want to answer questions about the horse or who was taking care of her. She claimed that she did not know the names or addresses. But the program director replied that she must give the information right away or she would have to stay longer at the program, and Polly gave in and answered these and other questions about friends and activities.

The program director admonished Polly that she must speak up or stay longer at the program. Polly pointed out that she had a guardian *ad litem* (GAL) and therefore would have a voice in court. The program director contradicted this: "No, you have no voice". She threatened to have the transporters back if Polly did not cooperate and said she could be restrained and taken somewhere a lot worse. She referred to "therapeutic schools" in Utah, which Polly knew to have been publicized for mistreatment of children.

Polly started talking about how she needed to call her friends and finally the program director permitted this. She managed to communicate to her friends that something was wrong. During the next week, which was supposed to be a "vacation", Polly went along with everything. She and her mother drove around the city and when Polly found a way to go alone to a restroom, she got to use a stranger's phone to call her aunt and tell where the B and B was located.

At this point, the COVID pandemic began and Polly's mother cancelled their flight back home, even though under the court order Polly was now supposed to go to her father. Polly argued and said she had to go back to school. The program director came and threatened to bring the transporters back. Much commotion ensued, with Polly and her mother going back and forth to a hotel arranged by the mother's friend and again to the B and B. The police and Polly's father were at the B and B. Polly's mother had no custody documents and the police read out the court order and warned the mother of possible felony kidnapping. While the police blocked the others, Polly and her father went to his car and left. Polly described her mother at this time as "berserk", flailing and stamping. Nevertheless, in her interview Polly noted that the court ordered her back with her mother and that she had no option but to run away, which she did. The remainder of her story is not presently for publication.

Vivian's Story

Vivian was 8 years old and in 3rd grade when her parents divorced. They lived in a small town in the Midwestern United States, where divorce was uncommon and much gossip followed.

To Vivian's father's displeasure, her mother was given 60% parenting time. The father encouraged Vivian to ask the guardian *ad litem* to make the division 50/50. Vivian described this as "guilt-tripping" and said she did it because she hated to see her parents hurting. The court agreed to the 50/50 plan. In the interview, Vivian said she did not remember what the rationale for this decision was, but she remembered that she asked her therapist if it was a good idea.

Two years later, Vivian's mother remarried. Her new husband was a professional with a practice in another state. Vivian and her younger sister liked him. Vivian's father hated him, though, and told the girls that their mother did not love them, but only the new husband. The father also made derogatory remarks about the man's ethnicity, which was different from his own. The girls wanted to move to be with their mother and their new stepfather; the mother had not yet made the move permanently but maintained a place to live where the daughters were.

By the time Vivian was finishing 6th grade, her mother was preparing to move to be with her new husband. The girls wanted to go too. According to Vivian, her father was angry and began physical and sexual abuse. But Vivian did not disclose because she did not want to get her father "in trouble". The court ruled against letting Vivian and her sister move with their mother, who maintained an apartment near the girls and had them with her week on/week off for the next two years. Vivian's father remarried at about this time.

Vivian still did not tell about the abuse. As she said in the interview, she did not "see a path forward". If she disclosed, there might be "a big fight", which she did not want. However, she felt her father was normalizing the abuse. He pushed Vivian's sister and grabbed her by the hair, as well as slamming Vivian into a wall. As for sexualized behavior, according to Vivian her father "groped" her, walked into the bathroom when she was in the shower, and told her to sit and talk to him when he was showering. He would unlock the bathroom door to get in.

Because of the arrangements for the girls, Vivian's mother was working only 50% of the time and could no longer afford lawyer's fees. The court again refused to allow the girls to move out of state. Vivian now "broke down" and disclosed what her father had been doing. She was terrified going back to his house. He had "gotten wind" of her complaints and now began to talk about parental alienation for the first time. The guardian *ad litem* told the girls "sometimes we have to do things we don't want to do."

The girls were at this time (the end of Vivian's 9th grade year) having one weekend a month with their mother in the state where they lived, another in the state the mother had moved to. Returning to their father's state after one weekend, they got off the plane and sat down in the terminal. Their father sent security to get them. Vivian told the policewoman what had been happening and she said, "that's abuse". The policewoman took the girls to the airport police station and they were allowed to stay with their mother or with their mother's friend while a child protective services investigation began. In a phone conversation, the case manager threatened the girls that they would be put in foster care.

Child protective services did an interview with Vivian's father while a detective watched through a one-way mirror. They were unable to confirm sexual abuse (unsurprising, because Vivian's statements did not involve physical penetration or anything that would leave evidence).

After Vivian's 9th grade year, the girls went for reunification therapy at a therapist's office. (Vivian called this "reunification therapy lite".) Their mother, whom they had been visiting in another state, dropped them off at the therapist's office. They were supposed to be there for an hour and then go on to their father's house. They tried to tell the therapist what had been happening, but felt they got no response. The girls would not get up to go. They were at the therapist's office from 9am until after 6 and were given no food or water. The therapist threatened that they would be sent to foster care and said they would probably be sexually assaulted when they were there.

They attended office reunification therapy with their father; the therapist was the father's personal therapist. When they told the therapist what their father had done, the father stated that he had been assaulted by his Cub Scout leader, so the girls should just forget the events the way he did. The therapist gave the girls a to-do list with items generated by the father, such as to stop talking about the abuse.

Vivian and her sister (now 15 and 13 years old) ended up "couch surfing" with friends of their father for the whole summer. There was a no-contact order against their mother. The court then let them go to live with a friend of their mother. The girls were afraid that if they went to school their father would come and pick them up there, so they did not go to school for the first two weeks of the year.

In the summer following Vivian's 10th grade year, a new reunification therapy order was made. Vivian's mother had not been allowed to be present at the court proceedings, so she did not know that the girls were ordered to an intensive reunification program in a western state. As instructed, their mother dropped them at the courthouse and left their bags with security. The case manager told the girls just to do what they were told. Youth transport service workers were there, and escorted by security, took the girls to separate cars. They were locked in "like prisoners" and threatened with worse if they did not cooperate. The transporters did not let them close bathroom doors. Vivian was told she could have dinner with her sister if she was "good". (Unfortunately, this dinner led to a bout of food poisoning.)

Next day, the girls were flown to another state where the reunification therapy was to take place. They met the program director, a psychologist known to have lost his professional license. The transporters accidentally took Vivian to the office of an associated lawyer, but then they went to a hotel conference room. Their father and his wife were there. The therapy leader read out parts of the court order. The girls stated why they did not feel safe. They were told that there was a moratorium on discussing the past history and that there would be a 90-day no-contact order against their mother. This was the first time they had heard the term "parental alienation".

The girls refused to cooperate on the first day of the program. Vivian felt their father was "painted" as a victim and the girls were blamed. The case manager threatened the girls with wilderness therapy, foster care, and even institutionalization, warning them that they might be sexually assaulted at some places they could be sent. They had to write a letter to their mother stating that they had chosen separation from her and wilderness therapy over the reunification program.

The girls slept in the same room, with the door open to their father and stepmother's room, and they were able to talk. They felt the reunification therapy staff could get away with anything and decided they must "fake it until you make it". But they found it was difficult to fake their reactions. Watching the usual videos, Vivian tried to listen and see if the messages could really be true. She felt the real message was "don't trust your own memories or sense of safety". Vivian told the therapists they were doing "reverse parental alienation", a communication that was not well received.

Asked in the Zoom interview what the goal of the treatment was, and what the girls would have to do to get out, Vivian said she thought it was to "form kids into the perfect victim for abuse". No one would believe them. When the therapists saw that Vivian was depressed, they took her into a small room and told her that if she was depressed she was not working hard enough.

At the end of the program, the girls answered questionnaires while staff members walked around behind them. The questions asked included "how did you feel you were treated at the workshop?" and "how is your relationship with your father now?".

After a "family vacation" near the program site, the girls went back to their father's house. Vivian was now 16½. She hoped the 90-day no-contact period would not be extended. For the first six weeks, the girls were not allowed to be alone, to close doors, or to have screen use. They had regular family meetings and watched videos similar to those at the treatment program. Vivian had to show "prosocial behavior" and could not just stay in her room. She was isolated from her friends but after six weeks was allowed to volunteer at the church nursery.

Vivian said the abuse continued. She could not tell anyone and could not escape if her father was angry. He would tell the girls that they had better be good because he was going to be talking to the reunification program director. When Vivian and her sister asked about the no-contact period, their father became angry.

Unlike some children in these situations, Vivian and her sister did not go to an "aftercare" provider. It was advised that they see such a person in another state, but the court did not agree. They saw a local therapist who realized the problem was coercive control and abuse; the therapist had initially believed the allegations of parental alienation, but turned around after seeing the facts of the case. Still, it was nine months before the girls saw their mother. Eventually, after various decisions by the court and the case manager, the girls moved out of state to live with their mother and stepfather.

Vivian says she now occasionally gets emails from her father, and he says he would make different decisions if it were to do over again.

Discussion

Although their ages at the time of the parental alienation allegations were similar, the girls who were interviewed could be expected to be closer to physical maturity than the boys discussed in the preceding chapter. This factor could affect their relationships with both fathers and mothers, and could possibly be read as meaning that the girls were ready to "reject" parents in favor of peers and romantic partners, or as meaning that the girls were possible sources of anxiety over either pregnancy or allegations of sexual abuse by parents. Although boys' reproductive maturity and sexual lives also create concerns for parents, those worries are generally less direct than those focused on girls, as boys' parents may feel that girls' families will have to bear the burden of unwanted pregnancies.

Other than matters of physical maturation, the boys and girls interviewed were rather similar to each other. Notably, they were all either oldest or only children. Those who were oldest expressed much concern about their younger siblings who were caught up in the allegations of parental alienation. Protection of a younger sibling may have been one motive for resistance to the wishes of a rejected parent.

Were These Interviewees Typical of Girls in Parental Alienation Cases?

As was the case for the young men interviewees, it is not possible to know whether these young women were typical or had been typical at the time of their experiences with parental alienation allegations and reunification therapy. It is quite possible that the only young women to come forward to be interviewed are those who have a specific set of personal characteristics or who have had a specific set of experiences with parental alienation allegations. The value of their narratives is a matter of establishing what some (but not necessarily all) of these experiences were like.

Were the Parents' Actions in These Cases Typical of Parental Alienation Cases?

Again, with this small set of interviews, it is not possible to establish a spectrum of parental actions or of treatment methods. However, the allegations of parental alienation and the behaviors of both the preferred and the rejected parents resembled each other for the boys' group as well as for the girls, and both resembled other published accounts of experiences with parental alienation allegations and with reunification therapy.

How Was Parental Alienation Identified in the Cases in This Chapter?

The young women who were interviewed did not seem to know how their avoidance of one parent had led to identification of parental alienation. They did not mention any of the other factors that are considered by alienationists to indicate a parental alienation case (Bernet, 2020; discussed in an earlier chapter of this book). These would have included having an earlier good relationship with the rejected parent, having no substantiated evidence of abuse or neglect by that parent, having evidence of alienating behaviors by the preferred parent, and specific actions by the child other than avoiding one parent. None of the interviewees mentioned these factors having been discussed or showed any awareness that identification of parental alienation has been related to those factors. (In one case, however, the interviewee noted that a witness had said that one of her parents "badmouthed" the other, referencing a factor often presented as evidence of parental alienation.) As far as the interviewees were concerned, the parental alienation identification usually came out of nowhere when *somebody said parental alienation.* This fact about the narratives does not, of course, show that other factors were not considered in evaluating these cases, but it is noteworthy that young women who have felt great concern about the use of parental alienation allegations would have been likely to look into the identification issue.

Had the Interviewees Had Any Adverse Experiences with the Parent They Wanted to Avoid?

One interviewee reported physical abuse which had led to an investigation and one mentioned pushing and shoving of herself and a sibling. One reported sexualized behavior on the part of the rejected parent, including intrusive behavior like coming into the bathroom uninvited. Most of the concerns were emotional ones, however, and the interviewees referred to a parent being "hostile" or overly strict and critical. One interviewee said her primary motive for asking for a changed parenting plan was that she was tired of the logistics of "week on/week off".

Interviewees who had been taken to a treatment program by youth transport service workers did have adverse experiences with those people and may have attributed those experiences to the avoided parent, who had arranged for the transport. The transporters were reported as threatening and scolding the children and as talking inappropriately about other distressing cases they had worked on. That the transporters served as "hired muscle" is shown by the statement of one young woman that a therapist threatened that she would bring the transporters back if she did not get cooperation.

Insulting or threatening treatment by therapists at the reunification programs could similarly have been processed as adverse experiences with a parent, who had approved of the program and was actually present at the time.

How Did Stepparents or Other Social Influences Affect These Cases?

One stepparent demanded that the child be made to treat her more "respectfully". In another narrative, the mother (who was eventually rejected by the child) had babysitters and various people living in the home for child care help; the child's objection to the habits of one of these people seems to have been the beginning of serious conflict. The same mother had a woman friend who was instrumental in arranging reunification therapy and associated travel plans. One stepparent was said to have organized their "strategies" and was highly intrusive in contacts with the stepdaughter's sibling. In several cases, the girls were very concerned about lack of contact with their friends and distressed about losing the phones that made contacts possible. One grandparent was seen as an important source of support.

What Were the Effects of Reunification Therapy in These Cases?

The interviewees who attended intensive programs recalled fear and distress at the reunification program; they remembered being threatened with other programs where they would be even more vulnerable. They found some aspects of their reunification therapy experiences artificial and off-putting although neither threatening nor dangerous. For example, the "family meeting" format and the requirement for complimenting each other, prescribed as part of their "aftercare", were experienced as tiresome and unhelpful. In one case, the program's response to a girl's depression was to tell her she was not working hard enough, a response with the potential for exacerbating her emotional difficulty. No interview spoke of the program they attended as having improved their relationship with an avoided parent. In one case, the interviewee felt that the program had eventually led to estrangement from both parents.

What Was the Timeline in These Cases, and What Does the Timeline Mean?

One factor alienationists reference in their posited identification methods is that children had good relationships with parents before the divorce and only began to avoid a parent some time after the divorce. This assumption, of course, mistakenly suggests that no changes would have occurred in the relationship if there had been no divorce or if the preferred parent had not "badmouthed" the now-rejected parent. Identification of a previous good relationship is, problematically, often based on videos or photographs of pleasurable events like birthday parties or unwrapping of Christmas presents. (Families are not likely to make the same records of parents spanking or shouting at a child, or of a parent drunk or violent.)

Establishing that there was a previous good parent–child relationship is difficult and was not done effectively in the cases of these interviewees. The children in all these cases were 8 years old or younger when their parents divorced. The existing relationships (good or bad) could not have remained unchanged as the girls got older—indeed, if this had been possible, the outcome would have been poor, as a good relationship between a parent and an 8-year-old is by no means the same as a good relationship with a 16-year-old.

Alienationists unfortunately seem to suggest that if a teenage girl, who when younger sat on Daddy's lap, now does not want contact with her father, the reason for this must be the behavior of the mother (or the reverse may also be proposed, with father's behavior changing the attitude toward the mother). The timeline, with early good times followed by later rejection, is taken as evidence of parental alienation. Actually, however, a wide range of factors should be considered as possible causes, acting either individually or collectively. The girl's physical maturation, social and psychological pressures toward autonomy, and the rejected parent's own attitudes and behavior all require consideration.

Earlier parent–child relationships and the timeline of negative changes are not clear in the narratives presented by young women interviewees and, even if well understood, would not give real evidence that one parent had caused parental alienation by his or her actions.

References

Bernet, W. (2020). Introduction to parental alienation. In D. Lorandos & W. Bernet (Eds.), *Parental alienation—science and law* (pp. 5–43). Charles C. Thomas.

Brouillard, C., Brendgen, M., Vitaro, F., Dionne, G., & Boivin, M. (2018). Links between the mother-adolescent and father-adolescent relationships and depression. *Journal of Clinical Child and Adolescent Psychology*, 47, S397–S408. https://doi.org/10.1080/15374416.2017.1350964.

Fava, M. Hwang, I., Rush, A., Sampson, N., Walters, E., & Kessler, R. (2010). The importance of irritability as a symptom of major depressive disorder: Results from the National Comorbidity Survey Replication. *Molecular Psychiatry*, 15, 856–867. https://doi.org/10.1038/mp.2009.20.

Yong, M., McCarty, C., Vander Stoep, A., & McCauley, E. (2022). Gender differences in the effects of academic achievement on depressive symptoms during adolescence. *Journal of Child and Family Studies*, 31, 3326–3341. https://doi.org/10.1007/s10826-022-02414-x.

6 The Parental Alienation Stories of Four Mothers in North America

The first chapters of this book have concentrated on young adults who, as children or adolescents, were part of child custody cases in which parental alienation was alleged. Some of them were ordered to attend intensive reunification therapies; others received various kinds of office-based treatment; still others spent much time and energy avoiding these treatments. These young people are subjects of much concern because the fear and even pain associated with intensive reunification therapies have the potential for disturbing development and causing long- or short-term mental health concerns. Being forced to have contact with a parent who is feared or deeply disliked can have similar consequences. The impact of reunification programs on children, who are essentially helpless to escape disturbing experiences, can be powerful, and is thought to be greater than the impact of similar experiences on older people.

However, the importance of reunification therapy's effects on older people must not be ignored. For every child who is said to be influenced by parental alienation, there is by definition one parent, the child's preferred parent, who is accused of having acted to alienate the child from the other parent. Intensive reunification programs demand that children be prevented from any contact with the allegedly alienating parent, initially for perhaps 90 days, but possibly for years. The allegedly alienating parent may also be required to attend therapy approved by alienationists, to do "homework" as assigned by the approved therapist, and to write a letter of apology telling the children that the parent is to be blamed for causing the child's avoidance of the other parent. If the preferred parent fails to comply with these requirements, or is said by the therapist to have been insufficiently sincere or to insist that they have not caused the avoidance, they may not have any contact with the child until he or she turns 18.

The situations created when preferred parents are alleged to have alienated children are deeply painful to the parents as well as to the

DOI: 10.4324/9781003454793-6

children. Parents separated from their children experience longing for contact or at least for the knowledge that the child is all right. If the rejected parent, who now has physical custody of the child, was known to be abusive or neglectful, or if domestic violence was part of the marriage, the preferred parent experiences real fear about what may be happening to the child.

There are additional harms to parents in these family situations. The parent alleged to have alienated the child must pay to attend the alienationist-approved therapist. If contact through supervised visitation is granted by the court, the supervisor must be paid, again by the preferred parent. Legal fees pile up, as few preferred parents are prepared to represent themselves in court (and even fewer are successful if they try). Preferred parents may find themselves selling their homes, often their only property, to pay these bills.

In recent years, a new potential harm for allegedly-alienating parents has developed. This problem derives from the relatively recent claim that parental alienation is a form of child abuse or "family violence" (Harman, Kruk, & Hines, 2018). The "family violence" argument is not based on empirical evidence but is a matter of redefinition by parental alienation proponents, who use it to claim that cases where parental alienation is alleged are not child custody, but are child protection cases, and therefore should swiftly result in separation of the child and the preferred parent. The implication here is that the preferred parent, alleged to have alienated the child, should actually be described as a child abuser. Child abusers, of course, are prohibited from working with children, so preferred parents who have been described in this way would not be able to work as teachers, child care staff, nurses, doctors, foster parents, and so on. Because many people doing those jobs are women, it appears that mothers are particularly vulnerable to an argument that has the potential for destroying careers and reputations as well as impoverishing parents.

The group of four mothers who were interviewed for this chapter are not presented as representative of mothers alleged to have alienated their children from the fathers. All had asked the present author either to testify in their cases or to consult with their lawyers, and had subsequently agreed to be interviewed about the details of their cases. As readers will see, the interviewed mothers cover a wide range of issues and outcomes and do not have a great deal in common other than being residents of the United States. Two of them managed to avoid losing contact with their children, but the other two experienced the brunt of determined parental alienation allegations. All were much impacted financially by the allegations.

As was the case for the young men and women in earlier chapters, identifying material for this group of mothers will be withheld as much as possible. Although it would be of real interest to include the names of custody evaluators who alleged that parental alienation was present, and the names of the reunification therapies they recommended, these will not be included because of the possibility that the information would identify the interviewee. This policy will be applied even in the case of one interviewee who has allowed herself to be named when discussing her case at a national conference.

Anna's Story

Anna's divorce was already in progress when a consultant brought in by her children's father stated that parental alienation was present, a conclusion that was reached without the consultant speaking to the two girls or to Anna. The consultant was paid $10,000, testified for an hour or two, and was not seen again in this case.

In actuality, the daughters had been 50/50 with their mother and their father, and according to Anna, there were no problems at the time. But the consultant stated that Anna had performed alienating behaviors, which were putting some snacks in the girls' backpacks when they were going to their father's house, and providing them with hair conditioner. He recommended that contact with Anna be prohibited until such time as the "relationship with Dad equals the relationship with Mom" and made the argument that parental alienation is a form of domestic violence. On the basis of these statements, the family court judge ordered, first, no contact of the girls with their mother, and then, supervised visitation. Anna had to pay the supervisor, and the company providing supervision sent a very young, untrained supervisor (whose reports could have considerable influence). A child protective services investigation reported that the girls' father was emotionally abusive, a conclusion that should rebut the allegation of parental alienation, but Anna's attorney advised her just to keep her mouth shut about all these issues.

A reunification therapist was engaged to work with the parents and girls in an office-based program. He had a few sessions with Anna but concentrated on the father and the girls. The therapist accepted the parental alienation allegation, but also thought in terms of "Munchausen by proxy" or Factitious Disorder, a disorder in which a parent causes health problems in a child in order to get attention and praise for caring for the child. Although this disorder was originally described with respect to parents who cause evidence of physical disorders (for instance, by adding some substance to a child's urine sample, or feeding the child inappropriately), the term can also be applied to apparent causing mental health disorders and has even been equated with parental alienation (Butz, 2020).

The reunification therapist told Anna to read the book *Divorce Poison* (Warshak, 2010), a popular book written by one of the creators of the reunification therapy Family Bridges. The therapist directed Anna to read the book carefully and said that they would discuss it chapter by chapter. Anna refused to do this.

The reunification therapist also directed Anna to write a letter to the children that would confess to her having caused the alleged adverse attitude to their father. He said it must be genuinely remorseful. Anna refused to do this, first because she felt it was not true, and second because she considered that the therapist would use this "confession" against her. She was particularly concerned because the children's father had accused her (incorrectly) of giving the children poisoned candy to give to him, this accusation had been stated by his lawyer in a court document to be "on good evidence", and Anna saw how a series of accusations could work even if none were true.

In a move that was legal in the state where she lived, Anna recorded telephone conversations. She sent the court the resulting information about the father, including his arrest record, psychological evaluation, and drug use. The therapist told her that if she did this any more, it would "adversely affect custody". (In her interview, Anna noted that this statement was a part of what she called "threat therapy".)

Anna realized that the lawyers did not understand parental alienation and that she would have to educate herself. She also realized that, speaking generally, judges will not take back the parental alienation label once they have applied it. She had to learn more about these issues and become capable of arguing for herself.

As months passed, Anna decided to tell her lawyer that she was going to stop doing things his way ("keep your mouth shut"). She recorded a session with the therapist. She had just learned that the Board of Psychology, the licensing and regulation agency in the state where Anna lived, did not support the idea of parental alienation or of reunification therapy. While recording, Anna asked the therapist to tell her what she had done that the Board of Psychology would accept as evidence that she had alienated the girls. She also asked him, "how are you billing this?", that is, what problem he was claiming to treat. The therapist did not provide answers to any of these queries.

Three weeks later, the court asked the therapist in what way Anna had caused parental alienation. He now replied "it's hybrid", meaning that both parents had behaved in ways that caused the children to have negative attitudes toward the father. He also said that the younger girl, who was "on the autistic spectrum", had been "brainwashed". After a lengthy settlement conference, the judge ordered that the children quickly go back to 50/50 time with each parent.

Anna's case continued with many of the chaotic events that appear typical of parental alienation cases. The reunification therapist was removed and replaced with a new therapist. The judge involved in the settlement recused himself and was replaced by a new judge. Unknown to Anna, the new therapist was talking to the father and to the director of an intensive reunification therapy program. To add to the chaos, the COVID pandemic shut down the courts for a period of time.

Two years after the beginning of this case, the girls' father asked for full custody and for an order to send the girls to an intensive reunification therapy program. The requested order also included a no-contact order for six months to a year because Anna had talked to the girls on the telephone. The settlement judge tried to persuade the father to drop this demand and noted that the father was taking the girls to Hawaii but not to therapy.

Anna now had to decide on a strategy to deal with the new demands. She had old records from the current therapist and could show how recently submitted material had inserted new statements into the old material. For example, the therapist said that Anna was "aggressive" and had a concerning attitude at a meeting, but Anna could prove that she had been out of state and had not been present at the meeting.

Building her defense against the allegations of parental alienation, Anna felt she could not prove herself "not guilty", so she had to attack the parental alienation "package". She wanted to get the current therapist on record in order to have grounds for an appeal. The therapist did not know Anna had the original records and could not answer the question, "why haven't you talked to the mother's therapist?". The therapist had not seen the girls for two years but testified that they should go to the intensive reunification program even though they were at this point doing 50/50 with their parents, without complaint.

Anna's lawyer told her that the new judge would not change the order for no-contact between Anna and the girls and for attendance at the intensive reunification program. Anna realized that the program was a "pretty package" for the judge and her only recourse was to "poke holes in the package". She developed a list of questions to be asked about the program, as they might be asked about any other treatment program:

Where is the intensive reunification program located?
Who is the owner?
Who did the intake form for the girls?

Where is the release for the therapist to talk to the director of the intensive reunification program?
What assessment was used?
Was it not the lawyers who first recommended this intensive reunification program?
Where is the staff directory for the program?
Who are the transport team?
What about cost and about any aftercare?

Anna's questions proved to be an effective defense. The current therapist was disciplined by the Board of Psychology after a complaint was filed. The court's judgment stated that "the court believes that [the intensive reunification program] attempts to cure or treat the harmful effects of alienation through education, and by, in turn, alienating the preferred parent...If the court accepts the premise that alienation is harmful, then it must by that same premise find [the intensive reunification program's] educational process may also be harmful."

A new reunification therapist was appointed but there were no meetings with the father and daughters and the father did not take a class he was told to take. The older daughter, by her father's choice, did not continue to visit the father at that time; she had been recording his outbursts and made a record of a line of cocaine she found at his house. Later, she resumed some contact, perhaps an hour at a time, but went home if he had an emotional outburst. The girls have remained in Anna's care.

Anna's current response to these past events seems to be a motivating anger that has helped her speak up to organizations and people that can fight the effects of parental alienation allegations.

Lisa's Story

Soon after Lisa's divorce proceedings began in 2016, parental alienation was mentioned as a factor in custody decisions. In her interview, Lisa said she did not take the allegations seriously. She was a teacher and said she "lived in a trauma-informed world" so none of the language used made much sense to her. She found the custody evaluation to be like a foreign language—for instance, she did not know the word "denigration". She simply disregarded most of what was said and done, and concentrated on her work and on homeschooling her two sons, who were not yet in their teens.

Lisa was puzzled by the psychological evaluation using a questionnaire. She was told she could agree, disagree, or leave the answers blank; one statement was "My mother is a good person". But when she left an answer blank, the evaluator told her that she had to answer, even though the instructions had said otherwise. She wondered later whether it would have made any difference to the case if she had taken the evaluation more seriously.

At the time of the divorce, Lisa's two sons were seeing a therapist, but their father threatened to sue that person for malpractice. Subsequently, the father arranged for the boys to see a therapist who is well-known to be a proponent of parental alienation ideas. This seems to have been the beginning of the parental alienation allegations, but there was also an incident in which the boys refused to get into the car with their father when they felt unsafe with his angry driving.

Lisa was ordered not to tell the boys what was happening in the court or otherwise. This was difficult, and she said they developed ways of communicating in metaphors so they would not have to lie about what had been said. A major issue arose with respect to the fact that the boys' father had at one point raped Lisa. The father told the evaluator that Lisa had called him "rapist" to the children. A major alienationist lawyer and his investigator were called in. Another local parental alienation proponent questioned the boys for several hours on whether Lisa had told them about this event; the father later castigated this person for not having been severe enough in his questioning.

The evaluator's report said that Lisa must give up and sign her agreement to the court order limiting contact with the children. If she did this, a no-contact period would be only 60 days, not 90. A problem with the order was that after being with their father, the boys would come home and tell Lisa what happened. If she asked any questions, this was seen as an alienating behavior.

A new parenting plan was instituted, with step-ups in time with the father every two months. Lisa asked for the local therapist to be present at each step-up decision. But the father did not want to wait two months. He met with the boys at the therapists's office, and the boys came home and said they had "held the line" on the two month provision. The father was angry in the car when driving them and said he would not wait. Lisa later called the therapist to discuss this, and the therapist said she was meddling and alienating.

Under the parenting plan at that time, the boys were to have one dinner a week with their father. The father went to the therapist and said he must have more time than that. The therapist then communicated to Lisa that in order not to be alienating, she must do what the father asks and be "encouraging" of his relationship with the boys. Lisa responded that she would do this if the judge ordered it, but this never happened and the idea was dropped.

The therapist felt that counseling and office-based reunification therapy were all that the boys needed, but the father wanted them to go to one or another of the intensive reunification therapies. The father spoke to the director of one of the major intensive reunification programs and wanted that person to talk to the judge and also to approve of any therapist to be employed.

While this was all going on, the father was living with a girlfriend who was "triggered" by the boys and got into physical altercations, ending in the police being called. The older son was suspicious of this woman, although he thought it best for his mother not to know about the situation. Another family member investigated the girlfriend's background and found that she had served a prison term for fraud. The father was also strongly influenced by another individual who told the boys that evil forces were at work; the boys declined to engage with that person.

There was also a community background on the other side, supporting Lisa and the children. A community network developed and members would attend court with Lisa and make eye contact with her. They loaned her money to pay for legal representation. They also helped arrange separate legal representation for the boys. The community members even met with Lisa's lawyer to be brought up to date on events.

Although the boys had their own legal representation, the legal aspects of the case were not easy to deal with. Lisa's lawyer did not want the boys to have a guardian *ad litem* and said that to find someone skilled in interviewing children they would have to go to a distant city. The lawyer did not want the boys to testify and said the judge did not like children testifying. This position stayed firm even though one of the boys, still in his mid-teens, was a witness of a serious car accident and testified about this event in another court.

An incident between the father and the boys was probably a deciding factor in this case, ending with the boys being able to decide their own "parenting plan". There was an altercation at the father's house and the police were called. The boys got away, but left behind a musical instrument much needed and wanted by one of them. The father refused to allow the instrument to be returned and claimed that the boys had self-injured in order to "get him in trouble" (and that this in itself was a sign of parental alienation). The boy's teacher said the boy could use her instrument, and the therapist ordered Lisa to take that (quite valuable) instrument to the father's house; the therapist said this would be a way for Lisa to tell the children that the father was trustworthy. Lisa refused to do this—and the therapist said that was all right, the boys trusted their father.

In Lisa's interview, she speculated on how she managed to cope with this situation and what might have been better decisions that would have more quickly freed the boys from the results of the parental alienation allegations. Lisa said she developed a way not to push against accusations, to look as if she was complying, and to learn the "rules of the game". It helped her to think of it as a game, even if one whose rules were wrong—if it was a game, it was not an existential threat. She needed to conserve energy, which she could have done better if she had taken the matter seriously from the beginning. She had to see what resources were needed in order to conserve them and not "feel crazy". Although Lisa managed to do these things, she feels that the long-term effect on her is a fear that "anything can happen". She cried with relief when her younger son turned 18.

Asked about the impact of the parental alienation allegations on her sons, Lisa says they want to go places where people do not know their stories. They have shied away from dating and do not want to "open up" in case someone twists their words. They feel vulnerable and do not share on social media as most people their age do.

Christine's Story

Christine's story of parental alienation allegations is very different from the two previous stories. Her narrative actually began years before parenthood, with her own abusive treatment by her mother and father. The theme of abuse was consistent through much of Christine's life.

Christine was married to someone else when she met her child's father at a meeting of a support group. The father (to be) was unwashed and homeless, living in his pick-up truck. Christine befriended the man and brought him home with her for Christmas, regarding him as also a friend of the then-husband. However, Christine had felt ambivalent about the marriage and thought marriage counseling was not working, and later filed for divorce.

Christine talked their new friend into taking a job with a company that required him to travel frequently. When he was not on the road, he stayed with Christine sometimes and seemed to be becoming a more responsible person. Because of various issues, the man went to a sex counselor and disclosed that loving feelings made him feel "dirty". Nevertheless, the two married.

Her new husband's increasingly abusive behavior brought back Christine's memories of her childhood and she felt that her "emotional space got smaller". Her husband would pick at her to start a quarrel and keep her awake at night, and sometimes she was forced to sleep in a closet. But she felt that life was short and she wanted to have children.

Christine had had a number of miscarriages and sought treatment for two years without a viable pregnancy. She proposed to adopt, but her husband's apparently affluent and powerful family did not approve. At that time, there were no surrogacy laws in the state where Christine lived. Christine and her husband met with a possible surrogate with whom they could use frozen ova. There were conflicts and financial demands during the pregnancy and the baby, a girl, was born a little early and stayed in the hospital briefly.

When the baby came home, she had some medical problems, and the husband used those to keep Christine terrified. However, he also said that the baby did not "feel like theirs" and that he felt like a baby-sitter for "somebody else's brat".

Christine's interview recounted many job and family problems before the child was five years old. Her husband was involved in various dishonest actions through businesses he had started. Christine herself had a job and had the child with a baby-sitter except for some times when the father would stay with her. During quarrels, the father would threaten that if Christine left him, he would take the child.

When the little girl started preschool, Christine applied for a job at the school, got it, and was sometimes able to interact with her daughter. Christine said she was not "ready to separate" at this time. When it was time for elementary school, Christine volunteered at the school a great deal and loved being with the kids.

From the time the daughter was 3, the husband refused sex with Christine. He soon had his own bedroom. He did not want Christine to work. They discussed divorce but Christine did not want the daughter to have to "go back and forth". She proposed that they stay in the same house but live separately, including dating discreetly if they chose to date, and coordinating their schedules to care for the child. When Christine went out, however, the father told the daughter that her mother was a whore and would leave and never come back. There was one incident when the father was screaming and smashing things when Christine was out on what he assumed was a date.

The father's drug use and emotional outbursts escalated by the time the daughter was in junior high school. He also began to "court" the daughter, bringing her flowers. He went into her bedroom and bathroom without permission even when she was using the toilet or bathing. He took her to various events and family gatherings and would not allow Christine to go along. Christine never discussed any of these issues with her daughter.

Finally, the father moved out, leaving the daughter with Christine. It was months later before the mother and daughter talked about their history. Meanwhile, the daughter had occasional visits with her father. She did not want to go because she felt her father did not really want her but was using her to get at her mother. The daughter would refuse to go to the driveway to get into her father's car (there was a restraining order prohibiting him from going onto the property). But, after a holiday visit, the daughter said she would not go again. She had started to show symptoms of post-traumatic stress disorder like trembling and nausea.

The divorce was finalized and the judge ordered 50/50 parenting. The judge would not permit the daughter to testify or meet with him in chambers. The counselors' testimony that there was no parental alienation was thrown out, and the judge stated that the therapists should not give the daughter (now 15) the idea that she could be allowed to have anything to say.

At a later hearing, a well-known alienationist, hired by the father, testified for several hours. The father had found an intensive reunification therapy, approved by this proponent, and he threatened the current therapist that he would have the daughter taken there. And indeed, youth transport service workers subsequently arrived to take the daughter from her school. The school staff had told the girl that they would warn her if anything was happening, but instead, she was called to the office and the transporters grabbed her. They drove her to a nearby major city and threatened that they would handcuff her if she did not cooperate. Her phone and possessions were taken away.

The girl was flown to the venue for the reunification program and went through the procedures; Christine was not present and did not describe this in her interview. However, she said the daughter had told her that she did her best to ignore the therapist. The girl would sing songs in her head and stare at a fishtank, which the therapist finally put away. She counted how many blue things were in the room, to distract herself. At night, she slept in a bunk bed with her father, though she was awake much of the night and searching for her phone, which had been hidden.

Afterwards, the daughter and father were to do a "family vacation" as part of the reunification program. They went to a nearby major amusement park. The girl did not want to go on rides where she would have to sit close to her father. Notably, the father left the girl by herself at the park for part of the day, according to Christine; she had no contacts on her new phone and no money. Christine was of the opinion that this was part of the reunification therapy and that the child's panic was designed to enhance the bond with the parent.

The treatment did not end with the reunification program and the "family vacation". Christine's part of the treatment began at this point.

As it was assumed that she had caused the daughter's attitude toward the father, she was seen as in need of related therapy. Christine had regular meetings with a man who was not a mental health professional and who had not received training in the relevant reunification therapy. He had "workbooks" with reunification program materials Christine was required to read and respond to. He "graded" Christine's work and passed it on to the judge, although confidentiality had been promised to Christine.

The daughter too continued to be "treated". As the COVID pandemic came on, she was in lockdown with her father. He graded her daily on her obedience, congeniality, and appearance of happiness, and himself on his use of discipline. He met on line with the reunification therapist. The daughter was told that if her "grades" (given by the father) were too low she would have to go back to the reunification program. She was not allowed to say "No" and was described as being a "brat" because she had not been disciplined enough. There were threats to put Christine in jail for contempt if the daughter did not cooperate. The girl spent most of a year isolated with her father. Then, after Christine was able to get a lawyer, 50/50 parenting time was restored.

Christine's daughter has turned 18 and is now back with her mother. According to the mother's interview, their relationship is good, although the daughter resents the efforts her mother made to "push" her to contact with the father. Asked about the impact of the reunification program and other events, Christine emphasized the effects on her daughter, including her fear and hatred of her father. The young woman is also fearful of any involvement with the court system and recalls being ignored by the therapists and the judge.

Marie's Story

Marie's story is also one of rocky beginnings. Marie became pregnant before marrying her child's father, who wanted her to terminate the pregnancy. The two lived in different states and the father did not want to bring Marie's belongings to his state. The father wanted Marie to sign a prenuptial agreement stating she would get none of his family money in a divorce unless they had been married for two years. He frequently criticized her expenditures as frivolous and wanted to manage what she ate while pregnant.

When the baby was born by an emergency caesarean section, the father told Marie he might not pick her and the baby up from the hospital. There was already a conflict about the baby's name, and the father argued with the nurses about changing the birth certificate that Marie had filled out. Thinking he would not pick them up to go home, Marie called her mother, who with some friends drove from a neighboring state—but as they arrived at the hospital, the father also pulled up. Marie decided she would go home with her mother for a few days to recover from the C-section. She soon got a phone call accusing her of having kidnapped the baby and saying she must return.

The couple went to court three months later, when the father filed for custody. Marie's mother got her an attorney. The father brought a secretly recorded tape on which he discussed with Marie his demands to have the tax exemption for the baby, to pay no child support, and for Marie not to leave the state with the baby. The judge did not accept that Marie had agreed to these things, but gave her full custody and permission to leave the state. The father was allowed a week of custody before he left for a period of professional training.

Marie went to live in a neighboring state and took a job that allowed her to transport the baby easily for visits to the father. Within three years, she had remarried and had another child, also a boy. The new husband had difficulty handling a preschool stepchild and a new baby; he did not like Marie to breastfeed. Marie's older child began to call his stepfather "Dad" and this increased Marie's conflict with her former husband.

Though the two fathers were at loggerheads, when the second marriage ended in divorce, they developed a better relationship based on their enmity against Marie. The fathers simultaneously filed for custody, in the different states where they lived. Neither was successful at that time.

The ensuing months and years were fraught with conflict. Marie felt that the two fathers watched her carefully, and she did not date for a long time.

The elder child always had trouble with going to see his father, and after he got a phone at age 9 or 10, would contact Marie when he was at the father's house. He told his mother he would run away, and texted "get me out of here". Marie took the texts to the school principal, who called in a psychiatrist and eventually a counselor, which made the child angry with Marie. The father continued to insist that the child must come to his house, and the counselor called him out on this—but also said that Marie must control herself.

When the elder boy refused to go to his father at Christmas, the father filed a complaint of contempt against Marie. The court ordered the visit and Marie dropped the boy off as ordered. However, the boy and the father began to fight and the boy called the police—who did not help. The father took the boy to a popular restaurant and kept him there for four hours, then took him to a hotel. He told the boy that if he would not come out to have dinner, he would not be allowed to play in a basketball game the next day. On the next day, however, the father dropped the boy off at the basketball game and left without telling anyone.

After that episode, the boy began to disclose physical and sexual abuse. Child protective services in the father's state began an investigation but closed the case, concluding that the allegations were unfounded (that is, had not been supported by any available evidence). The court ordered the father to relinquish his guns, but he refused and moved out of the state.

Up to this point, parental alienation had not been mentioned, but now the two fathers hired a psychologist well-known for support of the parental alienation concept. Marie was blindsided. She said in her interview that she had had no inkling of this possibility. She had legal representation, but her attorney refused to talk to a consultant who was brought in and eventually "fired" Marie as a client.

The psychologist evaluated both boys, and his report recommended putting each boy in his father's custody and initiating a 90-day no-contact period for Marie. The no-contact period was to follow reunification therapy in a program that functioned rather differently from most of the programs in that it actually did involve a "camp" where there were other families; both parents also attended. The court ordered that after the treatment, the older boy could come back to visit Marie if he had "behaved himself". However, he did not come back even when the no-contact period was over. He remains angry at therapists and will not see one. According to Marie, he is behaving irresponsibly and has had a tendency to angry outbursts.

The younger boy did not attend the treatment program, although all family members are expected to be involved. The court put him in his father's full custody, but Marie has him every other weekend. Marie did not say much about his present attitude or behavior.

In Marie's interview, she expressed sadness and anxiety about her present situation and those of her sons, especially the older one. She had a good counselor soon after returning from the reunification program, but that woman retired. A second counselor was trauma-focused but knew nothing about parental alienation; she left because of illness in her family. It has been hard for Marie to find knowledgeable help. Her church gives some support, but most of the congregation are older people and none of them understand Marie's situation. She has made contact with a support group for people who have lost contact with a child because of parental alienation allegations, One Mom's Battle, but says that although the people are very nice, they do not satisfy her need for a real friend or an effective counselor.

Unfortunately, Marie's family is now unsupportive. She moved in with her mother and father after she lost her house in the child custody conflict, but her father died after a long illness and her mother is now ill. There is conflict with her sisters. They exchange pejoratives like "narcissist" and actually had a fistfight the day after the father died.

Discussion

Are These Narratives Typical of Cases Where Parental Alienation Is Alleged?

The narratives in this chapter show great variability among alleged alienation cases, but were not especially chosen for this purpose. The differences appeared unexpectedly among the four mothers who volunteered to be interviewed. It is notable, incidentally, that there is no way to ascertain the accuracy of the interview material or to check it against objective measures. However, if the goal is to consider events as the individuals experienced them, this issue is not an important one.

By chance or otherwise, the four mothers interviewed seem to fall into two rather different pairs. One pair had, and were able to use, a variety of resources to fight allegations of parental alienation, and they did this successfully. The other pair lacked resources or were unable to mobilize the ones they had, and as a result they lost contact with their children for periods of time and were forced to deal with orders to participate in reunification therapies. The narratives suggest that one important resource for two of the mothers may have been the remains of a reasonably functional marriage in which the spouses had not used physical or emotional abuse or coercive control to force each other to cooperate. In the two cases where the marriage was said to have been dysfunctional from early on, and where drugs and alcohol played serious roles, there were fewer, or less usable, resources. Resources used in navigating the courts were crucial to the different outcomes.

The commonalities among these four mothers were real, if less obvious than some of the differences. All were surprised by the allegations against them and felt that the children had good reasons for their attitudes toward the fathers. All stated primary concerns with the children's feelings and wishes, and although annoyed by the claims made against them, did not put undue emphasis on their own reputations or emotions as they might be affected by the allegations. All sought some sort of social support, whether from community friends, their own families, or dating and remarriage. All made voluntary or involuntary financial sacrifices in order to hire legal or mental health help.

As was the case for the now-adult children in these cases, it is not possible to know how typical these mothers would be of a much larger potential sample of cases. It is a particularly interesting question whether this group of mothers, who were ready and willing to tell their stories, may be different from mothers who prefer to maintain their privacy and, perhaps, to avoid thinking about their experiences.

How Was Parental Alienation Identified in These Cases?

The narratives presented in previous chapters about the now-adult children, not surprisingly, stressed the participants' memories of their own behavior and that of the parent they wanted to avoid. The mothers' interviews also covered these issues, but their major concern was that they had been alleged to perform parental alienating behaviors that are proposed as providing evidence that a preferred parent has caused a child's avoidance of the other parent (Bernet, 2020; Freeman, 2020).

It was clear that the children in the cases described in this chapter had avoided one parent, or at least had attempted to negotiate with that parent and the court about their contact with the parent. (Such negotiation is considered improper by many parental alienation proponents, as it implies that the child has some power over the parent and is not wholeheartedly compliant.) The issue about identification of parental alienation would then involve three of the other factors in the Five Factor Model (Bernet, 2020). The most important of these, from the viewpoint of defense of the mother, would be whether she had indeed carried out alienating behaviors. If she had never done so, presumably parental alienation should not be identified, no matter what other factors were present, and prohibiting contact between the child and the mother would be unreasonable, as the mother could not be said to have caused the child's avoidance.

The list of alienating behaviors used by proponents of parental alienation is the one proposed decades ago by Richard Gardner when he initially described his view of parental alienation. More recent alienationists have claimed that the Baker Strategies Questionnaire (Baker & Chambers, 2011) uses observation of alienating behaviors to identify individuals who are alienating children; unfortunately, the only attempt to validate this questionnaire involved asking professionals to identify vignettes in which the behaviors were embedded, rather than to use the list in real cases.

One serious problem with the Baker Strategies Questionnaire and other attempts to use the alienating behaviors list to identify parental alienation cases is that the so-called alienating behaviors are also found in some form among well-functioning parents. Fathers may say about their wives, "I don't trust her driving in that crowded parking lot, she's too careless", and mothers may denigrate their husbands by saying in front of their children, "I am going to scream if your father leaves his dirty socks in the living room again". Both mothers and fathers may make it clear to their children that they do not enjoy contact with in-laws. Other alienating behaviors are also common, for example "interfering with contact" by insisting on supervising children's toothbrushing or bandaging a skinned knee. Behaviors of this type thus do not thoroughly differentiate parental alienation from other situations in which a child avoids a parent. Certainly one or two observed occurrences of these behaviors should not be claimed as evidence of parental alienation.

It might be possible by careful empirical work to find differences on the Baker Strategies Questionnaire between families whose children were thought to avoid a parent because of alienation and those who appeared to avoid for other reasons. This work has never been done, however, so it would not be possible to use evidence of alienating behaviors to argue that the mothers interviewed for this chapter had caused their children to avoid the fathers.

Adverse Experiences of Mothers and Children

When children have suffered abuse or seen their mothers abused, their avoidance of the fathers should not be considered evidence of parental alienation, according to alienationists (Bernet, 2020; Freeman, 2020)—assuming that an investigation has substantiated the abuse. Unsubstantiated abuse allegations, on the other hand, are not only rejected as justifications of children's avoidance, but they may actually be interpreted as evidence that there has been alienating behavior by the preferred parent who has made the allegations. Similarly, children's unsubstantiated allegations of abuse can be interpreted by alienationists to be evidence that the preferred parent has "brainwashed" the children.

Some abuse allegations are difficult or impossible to substantiate. For instance, sexual abuse that does not include penetration or cause bleeding, bruising, or infection may be undetectable unless it is accidentally observed. Emotional abuse, similarly, can be substantiated only if it is overheard or recorded in some way. Like allegations of other forms of abuse, these allegations can be interpreted as evidence that someone is denigrating or attacking the accused parent.

Allegations of serious abuse experiences thus can be used by parental alienation proponents to argue that a preferred parent is performing alienating behaviors, even though substantiated evidence of abuse is considered to rule out parental alienation in most cases. In some cases, however, a "hybrid" situation is held to exist, in which one parent has been abusive but the other is also attempting to alienate the children.

The interviews of mothers in this chapter showed that few, if any, allegations of abuse were made by the mothers, although the mothers' narratives reported many adverse events that did not rise to the level of substantiated abuse. These mothers were less likely than the children to call the police, to ask for investigation of abuse, or to complain of inappropriate behavior by the fathers. However, all the mothers reported events sufficiently frequent and adverse to explain why children avoided contact with their fathers. Some of the events had occurred while the parents were living together, but many of them followed the separation and were features of the relationships between fathers and children.

Adverse experiences for both mothers and children may result from alcohol and drug use or efforts at coercive control, all of which are described in the interviews for this chapter. Events that are apparently directed toward mothers are often observed by children and can have indirect effects on the latter.

Stepparents and Other Social Influences

All of the interviews with mothers indicated the presence of other adults who complicated the difficult parent–child relationship. New spouses, boyfriends, girlfriends, and dating partners played possible roles in relationship difficulties and in allegations of parental alienation. It seems unnecessary to point this out, as obviously the parents and children are not existing in a vacuum, but thinking about parental alienation has focused almost entirely on the biological parents and their offspring. These people are defined as "a family" on their own, in spite of their strong, family-like relationships with other people, and it is on the basis of that definition that reunification programs are often referred to as "family therapy" or "family systems therapy".

In one of the narratives in this chapter, a stepgrandmother played an important role and supported the children's position. In another, a spouse's parents were said to have influenced a decision about adoption. The children themselves—especially teenagers—may affect one parent's decisions and interactions with the other parent; in one of this chapter's cases, the children entered directly into negotiation with the father and did not reveal all that was happening to the mother. A parent's siblings may be supportive or overtly hostile to that person's position.

Parents' views and decisions about allegations of parental alienation (either made or experienced) may also be affected by "life coaches" and "parenting coaches" whose professional skills are highly variable. In one of the cases in this chapter, a father was strongly influenced by some self-help programs and wanted the children to take part in those programs.

The oversimplified view of children's avoidance of a parent as solely based on nuclear family relationships is mistaken and fails to take into account the multitude of social influences experienced by parents and by children.

Effects of Allegations of Parental Alienation

When young adults were asked in previous chapters about the effects their experiences had had on them, they answered exactly what was asked—how they had been affected. The mothers in this chapter's interviews had a rather different tendency. Their replies concentrated on how the children had been affected.

Three of the mothers said their relationships with their children had survived and even been strengthened by their experiences. Some referred to the children being "empowered" by their successful negotiation of the situation. One felt that her daughter had not yet talked about some of the events, and another had essentially lost meaningful connection with her son, whose behavior was of concern to her.

When these mothers talked about their own outcomes, there was some degree of pride in having overcome adversity and to some extent protected the children from harm. But there was also a sense of anxiety that they had not previously experienced. One mother said she now felt that "anything could happen", that she could no longer plan or expect her life to be controllable. There was also anger about the allegations and the wish to prevent others from having these experiences.

In addition to these psychological effects, of course, both mothers and children were affected in practical ways by allegations of parental alienation. Legal costs of hundreds of thousands of dollars were mentioned, and debts to friends and relatives were incurred. Houses and other property might be sold in order to raise cash. Savings and college funds could be badly depleted, with ill effects for both the mother and the children.

What Was the Timeline and What Is the Implication?

The method of identifying parental alienation called the Five Factor Model (Bernet, 2020) includes a focus on the timing of events. In order for a child's avoidance of a parent to be classified as parental alienation, there must have been an initial good parent–child relationship that has deteriorated from about the time of the marital separation. This timing is said to show that some actions of the preferred parent are likely to have caused the child's negative attitude toward the other parent.

Two of the mothers said little or nothing about the father–child relationship during the marriage, but noted worsening child attitudes associated with the father's later behavior and with court orders for their own contact with their children. The other two reported fathers' problematic attitudes as early as the pregnancy and birth of the children, and the development of children's negative attitudes over time during as well as after the marriage.

These timelines suggest that in some cases where parental alienation is alleged, there were poor father–child relationships to begin with, and thus parental alienation as defined by alienationists should never have been claimed to exist. In other cases, there are clear reasons for the children's negative attitudes that are displayed as they avoid one parent from whom they have experienced increasingly difficult behavior.

References

Baker, A., & Chambers, J. (2011). Adult recall of childhood exposure to parental conflict: Unpacking the black box of parental alienation. *Journal of Divorce and Remarriage*, 52, 55–76. https://doi.org/10.1080/10502556.2011.534396.

Bernet, W. (2020). Introduction to parental alienation. In D. Lorandos & W. Bernet (Eds.), *Parental alienation—science and law* (pp. 5–43). Charles C. Thomas.

Butz, M. (2020). *Parental alienation and Factitious Disorder by Proxy beyond DSM-5: Interrelated multidimensional diagnoses*. Routledge.

Freeman, B. (2020). The psychosocial assessment of contact refusal. In D. Lorandos & W. Bernet (Eds.), *Parental alienation—Science and law* (pp.44–81). Charles C. Thomas.

Harman, J., Kruk, E., & Hines, D. (2018). Parental alienating behaviors:An unacknowledged form of family violence. *Psychological Bulletin*, 144, 1275–1299. https://doi.org/10.1037/bul0000175.

Warshak, R. (2010). *Divorce poison*. William Morrow.

7 A Global Problem

Parental Alienation Allegations Against Mothers Around the World

The concept of parental alienation began in the United States at a time when there was a good deal of concerned discussion about divorce and about the women's movement. Fathers' rights groups were starting to organize at about the same time. As was noted in an earlier chapter, following the publications of Richard Gardner (1985, 2001), the parental alienation concept began to be applied in family courts in the United States. A conference of the Association of Family and Conciliation Courts (AFCC) in 2000 focused on aspects of the parental alienation concept (Doughty & Drew, 2022).

From the United States, use of the parental alienation concept began to spread to other English-speaking countries and then to become a global phenomenon (Doughty & Rathus, 2022). Parental alienation arguments have been used in child custody and parenting decisions in Australia, New Zealand, Canada, the United Kingdom, Italy, Israel, and Spain, among others. Most egregiously, Brazil for a time criminalized parental alienation and as of this writing continues to work on related legislation.

The use of the parental alienation concept in courts—not to speak of criminalization—is profoundly questionable in the absence of any means of identifying parental alienation cases with scientifically supported methods. The Five Factor Model (Bernet, 2020) lists criteria for concluding that parental alienation is present, but no evidence has been produced to show that this model differentiates between a group of children who have been alienated from one parent by the other, and a second group of children who avoid one parent for different reasons.

This chapter will present narratives based on interviews with five mothers living outside the United States. One of these women lives in Canada, two in the United Kingdom, one in Brazil, and one in Russia. All of them contacted the author after hearing of this project and all were interviewed virtually.

DOI: 10.4324/9781003454793-7

Lynn's Story

Lynn was living near a major Canadian city when she became pregnant by a boyfriend whom she never married. The boyfriend wanted her to terminate the pregnancy and ended their relationship when she was six and a half months along. Lynn let him come to the hospital to see the baby, a little girl named Molly, and later would take the baby to see the paternal grandmother. Lynn, the boyfriend, and the baby even traveled together—Lynn referred to this as the "fake family phase". But Lynn and her mother were raising the child.

When Molly was about four years old, according to Lynn, her father had a new girlfriend in the picture and began to change his attitudes. A year or two later, he gave a birthday party for Molly, but Molly called Lynn and asked to come home. Molly told Lynn that her father had been angry when she interrupted him on the phone, grabbed her by the arm, and threw her into the bathroom. Molly bumped her head and declared that she had been locked in, but in fact there was no external lock on the bathroom door. There was an investigation by child protective services, but it was closed as inconclusive.

From this point, Molly refused to visit her father, who said she had made up the story. The father would phone Molly and ask if she would come, but she would refuse, so he would not come to get her. Lynn did not force her to go, a fact that was used against her in later court proceedings—but she did encourage the child to go.

When Molly was six, her father applied to have her in his custody 20% of the time, to have this arrangement designated as joint custody, and to have her with him on weekends. A settlement conference a few months later ended with the judge directing Lynn to make Molly go to her father. The transfer was to take place at a nearby mega-mall. Lynn's lawyer suggested that a third party should take Molly to her father.

Molly was willing to go to the first visit. She thought her father might apologize for what he had done, but he did not. On later attempted visits, Molly would stand and refuse to go to her father, and the father would call Lynn to come and get her.

A children's lawyer (equivalent to a guardian *ad litem* in the United States) was assigned to Molly. She recommended that Molly and her father go to an office-based form of reunification therapy and suggested two therapists. When Lynn responded that she could not afford their charges, the court ordered that the fees be taken off the child support Lynn received. One therapist began working with Molly and told her that adults can make mistakes but now she must move on.

Following the settlement, the old pick-up pattern continued. The father would arrive at the house, Molly would go out to him, then would stall. The father would then call Lynn to come and get Molly. The father's lawyer told Lynn she should carry Molly and put her in the father's car. Instead, Lynn hid in the lobby of the building to see what happened when the father came to get Molly. She heard Molly crying and screaming; the father grabbed her and brought her inside and was yelling at her.

Lynn then called the relevant government agency, even though she had been told not to do this. The agency said they would investigate because of the earlier complaint.

The father's lawyer wrote to Lynn, saying that the father would not come to pick up Molly because it caused him too much anxiety. For the next eight months, the father did not visit. He called Molly twice during that time, on her birthday and on Father's Day. But after Lynn suggested it to him, the father started making more frequent calls. Lynn encouraged Molly to talk to him about the incident, but he declared that it did not happen (Lynn described this as "gaslighting").

In a settlement conference early in the next year, Lynn's lawyer failed to submit any required documents. The judge had supposedly confidential material from the therapists and, for the first time, used the term parental alienation. In a second conference a few months later, the judge listed three options that might be ordered: 1. The father walks away from the issue. 2. The father gets full custody. 3. Molly is sent to foster care.

There was to be no more continuance and the case was to go straight to trial. Lynn had been dropped by her legal aid lawyer and was now desperately trying to find legal help, as she found she had to represent herself. In her interview, Lynn said she had called between 70 and 90 lawyers, all of whom refused to take the case because they would have only two months to prepare. Costs of $1,000 had been awarded to the father and Lynn had to pay this at once. Lynn started scanning and collating material that she might need to use at trial. She asked the court for an adjournment but was refused.

Molly's father began to ask for full custody after parental alienation was mentioned. Offers to settle went back and forth until the trial date.

During the trial, Molly was not allowed to be in the house with Lynn because she might accidentally overhear something about the trial. She had to stay at friends' houses for a few days. Molly actually knew nothing about the trial until she heard her father and his girlfriend talking about the judge and the court order; then Lynn answered some of her questions.

At the trial, a well-known parental alienation proponent testified that there must be alienation because Lynn had no pictures of Molly's father in her living room; this was true, but Molly had pictures of him in her room. (Lynn cried while describing this part of the trial.) The expert witness stated that when Lynn tried to get Molly to hug her father, she was "injecting herself into the relationship", but when she did not, she was "not encouraging" of the relationship.

The trial took nine days, and the decision, very unusually, was released a week later. Molly's father was awarded full custody and all decision-making. Lynn was told to have Molly in her father's custody in 48 hours or the police would handle it. She could not afford an appeal and packed Molly's belongings; according to Lynn, Molly told her that she would be "traumatized for life".

Lynn borrowed money to pay for an appeal and had a lawyer for three months. Finally, the lawyer told Lynn the case was not appealable. In the two years since then, Lynn and Molly have had only Zoom visits supervised by Molly's father. Molly has been hospitalized three times, for suicidal ideation, self-harm, and head-banging. She has run away twice and told the police she would kill herself if she had to go back to her father. As of this writing, the situation remains the same.

Megan's Story

Megan is a British woman who split from her abusive husband when her son, Jack, was nine months old. There was some contact between Jack and his father, and Megan says that at one time the father tried to kidnap Jack from the grandparents' house.

When Jack was almost four, he told his nursery teacher that his father touched his bottom and it hurt. The nursery called Megan and said she must report this disclosure, or they would. There was a social care investigation, which Megan said the police were "happy to have social care do". But the investigation ended with a report denying any concerns.

The disclosures continued and Jack's behavior deteriorated. He began to see a play therapist. He would scream and run from his father, hide, or lock himself in the bathroom. In a few months he made more serious disclosures and said there were photographs of his bottom with a finger in it. The police and social care were again involved, but in court the judge ignored the report and gave the father custody for overnights and alternate weekends. There had been no medical examination.

In her interview, Megan said she felt her lawyer was in way over his head. He advised her not to mention any abuse she had experienced from Jack's father. Social care said Megan was emotionally abusive to Jack.

At the next hearing, a Cafcass (Children and Family Court Advisory and Support Service) guardian was appointed for Jack. The police suggested a medical examination and it was confirmed that Jack had anal thrush, a yeast infection that may be associated with sexual abuse.

Soon afterward, an Achieving Best Evidence (ABE) examination was provided for Jack. In this, a specialist interviews the child, putting questions in child language, and videorecords the proceedings. Jack repeated his allegations and described the bedroom where he said the events had taken place. The police also questioned Jack's play therapist. Contact between Jack and his father was stopped while this investigation went on.

In Megan's interview, she said the police felt they had enough evidence to arrest Jack's father. In court, however, the judge ordered the police to his chambers to explain why they had investigated Jack's father. He did not think they were right in this and ordered that there be no more police involvement. The judge ordered that Jack could stay in Megan's care but there must be contact with his father.

Jack's father declared that the child was schizophrenic. A psychologist was appointed and stated that Jack was abused and neglected and had received no love from his parents. The psychologist concluded that Megan had alienated Jack from his father, that Jack should go to live with his father, and that Megan should have five years of intensive therapy—but that the therapy would probably not work.

When he was six years old, Jack was removed from Megan's care and sent to live with his father. There was a one-year supervision order for contact with Megan. Initially, a social worker was the supervisor. Jack clung to Megan and refused to go to his father, who then rugby-tackled him to the ground and got him into the car. In a few months, the amount of contact was increased, and supervision then was by Megan's aunt, a professional who worked with children.

Jack's father next transferred the boy to a new school without warning, separating him from the school, friends, and sports he had enjoyed. A new social care team was assigned when Jack went to live with his father. Jack was still making disclosures at school and was violent with other children. Jack saw the school counselor six times in a short period. The social care team stopped Jack's contact with Megan but did not tell her the decision was based on Jack's disclosures to the counselor.

Jack's father diagnosed Jack as having a "tic of the eyeball" and found a doctor who said he did not see it but believed the father. Megan took Jack to have his eyes examined and was told there was no such thing as a tic of the eyeball, but that Jack did have a lazy eye and should have glasses. This led to accusations that Megan had breached a court order, because she had taken Jack to the eye doctor without the father's permission.

Megan began at this point, when Jack was about eight, to challenge the social care team more. One of the social workers told her that Jack's allegations against his father were the reason for the supervised contact with Megan; Jack had said he was "terrified" of his father, and the social worker felt he could not know that word but must be quoting a statement by Megan.

Conflicts and changes in visitation continued over several years as Jack remained in his father's custody. When Jack visits Megan, he tells her he will not go back to his father, but then becomes anxious and says he will have to go. He knows that he will eventually be forced to go, and feels that if he has resisted, his father will give him no food, no hot water, no permission to leave the house. When Megan has told the father that Jack is now old enough to need some autonomy, the father has said that he cannot be given any agency.

Jack's father assaulted him a year or two ago. He took Jack by the throat and said he would kick him until he couldn't walk for a week. The police came and the case was sent back to the original judge. Jack had to go back to his father for several days, and when Megan picked him up, he told her that his father had "apologized" by saying he did not say that about walking, but said Jack would not be able to talk for a week.

At a fact-finding hearing, Jack's father admitted and demonstrated what he had done. The judge attributed his behavior to the stress of the COVID lockdown and ordered Jack back to his father. The court made Megan stay in the courtroom while the father went to pick up Jack, who was with Megan's mother and did not know what was happening. Megan was told to call Jack and give him "emotional permission" to go with his father. She was given a four-line script to use in this call, which did not go well. As soon as Jack heard what was ordered, he threw the phone out of the window of his grandmother's car, grabbed the keys and threw those out too, then was violently sick.

Megan now feels that the only thing that can be achieved is "damage control" until Jack is 18 minus three days, before which time a barring order prevents Megan from going back to court. It has been recommended that a well-known British alienationist provide family systems therapy.

Ellen's Story

Ellen's story was rather different from the one told by Megan, involving not only a longer marriage but also Ellen's problematic health and her career as a medical professional. Ellen, a British mother, described her husband as charming, successful, good-looking, and affluent. They had known each other for three years when they married. Ellen was pregnant at the time and feeling uncomfortable, in response to which her husband was irritable because of the impact on their honeymoon trip.

After her daughter Mona was born, Ellen said, she herself became submissive and dependent on her husband. She gave up her career plans and felt that whatever went wrong was her fault. When Mona was about five years old, Ellen was suffering from medical problems including back pain. She was in and out of the hospital and had to get a nanny to take care of Mona. Ellen believes that at this point her husband realized that she could not be the "certain kind of wife" he had wanted, and decided to divorce.

Before the divorce proceedings, however, physical abuse became part of the relationship. Feeling that he "deserved more than he was getting", Ellen's husband smacked her around the head. He also became physically abusive with Mona, once holding her down on the bed with his hands on her throat until Ellen pulled him off. Ellen found she was not just "freezing" with fear of her husband, but "fawning" in her attempts to placate him. He had told her that if she left him, he would take Mona.

For two years, Ellen slept on the sofa. She was thinking about divorce but had no money. Her husband told her that he only hurt her because she deserved it, and when they were on holiday pushed this claim so far that Ellen went into the bathroom and started to try to hang herself with her bathrobe sash, an action that she described as trying to find surcease rather than actually to die.

By this time, Ellen had become estranged from friends and family. She saw that her father-in-law and brothers-in-law were also abusive. Her sister-in-law told her that if she left her husband he would certainly take Mona. Ellen went to a lawyer who said she should file for a non-molestation order. Not long after, she attended a child's birthday party with Mona and Mona's father also dropped in. The birthday child's mother asked Ellen to stay afterward, gave her tea, and said she had never seen anyone as controlling as Mona's father. This woman gave Ellen the telephone number of a divorce lawyer.

But money was still a problem. Ellen could not ask for legal aid because her name was on the mortgage of their home. She applied for a high-interest litigation loan (a service that existed in the United Kingdom but that is being reconsidered).

Divorce proceedings began when Mona was about nine. Ellen's husband refused to move out of the home. He contacted Ellen's parents who were in another country, and to whom he had not spoken for years, and they flew to London to express their concern for Mona. The husband visited friends to tell them his side of the story.

Mona's father wanted to take Mona to visit his parents on holiday in another country and wanted to go for two weeks, which Ellen felt was too much. The husband accused Ellen of interfering but did not use the term "parental alienation" at this time; instead, he referred to Ellen as "enmeshed" with Mona. He brought in a mental health professional whose emphasis was well known to be on parental alienation. The husband's lawyers worked on many cases in which this parental alienation proponent was involved.

At a hearing about the proposed holiday visit, the district judge said Ellen was trying to stop Mona from having contact with her father. It was negotiated that Ellen would drop the non-molestation order, Mona would go with her father for a week, and the father would not harass Ellen.

Ellen said that following this she was terrified but did what she could to support Mona's father—making dinner for him and Mona, picking him up once when he fell asleep on the underground. Nevertheless, the father was angry when Mona complained about his rigidity and they were in court often. The parental alienation proponent was in the background, and the judge described Ellen as "malicious".

A psychiatrist associated with the parental alienation proponent recommended "flooding" or intense exposure of Mona to her father for ten days. He told Ellen, Mona "will love you a bit less and her father a bit more". A private social worker who observed this treatment described Mona as "traumatized" and said she was screaming that she wanted to die. When Mona came home she whispered to her mother, "I never want to see him again".

Some time later, Mona was sick with fever and other symptoms for ten days. Her father said Ellen was sabotaging their contact. A quarrel ensued in which Mona ran away from her father and he caught her and carried her screaming in a "fireman's lift". Mona tried to lock herself in the bathroom but her father held her down on the floor, and (to use Ellen's description) "assaulted" her. The police came, and when they saw how frightened Mona was, they arrested the father, who was then bailed out.

At the next hearing, the psychiatrist had emailed the judge saying that Ellen was a flight risk and might kill Mona or herself. The judge gave Mona's custody to her father, although his existing bail conditions meant that he could not take her. Instead, he moved his parents into his flat so Mona could go there. The judge directed that Mona be taken right away. Ellen was told to call Mona and tell her what was to happen but not to show any distress or the call would be cut off. The social worker subsequently said she saw signs of abuse in that Mona put her stuffed bunny on her mother's bed as she prepared to leave the flat; the social worker saw this as an attempt to comfort the mother and said it meant that Mona had been emotionally abused by being parentified by her mother.

Mona stayed with her father and his parents for years but continued to say she wanted to go back to her mother. Ellen was ordered into therapy with alienationist practitioners who wanted her to "confess" that she had worked to alienate Mona from her father, which she refused to do. In the course of the therapy, Ellen begged to have Mona's voice heard, but was told it could not be heard because it was not really Mona's voice—it was just an echo of Ellen's voice. Ellen was also told that she exaggerated the domestic violence and that she should not talk about it but should focus only on the present and future.

Mona returned to her mother when she was older and both mother and daughter are now activists in domestic violence and parental alienation causes.

Nadia's Story

Nadia's story of parental alienation allegations is complicated by its having taken place in several countries with different legal and cultural positions. Nadia is a Russian woman whose experiences with such allegations were primarily in Spain. According to Nadia, the concept of parental alienation was little known in Russia at the time her narrative begins, although the idea was subsequently introduced and is better known in Russia today.

Nadia had training in linguistics and in social sciences involving cultural differences. She was beginning to study Spanish when she met her husband-to-be, a South American man who was traveling in Russia. She initially wanted to speak Spanish with a native speaker, but eventually went to Spain to visit him. She had an offer to be a tour guide in Mexico but this did not work out. Nadia's boyfriend wanted her to come with him to visit his native country and they decided they should marry in order to simplify the documents required.

Nadia became pregnant almost at once (in her interview, she said everything happened "too quickly"). When they arrived in South America, she felt her husband was "no longer the same person" but had taken on the role of the *paterfamilias*, the authority and manager of the family. Nadia was aware of the cultural differences between herself and her husband but became puzzled whether his behavior was simply abusive or was culturally prescribed. She felt that her choice was either to conform to the role of a "Latin American wife" (as she saw it) or to go back to Russia.

The couple moved to Spain with their toddler daughter, where the husband wanted to reside, thinking the move would provide a solution for some business problems. The first year was difficult, according to Nadia, because they had to obtain a Spanish residence visa for Nadia and the little girl. Nadia took her daughter for a visit to Russia and later regretted that she had not just stayed there, but at the time she was worried that having no father would be a problem for the little girl and felt that she must simply accept whatever her husband did.

Living in a remote village, Nadia was often without a car or help when the child was sick. She did her best to placate her husband, though she found it intolerable when he hit her or threw things. The little girl had tantrums and tried to hurt herself or to hurt Nadia. The father would wake the little girl to make sure she was present at marital quarrels. Nadia was devastated at his threats to take the child away.

Nadia said in her interview that it was hard for her to realize that this behavior was abusive. The term abuse was not much used in Russia at that time, nor did Nadia know the concept of narcissism, which she now applies to her daughter's father.

Living in Spain, Nadia said, made cultural factors a significant part of the marital problems. The Spanish judicial system, in her opinion, was always pro-authoritarian. After Franco died in 1975, there was a long transitional period with divorce as a new option and some awareness of women's rights. During the Franco period, according to Nadia, there were asylums for women who did not conform, and nuns who acted as "moral police" as part of a public institution founded in 1941 and continuing until 1984. Newborn babies were taken from women seen as "liberals" or "Communists" and given to supporters of Franco's dictatorship, so the idea that mothers and children could or should be separated was accepted. Nadia felt that these historical and cultural factors were at work in her experiences with allegations of parental alienation in Spain.

Nadia started her divorce proceedings. She went to the police when her husband hit her on the face. She could have asked for a protection order, but she "did it wrong". When a complaint is made, there is supposed to be a hearing withing 72 hours if the woman wants a protection order. However, 40% of requests for protection orders are refused, and if a man appeals, the order may be removed even after it has been made. According to Nadia, mothers who asked for a protection order were often reported as "alienating" by social workers in later custody proceedings. Nadia was told that a protection order prevents the father from seeing the child. And she was unfamiliar with the system, so she did not ask for one—a mistake that did, however, temporarily keep Nadia from being accused of parental alienation.

A parenting plan was put together by the lawyers. Nadia believed that her daughter loved the father but that he was not doing regular care things like bathing her, when the child was with him. The little girl had a very irritated skin rash in her groin.

Nadia's lawyers advised her not to speak of domestic violence. She accepted the parenting plan and the advice of family mediators but did not notice the allegation of parental alienation that was made. The mediator told her that she, Nadia, was using "emotional energy" and that the child could telepathically receive Nadia's negative thoughts about the father because of the connection established before she was born. The mediator's report to the court said that Nadia had established a "cult" and Nadia felt the report suggested that she not only "brainwashed" the child but performed some sort of "black magic" by "putting obstacles in the way of father–child contact", as a social worker's report put it.

The COVID lockdown started when Nadia and the father were about to start shared custody, and as a result the daughter was with Nadia for most of two years. There was a drastic change in the girl's behavior as shared custody began and as Nadia moved in with a new man who had a daughter the same age as Nadia's. Nadia advised the man not to talk to her ex-husband, but he did and was accused of starting a fight. Nadia ended the relationship as too complicated to deal with.

Following the divorce, Nadia's daughter began coming home with more of the groin rash and saying that it hurt. Once, she said that her father beat her and left her for hours in a rooftop garden in the winter. The next time she went, she came home and said "I lied". A psychologist who was involved suggested that Nadia had influenced the child's thinking through telepathy. The little girl began to wet the bed regularly even though she had been dry for years. She began to have terrible nightmares and to say, as she had when much younger, that her father was a wolf and "will kill us".

Nadia found a forensic psychologist who was willing to break the rules and see the child without the father's permission. The child, now five years old, was afraid to talk and thought her father was listening; she said "he knows everything". When asked where she slept at her father's house, the little girl began to cry and to look for a way out of the room. In a second session, the child said she wanted to talk to the psychologist with Nadia out of the room because "she cries".

The little girl also told a court psychologist details of abuse that Nadia did not know. Nadia in fact was not sure that the sexual abuse had really happened, until one day while she was reading a story the child asked, "when Father's thing rises up, why is there a round red thing in the top?". Then Nadia believed her.

Nevertheless, it was alleged that Nadia had caused the child to be alienated from her father. Nadia took the child to visit her grandparents in Russia and left her there temporarily, and the father brought an action for parental kidnapping, a crime. Nadia returned to Russia to avoid being prosecuted. In Russia, she applied for and received an order for custody of her daughter, which was granted because the father refused to talk to the lawyer or participate in the proceedings. The father requested an international criminal warrant for Nadia's arrest, while the sexual abuse investigation is ongoing. This is where matters rested at the time of this writing.

Maria's Story

Maria is a Brazilian mother whose experiences with parental alienation allegations were much complicated by a 2010 law defining and punishing acts considered to be parental alienation. This law has stood in spite of criticism and recommendations by the United Nations that Brazil alter this law because of its impact on women and children.

Maria has in fact experienced two situations in which she was alleged to have alienated children, about ten years apart. In the first situation, she was 21 and became pregnant when involved with an older man. Her family insisted that she live with the man in spite of violence and other problems.

When the child of that pregnancy was two years old, he had serious constipation, said his anus hurt, and had a kidney infection that might have come from exposure to feces. The toddler asked Maria to put her finger in his anus and said his father would do this.

Maria became sick with headaches and depression and was treated with antidepressants. Finally, her parents told her she should leave her son's father, but the man called the police and claimed that Maria's father wanted to shoot him.

When he reached school age, Maria said, her son was a "zombie", "out of control", and that he talked about suicide. The school called her and told her she and the boy must go to therapy. He could not communicate any more and jumped dangerously from the stairs and a window. He attended the psychological clinic twice a week.

The boy's father had visitation but would rarely pick him up for a weekend. The boy was distraught but refused to talk after visits. A clinic psychologist told Maria she must insist that he tell her what had happened. The boy then reported having a bar of soap put into his anus and also referred to a toothbrush being used. Maria told the psychologist, who scheduled a meeting with a "roomful of people". They wanted Maria to file a complaint; she did not want to because she feared later consequences for her son. The clinic staff said the probability that the boy had made up this story was "none". Nevertheless, Maria was afraid of filing a false complaint and causing even more trouble. The judge of the family court gave the father supervised visitation with an aunt as the supervisor.

The father filed a custody demand. He also became the head of a fathers' rights group and passed on to a judge material written by Richard Gardner about parental alienation. (Gardner's ideas are discussed earlier in this book.) The later law about parental alienation was written by the judge who received this material, according to Maria.

In the next few years, the father was convicted of child sexual abuse. When out of prison on bail, he advocated for the parental alienation law. In 2011 his sentence was vacated, with the court of appeals deciding that there had not been enough proof to meet the standards of criminal law. According to Maria, the discussion equated parental alienation with the implantation of false memories and suggested that Maria could have created false memories not only for the boy but for the psychologists.

In 2011, the boy's father brought a suit against Maria for parental alienation. The family court allowed visitation, but said he must have six months of visitation before an overnight visit was allowed. The father did one visit, bringing along some of his relatives, then "disappeared". The family court judge said that the son, who was by now 13, could "defend himself" from abuse if necessary. Further litigation occurred following conflict over the boy's passport which he needed for a trip. When the Brazilian parental alienation law was approved, news media published details about the case, including the boy's name; the father was at the time appealing his conviction and claiming that the case was a striking example of parental alienation.

Maria's son was 23 at the time of the interview. He receives government benefits because of his emotional issues, and did not graduate from high school but did get the equivalent of a General Education Diploma (a United States designation for an examination to be taken by people who want to be credited as high school graduates). He was not able to pass college courses and is looking for a job.

Maria's second encounter with allegations of parental alienation occurred when she had a second son, ten years younger than the first. She had moved to a new town and met her second husband there. Once again, she became pregnant quickly. The husband became more violent and drank more, and Maria left him when her child was a month old; however, her mother-in-law came and begged Maria to take the man back, and she agreed.

The second husband told Maria that he would work with the first husband. When the child was four years old, the second husband was increasingly violent and Maria was afraid to confront him. She got a lawyer to establish visitation and child support. The second son's father was very angry when called to court and went back to his own home country for two years. Then he returned, bringing along his mother and sister, and retained a lawyer—immediately alleging parental alienation by Maria. The family court judge gave him visitation, but said he must have three months of visits before having an overnight visit. The boy's father again returned to his own home country. He said he would give Maria full custody if she would drop the child support demand. At the time of the interview, the boy was to wait by the phone at a certain time each week, but the father did not usually call him.

In her interview, Maria again emphasized the role of Brazilian laws and court functioning in allegations of parental alienation. But she also noted that "the court is a more dangerous abuser than the abuser". Much of the danger, she suggested, comes from the actions of social workers who are officers of the court. According to Maria, these are people who have had the best scores on civil service examinations. They have the power to take children from parents, place them for adoption, or institutionalize them.

Discussion

As with other narratives in this book, these stories have not been checked against any objective criteria, and they are based on the interviewees' memories and interpretation of those memories, as well as on the interviewer's choices of questions and decisions to include certain information. Some details of the interviews had to be omitted to ensure confidentiality for the participants. The questions that follow are discussed in terms of the information provided in the interviews and summarized in this chapter.

Are These Narratives Typical of Cases Where Parental Alienation Is Alleged?

Because so little systematic study of parental alienation allegations has been done, it is difficult to know whether these are typical stories. Taken at face value, these "global" narratives seem more intense than those provided by interviews of mothers in the United States, and more often reference physical and sexual abuse of either mother or child.

None of the children were sent for intensive reunification therapy (though this was advised in one case), as far as can be told from the mothers' interviews. Some of the children received undefined types of therapy, including one who was treated with "flooding", a term that usually means intense exposure to a feared object. The usual intervention was enforcement of contact between the children and their fathers, sometimes essentially a custody reversal with the child spending long periods in the father's home, at other times simply an approximation of 50/50 shared parenting. This took place even in the case of a father who was being investigated for child abuse but was able to have his own parents care for the child, and another father who had in fact been convicted of child sexual abuse.

A mother who was ordered into therapy reported that the thrust of the treatment was to persuade her to acknowledge that she had caused the child to have a negative attitude toward the father. Her unwillingness to do this was used as a reason to prohibit her from contact with the child.

How Was Parental Alienation Identified in These Cases?

Most of the mothers who were interviewed for this chapter were not clear on the methods that led to their children being identified as parental alienation cases. Some said that parental alienation had not been alleged until the divorce proceedings had moved along for a while. One noted that when she asked for an order of protection against her husband, she was given a form warning her about parental alienation.

The children in these cases resisted contact with their fathers or showed distress during and after contact with them. In some of the cases, there were physical altercations and attempts at running away. These factors are basic criteria for identification of parental alienation, though they cannot stand alone as indicators (Bernet, 2020).

In several cases, the children's schools contacted the mothers about children's behavioral problems and suggested that sexual abuse might be causing the difficulties. When the mothers reported these issues and asked for evaluation, pointing to the fathers as the possible abusers, the fathers called the reports false allegations. The use of false allegations of physical or sexual abuse is considered an alienating behavior that may be carried out by a parent who intends to limit contact between a child and the other parent, according to alienationists (e.g. Gardner, 1985), so the existence of unsubstantiated allegations may be presented as evidence of efforts at parental alienation, although it is well known that non-penetrative sexual abuse can be impossible to substantiate. Expression of concerns about sexual abuse may thus be taken as evidence to identify parental alienation.

It does not appear that any of the cases in this chapter were evaluated for parental alienation in any systematic way. Instead, at some point, *somebody said parental alienation*, and the case proceeded from there.

Adverse Experiences of Mothers and Children

This group of mothers reported a number of adverse experiences connected with marriage and parenthood. Several had unplanned pregnancies and some left the fathers soon after their babies were born, but remained in contact with them. All of the marital relationships appeared to involve coercive control, and most involved some level of domestic violence and alcoholism, but some of the mothers stayed in their marriages for years. Financial difficulties were sometimes the reason for staying with an abusive husband, and even when separation occurred, financial problems precluded effective legal representation or supportive psychotherapy.

The processes of fighting for acceptable child custody decisions were wearing for these mothers. Without legal training, and often without counsel, these mothers had to deal with police and judicial authorities while aware that errors on their part could mean that they might have no contact with their children. For example, if the children in some way learned about legal proceedings or judicial opinions, the mothers could be claimed to have intentionally given this information as a form of parental alienating behavior, an argument that would support parental alienation allegations against them.

A powerful adverse experience resulted from the mothers' awareness that their children were in distress and that the mothers could do nothing about this; indeed, any efforts to help or comfort the children would be interpreted as parental alienating behaviors, thus threatening further reduction in mother–child contact and further exposure to abuse for the children.

According to their mothers' descriptions, the children of this group experienced a range of adverse events. In the cases of sexual abuse, these would have included not only the abuse itself, and possible painful aftermaths, but also multiple medical examinations and exposure to investigating strangers. There were several reports of rough treatment of children by their fathers, the latter using physical methods to force child compliance.

Social Influences

In two of the cases described in this chapter, it was clear that the parents of either the mother or the father played roles in the custody conflict. In one case, her parents pressured a young pregnant woman to go and live with her child's father; in another, the father's parents moved into his apartment to take care of the child, whom the father could not contact because of an investigation for abuse. One father brought his mother and sister from his home country to support his custody claims. One of the mothers had taken her daughter to visit her own parents in another country but brought her back out of concern that she would have no father; she later returned with the child to her parents' country. Although one of the mothers in this group remarried briefly, none of them mentioned roles played by stepfathers or stepmothers in the custody conflict or in the allegations of parental alienation.

One of the mothers mentioned her current involvement with a protective parents group that has supported her not only in her personal struggle but also in efforts to change laws and judicial decisions. One of the fathers was described as a leader in a fathers' rights group that supported the use of parental alienation allegations.

Cultural issues were named by some of the mothers as significant factors in their cases. For example, one woman alluded to the authoritarian history of the country where she lived during the custody conflict. Another lived in a country, Brazil, that has passed a law making parental alienation a criminal offense punishable by imprisonment and by termination of parental rights; for her, allegations of parental alienation had serious implications even beyond her concerns about her child's experiences.

Some culturally determined positions of the judiciary also had significant effects on these mothers' experiences. Custom and culture are determinants of issues like the age at which a child might testify in court or be heard in a judge's chambers; when judges believe that children should not be heard, they are likely to accept the argument of parental alienation proponents that children simply repeat what a parent has told them. How seriously abuse is taken is also a cultural issue, as more authoritarian groups are more likely to consider physical punishment necessary for discipline and to regard as punishment some actions that might otherwise be considered abusive. Similarly, sexual abuse may be considered more, or less, serious for boys than for girls, and more, or less, serious for older than for younger children, as seen in the implication of the Brazilian judge that a 13-year-old could "fight off" a sexually abusive father.

Cultural issues also influence the institutions that are involved in allegations of parental alienation. Police responses to a conflict between separated parents may focus on expectations about men and women rather than on impacts on children. One mother noted that in her country social workers employed by the courts have enormous power to take children away from parents.

Finally, changes in culture create changes in the handling of child custody conflicts. The assumption that mothers would have custody of young children, and that fathers would pay child support, has disappeared. This change has come about in part because of the women's movement's successes in supporting employment and financial independence for women, and the backlash of the fathers' rights movement and its arguments against child support requirements and maternal custody. Allegations of parental alienation can be used to manipulate financial settlements at the time of divorce, and the more custodial time a parent has, the less child support that person owes the other parent.

Effects of Allegations of Parental Alienation

This group of mothers appeared to be most intensely affected by the fact that allegations of parental alienation endangered their relationships with their children. This was a realistic concern, because separations as lengthy as years were experienced by at least one. They were also concerned about financial loss and lack of professional progress that resulted from the need to spend time and money fighting the allegations. Although some of the mothers did work that involved children, none of them stated concerns that they might lose opportunities or professional licensure because of the parental alienation allegations that might label them as abusers.

What Was the Timeline, and What Does It Imply?

Conflict between fathers and mothers began early in all the cases described in this chapter. Some never lived together or separated soon after the child was born. Some of the pregnancies were unplanned and the fathers wanted termination. In all the cases, concerns about sexual or physical abuse of the child arose before the child was of school age. It appears that there were no early, well-functioning, father–child relationships in this group; one father had a family-like relationship with the child but did not live with the mother and child.

Proponents of parental alienation ideas state that one of the five factors by which they identify parental alienation is that a parent and child once had a good relationship, but following separation or divorce of the parents, the relationship has deteriorated (Bernet, 2020). In none of the cases described in this chapter did there appear to have been a good father–child relationship in the child's early life. For that reason, it would seem that parental alienation should never have been alleged against the mothers to begin with, much less used to make decisions about child custody and parenting plans.

References

Bernet, W. (2020). Introduction to parental alienation. In D. Lorandos & W. Bernet (Eds.), *Parental alienation—science and law* (pp. 5–43). Charles C. Thomas.

Doughty, J., & Drew, M. (2022). History of the parental alienation belief system. In J. Mercer & M. Drew (Eds.), *Challenging parental alienation* (pp. 21–39). Routledge.

Doughty, J., & Rathus, Z. (2022). International expansion of the parental alienation belief system through the UK and Australian experiences. In J. Mercer & M. Drew (Eds.), *Challenging parental alienation* (pp. 40–62). Routledge.

Gardner, R. (1985). Recent trends in divorce litigation. *Academy Forum*, 29(2), 3–7.

Gardner, R. (2001). *Therapeutic interventions for children with parental alienation syndrome*. Creative Therapeutics.

8 Three Fathers Who Were Alleged to Have Alienated Their Children

Gender conflicts have been at the heart of discussions of parental alienation, so the existence of possible gender differences is essential to this topic. The parental alienation concept, as presented by Richard Gardner (1985), developed in the context of changing gender roles in the Western world toward the end of the 20th century. Women's civil rights, for example holding credit cards in their own names or deciding not to take a husband's family name upon marriage, were still evolving; in fact, women in Switzerland only got to vote in 1971. It may have been in response to these social changes that numbers of fathers' rights or men's rights groups increased during this period and later.

Changes in perspectives on child custody and child care came in step with changes in gender roles. Whereas the "tender years doctrine" of decades past had automatically placed young children in their mother's care following divorce, a practice that usually resulted in the mothers having physical custody of the children long beyond early childhood, there more recently emerged a new standard of custody decided "in the best interests of the child" by family courts. Fathers' rights groups were active in discussions of custody policy and emphasized the importance for children of contact with their fathers. These groups noted that mothers are not always ideal caregivers and argued that fathers could do just as well as mothers, and therefore should be given serious consideration for full custody.

Another relevant social change was the gradually increasing public awareness of same-sex couples, many of whom had children by adoption, surrogacy, or sperm donation. Research concluded that children of same-sex couples did well and were quite comparable to those of male–female pairings. These findings contributed to the understanding that exposure to traditional gender roles, or even to both men and women, was not a necessary factor in determining the best interests of children. Being with a father for the sake of being with a father, or being with a mother for the

DOI: 10.4324/9781003454793-8

sake of being with a mother, were elements that did not need to play a part in decisions about a child's best interests.

Although arguments about gender roles diminished somewhat with time, a second gender conflict became—if anything—more intense. This was the increasing concern about gender-related violence, with continuing research work on interpersonal/domestic violence (IPV/DV). Although research on this topic consistently found that women were more likely than men to be injured or killed in episodes of domestic violence, and that men were more likely to be perpetrators of domestic violence, groups associated with the "men's movement" continued to argue that women were as violent as men and as responsible for serious aggression against domestic partners. The efforts to portray men and women as equally violent were relevant to questions about child custody, as mothers who had been subjected to domestic violence begged courts not to send their children to their fathers for fear that the children would be abused; the counterargument was that the mothers were themselves just as likely to treat the children with violence. The gender conflict about violence was reflected in claims that mothers were more likely than fathers to attempt to alienate children from the co-parent by performing alienating behaviors like "badmouthing". Gardner (2001) suggested that the proverbial fury of women scorned led divorced women to try to turn their children away from relationships with the fathers. Other authors wrote of "malicious mothers" who punished their former husbands by making the children hate them or who falsely accused the fathers of physical or sexual abuse of the children.

All of these notional gender differences are possible, but a profound lack of information about real cases makes it impossible to know which of the claims just described come close to describing the real-world situations. Although it is known that women are more likely to be injured or killed in domestic violence, we do not really know whether women equal men in episodes of violence but are less successful in harming men. With respect to parental alienation, we similarly do not even have estimates of numbers of men and of women making parental alienation allegations during litigation; we are even farther from knowing whether men or women carry out more of the actions called alienating behaviors.

Although the earlier chapters of this book reported the stories of about equal numbers of young men and women, more recent chapters have focused on mothers alone. Doing so may have appeared to readers to support the claim that mothers are the ones who alienate their children from fathers and make false claims of abuse, and mothers are thus the ones appearing in court upon allegations of parental alienation.

Whatever the reason, the approximately 100 cases in which the present author has been involved did much more frequently involve mothers alleged to have caused children to avoid their fathers. But that fact does not mean that fathers are never accused of alienating children from mothers, and perhaps 10 of the 100 cases seen were cases where fathers were alleged to have caused their children to avoid their mothers.

This chapter will present the narratives of three of those fathers alleged to have alienated their children from the mothers. The author of this book had been involved in one of the cases and had been in contact with the children; in two others, circumstances led to invitations to the fathers to tell their stories about parental alienation allegations. Some other fathers in the group of ten mentioned earlier could no longer be reached and one had concerns about ongoing litigation that made him reluctant to be interviewed.

These fathers' stories should be considered in the context of historical and social change as discussed earlier in this chapter, as well as with the understanding that parental alienation allegations against fathers are either less common than allegations against mothers, or involve stories that some fathers do not want to share.

John's Story

John is the father of two young adults and lives on the eastern seaboard of the United States. His first statement in the interview, after affirming his pride in his children, was a quotation from his lawyer, who had told him that "the business model is that alleged parental alienation is the same as real parental alienation" (echoing the title of this book to the effect that all that may be needed to start allegations is for *someone to say parental alienation*).

John and his children's mother had divorced when the children were in elementary school, following the disclosure of an affair on the mother's part. John did not spend much time talking about the marriage or the divorce; his focus was on the allegations of parental alienation and the resulting impact on his and his children's lives.

The mother tried to allege parental alienation against John a few years after their divorce, but was unsuccessful in gaining custody of the children, as the court decided there was no alienation. It was true, however, that at least one of the children was very angry with the mother because of the affair and other events.

Later, when the children were 14 and 16, the mother began to work with a lawyer-psychologist who was a disciple of one of the major alienationists. John felt this woman was motivated by power and money and described what he recalled as a look of triumph she gave him when the court ordered the children taken away and sent to an intensive reunification program. John said he found that he had "fewer rights than a pedophile" in this situation and could not get questions answered.

According to John, the same counselors who had been involved in the early attempt to allege parental alienation stayed on behind the scenes and re-emerged three years later when the second and successful attempt took place. The counselors had not seen the children for three years at this point but wrote a new report glossing over that fact. The judge, as John recalls, said that the bottom line was that the children needed their mother. The judge demanded cooperation and said that without it, John would go to jail and the children to foster care or a juvenile detention center. There was to be a 90-day period of no contact between John and the children.

The older child, then 16, spoke to the judge and asked what he would do if he were in their position. "If you lived with Dad who never said anything bad about Mom, but were sent to Mom who says bad things about Dad?"

John noted that the record of this hearing is still sealed although years have passed. In the state where John lives, judges are appointed by the legislature for six-year terms, and the judge in question was recently preparing for reappointment. The appointment commission "grilled" the judge (John's word for it) about this case, and the judge argued that they did not know the children were to be sent to a program in a distant state, but just trusted the counselors. The commission wanted to unseal the record but the mother in this case would not agree. As a result, further information about judicial decisions is not directly available.

The children were taken from John in August and shortly began the school year. Although John was prohibited from contact with them, he had contacts in the school system who passed information on to him. He found out the children were to be taken to the reunification program only a week before it happened. A school official called (risking their job) to tell John when the children went away.

John tried several legal steps, and those steps delayed the children's trip to the treatment program, but in October of that year they were transported to an intensive reunification program in a Western state. The older child, according to John, was in "complete paranoia" and believed that her backpack was bugged. The younger child hated the situation but was calmer.

John got a new attorney, a former federal prosecutor, soon after the children's trip to the reunification program. According to John, they made it clear that they would go to trial in order to get the children back. And, John said, the opposing attorney knew they had the money to do it. The lawyers discussed making a deal and proposed to depose everyone including the mother with the intention of asking for the order to be vacated. (In contrast, John felt, many parents lack the resources or confidence to fight these situations and simply try to placate the judge and opposing side.)

During this time, the children were with their mother and her new husband, and they later told John about their experiences. The new husband told them he was just as important in their lives as John was. They had "family meetings", as required by some reunification programs, every night, and could not leave until they said something nice about their mother and stepfather. (John noted the children's skill at sarcasm even at that age.)

The children had counseling with a practitioner approved by those who had identified them as having been alienated from their mother by John. John had five meetings alone with that counselor, who had him watch the standard reunification videos like "Welcome Back, Pluto". In the interview, John described the whole thing as "a farce".

John attended one of the children's sessions, and recalled that the children were "very savvy". They kept everything positive and light, saying "it's okay but we'd like to see you", avoiding any positions the counselor could interpret as indicating parental alienation.

Back in court, John's attorney asked for the order to be vacated. The judge said they only had wanted the children to have both parents. A month later, the older child, who was now 17, found that they could emancipate themselves. They notified their mother they were going to John. The mother wanted to sue, but backed down when told she would be deposed. There remained a question about payment for the reunification program, which amounted to $38,000; the mother was to pay only half, but also backed down on this when a deposition was proposed.

According to John, the mother now posts on the internet that Jesus will make sure the children are with her through eternity. The children, John says, recognize that this is both absurd and sacrilegious.

Keith's Story

Keith is a father living on the west coast of the United States, whose two children were ordered to attend a reunification program in another state. The marriage had apparently been more than adequate but was "good until it wasn't", possibly with the advent of a third party into Keith's wife's life. Keith reported that he was very fond of his mother- and father-in-law, who have continued to be supportive and who now do not speak to their daughter.

Keith's daughters were in elementary school when the divorce occurred and spent some time with mother and with father in a 50/50 parenting plan. However, there were complications. After a few years, the mother's boyfriend moved in; he happened to be an athletic coach for the older daughter. There was psychotherapy for the mother and the daughter, but the daughter told Keith of physical abuse by her mother, as well as yelling and name-calling by the mother. Eventually the daughter left to live with her father, and the younger girl stayed at the mother's house. Altercations continued, though, especially when the older girl visited her sister. Both girls reported to the police that the boyfriend had done inappropriate touching. Keith is now not sure about what happened; he says the boyfriend had "inappropriate boundaries" but that the girls may have misinterpreted some things.

According to Keith, reports from child protective services were muted because the girls' mother threatened criminal harassment charges against the investigators. As Keith said, the sexually problematic complaints may or may not have been quite accurate, but some physical abuse like grabbing and pushing does seem to have occurred.

Both girls left to stay with Keith, and after some months he applied to the family court to stop paying the child support he had been giving his former wife. This was the beginning of serious litigation including two trials based on the theme of parental alienation. Keith expressed frustration and concern about the fact that in the course of these trials, an opponent of the parental alienation concept was discounted in the judge's orders on the grounds that she had not interviewed the children, whereas a proponent of parental alienation, who also had not interviewed the children, was used as the basis of continuing isolation of the younger daughter.

The family court considering Keith's case ruled that the girls should be taken to a reunification program in another state and that youth transport service workers should transport them. (More details of this story are given by Barnett, Riley, & "Katherine", 2022). When Keith's daughters returned from the reunification program, the elder, who was 17, successfully petitioned for emancipation and went to live with her father. The younger girl stayed with her mother and moved to another state, remaining isolated for years from her father and sister. (The girls have recently begun to talk again.)

It is of course impossible to know what outcomes for this family were caused by parental alienation allegations or by reunification therapy, and what were caused by the entire situation or by unknown factors. The daughters remain somewhat estranged from each other, and the younger daughter will not talk to Keith at all. According to Keith, the girls' mother now apologizes for causing chaos but says she "had to do it".

Keith himself has now thrown much of his energy and resources into opposing the use of reunification therapies and of other aspects of parental alienation concepts. At the time of this writing, he is celebrating the passage of some state laws that comply with a model law that prohibits the removal of children from a protective parent's home for treatments focused on improving their relationship with a parent they want to avoid. Keith has been active in parents' groups that are concerned about parental alienation allegations and their consequences for children and for parents.

Keith proposed in his interview that because some reunification programs refer to themselves as "psychoeducational", parents who become involved with them should ask questions as if the program were a residential medical facility or a private school for their children. For example, parents should be sure to find out the address and actual physical venue of the program and the names, training, and licensure of the staff. Keith also encouraged parents to concentrate on what their state laws say about custody changes and to have legal representation with willingness to ask questions about the results claimed by reunification programs. Improving the future for families where parental alienation is alleged seems to be more important to Keith than indulging anger over past events.

Alan's Story

Alan is a father living in a rural area of the United States. His story involves two parts: the narrative of marriage, divorce, and parental alienation allegations, and a backstory that explains some part of what happened. Alan's interview was a little unusual in that he was able to provide a good deal of information about testimony at the trial and how the court's original decision unraveled.

Alan was in his 20s when he met his wife, who was about the same age and had been married before. Their relationship was gratifying, and they married and had a baby girl. During the pregnancy and the first year of the baby's life, all went smoothly. But a second pregnancy when the daughter was about a year old, while physically unproblematic, was accompanied by psychological and behavioral changes. Alan described this change in his wife as "like a switch flipped". His wife became irritable and had what Alan called "insane reactions" of heightened emotionality. These were especially bad on birthdays and holidays. According to Alan, her "meltdowns" also occurred every three days "like clockwork". The trigger for these episodes would be something simple like the butter being left on the kitchen counter.

Alan's wife would also attack him physically at times and would push her way through the children to get at him, if necessary. (She did not attack the children.) After this had been going on for some years, Alan felt an episode at Thanksgiving had been "one too many", and for the first time he mentioned divorce.

A dramatic event soon showed Alan what he was dealing with. He was on his way to work, ten miles from home, when he had a call from his mother-in-law. Alan's wife was threatening suicide. Alan returned home, where he found police and an ambulance already there. Alan's wife was taken to a hospital not far away, where she agreed to commit herself to the psychiatric facility.

Convinced that divorce would follow, Alan worked toward improving his own social support network and began to consult counselors from his church. He filed a motion asking the court to give him exclusive possession of the marital home to assure the children's best interests. Alan also searched for medical or other records that might shed light on his wife's behavior. He discovered that in the course of her previous marriage she had spent time in a psychiatric hospital; she had never told him this.

When the wife was discharged from the hospital, she was taking lithium and was much calmer. But she also started an affair with a married man. When distressed, however, she would call Alan and ask him to help her—for example, if something disturbed her while out shopping. The separation was amicable at the beginning. Alan would bring the children over for visits and would stay for dinner. He paid for her apartment and medical bills, until she became aggressive with him. The couple had shared phone and email accounts, and as a result Alan could see the correspondence between the wife and her boyfriend, who stated that he would make Alan pay for everything.

When the children were 12 and 10 years old, Alan began to date a woman he had known from childhood, and they are now married. Alan's children lived with them.

The children were afraid of their mother, who had long been a scary person to them because of her emotional behavior. After she started on lithium, she was calmer but the children were wary. Alan told her to "just be there" and let the children get used to her but she was impatient to have them with her, even though she did not actually have space for them to live. The maternal grandparents came to stay with the mother for Christmas and invited the children to visit for Christmas Eve. They brought along favorite toys, a train set and a large number of stuffed animals. The children called Alan to say goodnight and left the phone open so he could hear the children's mother and grandmother fighting.

Alan drove over to get the children and the grandparents rushed them out to the car—too quickly to bring the trains and animals, which their mother refused to return for some time.

The children's mother during this period tried a variety of different counselors and dropped each if not pleased. She was convinced that if forced to be with her, the children would love her.

The mother and her lawyer began a series of efforts to have the children sent to a specific reunification therapy program and to have contact between the children and Alan prohibited for a period. There were three attempts, with different outcomes. First, the court refused to order the treatment. Second, although the court ruled against ordering the treatment program, a counselor recommended by the program director came into the picture.

The third and final effort was the one about which Alan provided most information. The children's mother alleged that their reluctance to see her was a matter of parental alienation—that Alan had persuaded the children that their mother was dangerous, and they avoided her because of the attitude he had made them develop. She asked that the court order the children into an intensive reunification program, prohibit contact between the children and Alan for 90 days or more, and require follow-up therapy for the children with a practitioner approved by the program director. Such an order would also require that Alan attend treatment with an approved practitioner, pay for all the treatment, and write a letter of apology to the children taking responsibility for all the family's troubles.

Both sides retained expert witnesses to testify about the case and the reunification program. Alan's expert spoke briefly and argued that no empirical evidence showed that the suggested program was either safe or effective. The mother's experts were, first, the director of the proposed reunification program, a social worker, and second, a physician who had left his original specialization in emergency medicine to be an expert witness in cases where parental alienation was alleged. Each of these witnesses spoke for about an hour and a half with little interruption from the lawyers.

The program director countered that Alan's expert's testimony was completely wrong, totally unscientific, and biased. She stated that the testimony contradicted 1,100 appellate courts' decisions but did not argue that appellate courts were arbiters of psychological treatments. She presented the book *Parental alienation: Science and law* (edited by Lorandos and Bernet, 2020) and stated that it was "600 pages of science", although a good deal of the book is legal commentary. The director also used the term "evidence-based treatment" to describe her program, in direct contradiction to Alan's expert's discussion of the evidence for the treatment. In this testimony, the director cited Salvador Minuchin, a founder of family therapy, and referred to her program as "experiential therapy". In addition, she stated that her reunification program had nothing in common with other reunification programs and referred to the program and the concept of parental alienation as having international support (which is of course true, as Chapter 7 of this book shows).

The judge at this point asked about lack of evidence for the reunification program's effectiveness and noted that Alan's witness had pointed this out. The director replied that her program was 100% effective if the children did not have contact with their preferred parent. She cited a research publication that had recently appeared as evidence that her program was both safe and effective. Neither lawyers nor the judge queried this statement.

The physician expert referred to the authority of the Parental Alienation Study Group (PASG), a community of parents and professionals who support parental alienation concepts and promote the use of reunification programs. The judge asked this witness if the expertise involved were that of clinical psychology; he answered that it was behavioral medicine. The physician expert noted that "children are good liars" and pointed to his chapter in the book referenced earlier as evidence of expertise. He described Alan's expert's testimony as "ideological" and "not science-based" and commented that there was a need to educate the court. He also noted that intake into the proposed reunification program requires "someone who knows what to look for" in cases where parental alienation was alleged.

The judge agreed with the testimony of the reunification program director and the physician and ordered the children to go to the reunification program. But, behind the scenes, a different story was unfolding. The children's mother was changing her mind about the order she had requested.

According to Alan, he was receiving information from childhood friends of his own and friends of his current wife. They said that the children's mother, who had recently bought a house with her new fiancé had never told the fiancé either about the legal costs, the costs of having the expert witnesses testify, or her plan to have the children live with them in that house. She had maxed out several credit cards to pay the lawyers. She thought she could make Alan pay all the fees, so had not prepared to pay them or readied the bedrooms for the children even when it was three days before the children were scheduled to go to the reunification program.

When the mother's fiancé found this out, he called Alan and said the reunification program was the "stupidest thing he ever heard of". He insisted that the children's mother must recant. Her lawyer wanted to withdraw from the case. At a Zoom hearing, the judge made the mother explain what had happened and berated her for wasting the court's time. The lawyer was allowed to withdraw and later sued the mother for his fee. The couple later abandoned their house and moved out of state; the children have since had no communication with their mother.

Alan has adopted his second wife's youngest daughter and they and the children live as a family.

Discussion

Were These Fathers' Cases Typical of Cases Where Parental Alienation Is Alleged?

In the majority of cases, parental alienation is alleged to have been done by a child's mother, not the father. Only about 10% of the cases seen by the present author involved allegations against fathers. Thus, the fathers' cases cannot be thought of as typical of cases where parental alienation was alleged and reunification therapy and prohibition of contact were recommended, simply on the basis of gender differences. The fathers' cases were also different from many other cases because of factors related to gender: the fathers had financial and educational resources and confidence in their dealings with lawyers and courts, in ways not as often found among similar groups of mothers. The exorbitant costs of reunification therapies could be absorbed by this group of fathers, as could the expense of legal fees and custody evaluations. As a result, although the fathers were quite distressed by their situations, they were not frightened into compliance and did not make decisions because of the risk of losing homes or other property. They were able to, and did, continue their legal fights as the children wanted.

In Alan's case, two unusual circumstances arose. One was that the extensive testimony of the reunification program director, although it was followed by the court's decision to order reunification therapy, revealed some thinking that might be helpful in other cases and that was actually questioned by the judge. The second was the very improbable situation in which the children's mother had concealed her plans from her fiancé, and revealing the plans led to her wish to have the court order retracted.

The fathers' cases differed in the history and nature of the mother–child relationships. In Alan's case, the younger child had never had a calm relationship with the mother, and the older had had such a relationship only for the first year or so of their life. In John's case, the mother–child relationship had been rocky from early on and the children were very angry at the time of the divorce; the mother also had other children with whom she did not have much contact. In Keith's case, the children's conflict with the mother seems to have increased after the divorce and may have been exacerbated by their relationship with the mother's boyfriend. These differences are similar to the variety of relationships found in cases where mothers were alleged to have caused children's resistance to contact.

How Was Parental Alienation Identified in These Cases?

None of the fathers reported any formal procedure by which their children were evaluated as resisting contact with their mothers because of parental alienation. (It is possible that such evaluations did occur, but the fathers were not aware of them.) Such a procedure would presumably have applied the Five Factor Model, looking at child resistance, presence of a good prior relationship between parent and child, absence of substantiated abuse, evidence of parental alienating behaviors, and presence of certain child behaviors.

What would an evaluation using the Five Factor Model have shown? In all of the three interviews with fathers, the children did resist contact with their mothers. In two of three cases, the prior relationship with the mother was a poor one. There were no abuse investigations and therefore no substantiated abuse; Keith's daughters reported that their mother's boyfriend was abusive, but this claim was not investigated. None of the available evidence showed parental alienating behaviors by the fathers, or relevant child behaviors—although it is possible that the fathers did not know or did not mention these. With this minimum of information, it seems reasonable to conclude that application of the Five Factor Model would not necessarily have led to allegations of parental alienation in these cases.

One of the expert witnesses in Alan's case made the remarkable statement that to identify parental alienation you need "someone who knows what to look for", suggesting that parental alienation cases are not obviously different from other cases where children resist contact with a parent, and perhaps that efforts to find significant factors are needed for legal success. It may simply be that in these cases, *someone said parental alienation*, and that was sufficient to start the legal process on its way.

Were There Adverse Experiences Associated With Allegations of Parental Alienation in These Cases?

In two of the cases, there were adverse experiences for the fathers and the children starting well before the divorces. For John, his wife's affair and the impact on the children were distressing even before parental alienation was alleged. For Alan, his wife's mental illness was frightening to the children and made his life unpredictable, with family violence and the need to protect the children causing much difficulty. Alan's wife's post-divorce suicide threats and psychiatric hospitalization heightened the stress. According to Keith, on the other hand, the early adverse experiences for himself and his daughters were relatively light except for the divorce process itself; the later experiences, following the divorce, included concerns about the mother's boyfriend and his behavior toward the girls as well as difficulties about financial demands.

Keith and John both experienced the anxiety and helplessness of knowing that their children were taken by transporters to reunification programs that kept them isolated and prohibited all contact with the fathers. Returning from the treatment programs, their children were still prohibited from contact, leaving the fathers unable to do more than imagine what the children's feelings and experiences must be. These pressures were relieved for John when he managed to negotiate the legal system and when the oldest child, then 17, declared her intention to be emancipated (as was legally possible in their state). Keith had a similar experience with his eldest's emancipation, but remained out of contact with the younger sister and in fact spent many years without communicating with her; he remains, at the time of this writing, unhappy with her unwillingness to talk to him.

Alan's post-divorce adverse experiences were different from the others because his children's mother was forced by circumstances to change her mind about sending the children to a reunification program. However, Alan had reason to anticipate the use of such a program not once but twice, and as he found out about the program's practices was greatly distressed. His concern was amplified when he was forbidden to inform the children when they were to go to the treatment program and essentially given the choice of betraying his children's confidence by failing to warn them, and risking fines or imprisonment for contempt if he did warn them.

The financial adverse experiences associated with parental alienation allegations should not be minimized. Each of the fathers in these cases paid, or risked paying, multiple thousands of dollars. Expenditures of USD 500 or 600,000 are not unusual in cases where parental alienation is alleged. Financial harms can decimate college funds, interfere with responsibilities toward aging parents, use family resources that would pay for music lessons or orthodontia, force the sale of a family home, and draw heavily on a parent's retirement savings.

Were There Stepparents or Other Social Influences in These Cases?

Stepparents and other relatives or social contacts can act to ameliorate or to worsen family conflicts, including problems associated with allegations of parental alienation. Such influences were present among the fathers who were interviewed.

In John's case, the presence of their mother's boyfriend affected the children's attitudes even before the divorce occurred. The children experienced the intrusion of the boyfriend in the mother's distraction and changed expectations of them. Disclosure of the mother's affair followed the accidental finding of a phone in the oldest child's jacket when she and her father went for a walk, and as this was followed by conflict and divorce proceedings, the child's attitudes and relationships with both parents must have been affected by the event and in turn affected her father's concerns. The mother's other children, of whom she did not have custody, were shadowy figures whose existence may have reminded everyone that mothers and children might have quite intermittent relationships.

Following the divorce, the mother's new husband told the children that he was now as important as their father, a position that must have been met with distaste by children who already resented the man as the cause of their family break-up. It is possible, though not clear from John's interview, that the stepfather was instrumental in pressing for reunification therapy and prohibition of contacts between the children and John. These factors suggest that, indeed, a social influence other than the parents and children was at work in creating allegations of parental alienation, with consequences in specific court orders.

Keith's interview did not make it clear whether his children's mother had been involved with another man before their separation. The early post-divorce period seems to have been relatively peaceful, with 50/50 parenting arrangements. More difficulties arose when the children's mother had her boyfriend move into her house and be present when the girls were with her. There was an unusual complication because the boyfriend already had something of a relationship with one of the daughters, as her athletic coach. The boyfriend was later at the heart of disagreements between the girls, especially the elder, and their mother. The girls said he had grabbed or touched them inappropriately. These statements were bound to be of concern to Keith but could easily be interpreted as false allegations when considered from the parental alienation perspective; such an interpretation would be consistent with the argument that Keith was alienating the girls from their mother by encouraging them to claim that the mother's boyfriend had sexually abused them. Again, as in John's case, it appears that in Keith's family, a social influence from a third party contributed to allegations of parental alienation.

In Alan's very complicated case, several people other than the children's mother and father helped to influence the family situation. Alan's mother-in-law was aware of her daughter's emotional fragility and was the one to warn Alan about her suicidality and to help arrange for her psychiatric hospitalization. The mother- and father-in-law were also present during the high-conflict Christmas visit to the mother and helped by rushing the children to Alan's car when he came to get them. Their support of Alan and concern about their daughter may have encouraged the latter to see her situation as risking loss of contact with her children and to pursue the remedies she hoped for in allegations of parental alienation.

The mother's fiancé in Alan's case was apparently uninformed about the reunification program, its cost and its aftermath, as he was surprised and uncooperative when he found the children were to move into the house they had bought together. The fiancé had a major effect on the case when he made direct contact with Alan and arranged a meeting to talk about the court's order and the subsequent parenting plan. The fiancé's judgment of the reunification program as nonsense, and his refusal to allow the children to move in, were major factors in forcing the mother to refuse the order she had asked for and to abandon her plans for living with the children. In Alan's case, then, social influences were at work throughout the post-divorce period and especially as the court's order for reunification was about to take effect.

What Were the Effects of Parental Alienation Allegations on the Fathers Who Were Interviewed?

All of the fathers expressed their worries and concerns about their children's actual or possible experiences with reunification therapy and the associated period of contact prohibition. These problems were major issues in the fathers' lives for months or years and apparently were not fully resolved even when the children returned to normal contacts with their fathers. As an example of a concern, John mentioned the case of Nathan Grieco, a 16-year-old who had committed suicide when forced to live with his abusive father.

Experiencing allegations of parental alienation led to financial challenges for all the fathers interviewed, but all of them apparently were able to meet challenges like payment for legal representation. None of the fathers mentioned having had to sell their home and move to a less expensive area, or having had to borrow money from friends and family, as did some of the mothers described in other chapters. However, Keith, when his children were living with him, filed a motion for decreased child support payments, and he felt that this request was one of the factors that triggered allegations that he had alienated the girls from their mother. For all the fathers, the financial exigencies of parental alienation allegations would cause indirect financial harm to their families and possible difficult decisions about how money should be used.

None of the fathers interviewed for this chapter had a profession in which much contact with children was required. As a result, none felt or was threatened with loss of jobs or licensure based on the argument that parental alienation is a form of child abuse. As women are more likely than men to do jobs like teaching or nursing, in which contact with children may be a critical part of the work, it is probably the case that more women than men are exposed to this form of harm from parental alienation allegations.

Unlike some of the mothers discussed in other chapters, none of the fathers stated that their experiences of parental alienation allegations had altered their ways of thinking about the world or made them feel vulnerable or anxious. However, it is also true that these fathers' situations did not include possible sexual or physical abuse by the other parent, unlike some of the mothers' experiences, and therefore the fathers' cases may not have been as psychologically disruptive as those recounted by some of the mothers. In addition, none of the fathers mentioned that they had been ordered to write letters of apology to the children or to declare that they, the fathers, alone were responsible for family conflict and for the children's negative views of their mothers—orders that produce enormous stress in those who receive them, as they struggle with the choice of lying to their children or of having no further contact with them.

What Was the Timeline of the Fathers' Cases and What Does This Imply?

Proponents of the parental alienation concept have stressed the idea that parental alienation cases show good early relationships between parent and child, with the relationships deteriorating and moving toward rejection after separation or divorce. The implication, of course, is that after separation, a parent has the opportunity and motivation to negatively influence the child's attitude toward the other parent—in other words, to cause alienation. A child who has always had a poor relationship with a parent is, by this assumption, not to be considered to have been alienated.

There are many difficulties with this approach to identifying parental alienation cases, but one of the most serious problems is the difficulty of establishing evidence of a good or poor relationship. Parents do not usually make records of family shouting matches or semi-abusive punishments, but concentrate on recording happy times at birthday parties or holiday trips. In addition, the parental behavior that indicates a good relationship with a young child may be substantially different from behavior showing a good relationship with a teenager, so old records may not indicate anything about changes in the relationship following divorce.

In the cases of the interviewed parents, the timelines did not indicate that there had been good mother–child relationships before the divorce. In John's case, the children were angry and upset with their mother when her affair became known prior to the divorce. In Alan's case, one of the children had been exposed to the mother's frightening behavior from the toddler period on, and the other had had this experience since birth. Only Keith failed to mention significant problems between the mother and the children before the divorce, and in Keith's case the later presence of the mother's boyfriend appeared to be a significant factor affecting the children's attitudes. These timelines and related factors raise serious questions about whether there should ever have been allegations of parental alienation in the first place.

References

Barnett, A., Riley, A., & "Katherine". (2022). Experiences of parental alienation interventions. In J. Mercer & M. Drew (Eds.), *Challenging parental alienation* (pp. 63–86). Routledge.

Gardner, R. (1985). Recent trends in divorce litigation. *Academy Forum*, 29(2), 3–7.

Gardner, R. (2001). *Therapeutic interventions for children with parental alienation syndrome*. Creative Therapeutics.

Lorandos, D., & Bernet, W. (Eds.) (2020). *Parental alienation—science and law*. Charles C. Thomas.

9 Two Fathers Who Reported Positive Results From Reunification Programs

All of the interviewees in the other chapters of this book felt themselves to have been negatively affected by allegations of parental alienation and either by the experience of reunification programs or by the fear that they would have to attend such programs. Even Marla, who will be discussed in the next chapter, a mother who felt that she was the one who had been affected by alienating behaviors on the part of her children's father, did not think her son's reunification treatment had been at all successful (although she still thought that a more intensive program could have helped). This chapter will be different from the others in that it will focus on two cases where fathers had strongly positive feelings about identification of their children as alienated and about the outcomes of reunification treatments.

It is important for this book to examine these two fathers' interviews and to see how they contrast with other parents' comments. It would be unfair, unrealistic, and unscientific to assume that all parents and children in parental alienation cases are unhappy about their experiences and outcomes. It is not surprising that people with complaints should be eager to make themselves heard, or that people who have contentedly gone on with their lives should not bother to give interviews about past events—but surely if everyone who has experienced parental alienation allegations were displeased with their experiences, there would be fewer and fewer cases where alienationist concepts were employed, and this does not appear to be true. It would be astonishing if there were no cases in which parents felt that allegations of parental alienation against their co-parents had been accurate and the outcomes of treatment positive.

It is sometimes argued that there is "no such thing as parental alienation"—that in fact all cases where children avoid a parent are caused by factors other than the co-parent's efforts to cause alienation. Because mistaken allegations of parental alienation can have serious negative impacts on families, it is understandable that such a claim would be

DOI: 10.4324/9781003454793-9

made. However, in the complete absence of foundational research about parental alienation (indeed, even about children's avoidance of a parent), it is not logical to claim the unprovable nonexistence of a phenomenon. Human beings do many unpredictable and bizarre things, even stranger things than trying to influence a child's attitude toward a co-parent. Until we have empirical research showing how frequently parental alienation occurs, and under what circumstances it may be likely, it would behoove us to assume that narratives about parental alienation, as told by affected people, are equally accurate whether they take a positive or a negative approach to alienationism. (This does not mean, of course, that every legal case arguing that parental alienation has occurred should be given the same value.)

Most of the interviewees discussed in this book were people who had been in touch with the author in the past, although some were now-adult children who knew of the book project through other sources. That group had universally had some (or many) objections to the use of parental alienation concepts and related reunification treatments and were ready to discuss their experiences. Finding interviewees who had positive views of parental alienation concepts, and felt they had good outcomes from reunification programs, was not so simple. The author took advantage of membership in a listserv for professionals involved in child custody cases to ask to be put in touch with clients who had had positive experiences with reunification programs designed for cases of parental alienation. Only two responses came, and fortunately both of the individuals, both fathers living in the United States, were willing to participate in interviews. This chapter relates their narratives.

Ryan's Story

When Ryan met his wife, Barbara, the mother of his daughter, he was going through a job change and living first with his parents on the eastern seaboard of the United States and then in a house with some roommates. The meeting, in the early 2000s, was through an online dating platform. Ryan's wife-to-be was from an affluent family and was worried about stalking and kidnapping; she made it difficult to contact her, but a relationship developed nonetheless.

After the couple had been dating for a year, Ryan was clearly uncomfortable in his living situation, and Barbara suggested he move in with her. She soon made it clear that she wanted to marry, and as Ryan later told the story, he felt he had the choice of marrying her or having to find a new place to live, and he chose marriage.

The couple went for counseling before getting married, and Ryan in his interview said that at that time there were two "red flags" suggesting that the marriage was not necessarily well-advised. The first had to do with Barbara's display of anger when the two were doing work on some houses she owned. The second "red flag" came from her attitude when the Roman Catholic priest who was counseling them gave the opinion that they had not known each other long enough; she said he was giving them a hard time and proposed that they go to a priest in another town where she owned property, and they were in fact married in that place. But Ryan recalled that there were many problems about the wedding planning, with disagreements about the number of guests and whether children should be invited.

Ryan felt, also, that his wife's past history was relevant to the problems they had. She had not been brought up Roman Catholic, but had converted. She was adopted at an early age, having been born to an unmarried couple who later married and had another child, but who did not respond well to Ryan's wife when she later reached out to them. Barbara's adoptive father said that as a child, she did not "cling", according to Ryan's interview. When the marriage was going badly, Ryan was in touch with the adoptive father, who told Ryan he must "put his foot down"—an action that apparently caused more friction.

In his efforts to understand what had happened in the marriage, Ryan said he looked for and found two men who had previously been in serious relationships with his wife. One of them had bailed out a week before the scheduled wedding. Ryan felt that their stories were similar to his own and that the wife's difficult behavior had shipwrecked the marriages and also foretold the child custody problems.

With regard to the period of their married life, Ryan said he felt his wife wanted to be part of Ryan's close-knit family but did not know how to do it. Their daughter was born after a year of marriage, and little things began to be problematic. For example, Ryan's parents had owned a house in a popular beach and boating area where Ryan's wife loved to go boating. The parents sold the house and the boating possibilities were reduced. Ryan felt that Barbara felt very much entitled but did not appreciate what was given to her. She was angry much of the time. Ryan began to experience some serious business difficulties and the wife proposed that he close his office and work from home. He did not want to do that because he felt he would then have no way to escape her anger, but was forced to do it by his financial position.

Ryan described himself as a "stay at home Dad" and said he did much of the child care. Barbara breastfed but Ryan was often up at night. He put the child to bed, sat with her in a rocking chair and played music.

Later he did various activities like fishing and crafts with his daughter. Ryan draws and paints, and he noted that the now-adult daughter is an art major.

Ryan and his wife were married for 10 or 11 years before the situation worsened and the wife agreed to go for counseling. Several events prefigured this crisis: Ryan's sister, Barbara's mother and brother, and their dog all died in a short period of time. Although she agreed that counseling was needed, Ryan's wife insisted that he promise not to tell his family what they were doing and in fact not to talk to them until the counseling was finished. She threatened to take away his car (which she apparently owned) if he did not obey this rule.

Ryan did not say much about his wife's relationship with his parents, but he described an event that occurred toward the end of the marriage. Ryan's parents wanted to see their granddaughter before they went to Florida for the winter and they filed a lawsuit asking the court to order this. An agreement was reached by mediation in which the grandparents could have dinner at a restaurant with the girl (now about ten years old) at a restaurant while Ryan and Barbara sat at a nearby table. In his interview, Ryan did not make it clear whether there had been a long-standing disagreement about contact with the child, eventually leading to the lawsuit, or whether this was a way in which his family tended to respond to conflict.

When the daughter was about ten, Ryan decided he wanted a divorce and needed to get his office out of the house. Barbara began behaving violently and Ryan began to record her behavior of yelling at and hitting him. A neighbor also overheard the wife and was willing to testify when the divorce went to court. Ryan noted that the wife did not yell at or hit the daughter and was in fact very protective of her; the child never saw her mother hit or yell at her father, according to Ryan.

When the divorce was final, the court ordered supervised visits until an evaluation was done, because of the couple's history of violence. Ryan wanted full custody of his daughter. He was worried about badmouthing and brainwashing—alienationist terms he had never heard but learned about in the course of the divorce. The (now ex-) wife said he had lied in court and that the findings were "rigged". In Ryan's interview, he described his surprise at the use of the parental alienation concept and said he would never have thought anyone would say this.

At this point, Barbara said she wanted psychotherapy for the daughter, who was not speaking to Ryan. Ryan, who had not really wanted therapy, now suddenly felt it was needed. The first therapist they sought declined to go on because his training was not adequate for the extensive problems he saw in Ryan's family.

Although Ryan and Barbara had a 50/50 parenting plan, the daughter was clearly not amenable to contact with her father. According to Ryan, beginning when she was about 10½, when the girl was at his house she would hide in her bedroom and refuse to come down for meals. By the time she was 11 her negative attitude became very strong and she resisted coming to Ryan's house. When she was there, she would avoid Ryan and take long showers—which he dealt with by turning off the water. While they were waiting for a new evaluation to be done, Ryan went some weeks without picking up the daughter from the school bus, after she had been refusing to come with him.

The new evaluator made a point of talking to everyone in the family as he assessed the situation. Ryan also found a new therapist for himself during this period. Following the evaluation, the evaluator recommended taking the daughter to a reunification program in another state. The court ordered the mother to take the child to the program; Ryan had at this time not seen his daughter for several months.

At the program, a rental house was provided for Ryan and his daughter. A staff member from the program slept at the house the first night, and security was provided to prevent the girl's mother from interfering. The program plan was to introduce Barbara into the interaction on the fourth or fifth day of the program. She was "getting her own therapy" at the program and planned to be the one to take the child home. Ryan and his ex-wife were asked to write letters of apology to each other and to read them to each other, without the daughter present, and they did this. However, on the last day of the program, the mother refused to comply with what was being asked of her, and was thrown out of the program, so Ryan took his daughter home after all. Ryan felt that the program was a turning point for his daughter and himself, as they ate together for the first time in a while.

On returning home, Ryan found a new therapist, whom he described in his interview as "a godsend". The previous therapist had used what Ryan called "hardball tactics" and had told Ryan not to give up any parenting time. The new therapist had a more nuanced approach. The new therapist initially tried to work with Ryan, his daughter, and Barbara at the same time but this did not work out; Ryan said in his interview that his ex-wife was caught lying. Eventually, only Ryan and his daughter attended therapy. The therapist said approvingly that Ryan was reaching out and trying different approaches.

However, when the daughter graduated from middle school, she was still not speaking to Ryan. At the graduation ceremony, Ryan took pictures from a distance and felt very awkward. Ryan's father also came to the graduation and there was badmouthing of Ryan's whole family by Barbara.

When the daughter was about 16, she began to have private time with the therapist, and Ryan saw this as very beneficial. The therapist encouraged the girl to take trips with Ryan, and she accompanied him on a vacation to Baltimore and Washington—Ryan provided her with a private room. Later on, they went to Cape Cod. The daughter wanted to see the lighthouses but she still refused to sit beside Ryan in the car. These steps forward were interrupted by the year of the COVID pandemic, which Ryan felt his ex-wife used as an excuse. (Ryan himself has not been vaccinated but believes he could treat the disease with ivermectin, the antiparasitic drug.)

Eventually Ryan felt he had negotiated a milestone when he rented a house at the seashore and his daughter and a friend came for one weekend. They ended the therapy soon after, although at the time of this writing, several years later, the daughter still will not hug Ryan. Ryan also bought a house in a southern state and successfully got his daughter and three of her girlfriends to come to visit; he took the girls anywhere they wanted to go. Finally, two years before the interview, the daughter did not fight making the visit and brought a group of girls for the weekend, which Ryan felt went very well.

Thinking it all over, Ryan noted that asking for full custody seemed to get "a bad look from the court". He also felt it was essential to have "good doctors". He referred to a therapist who had come out of the office to sit in the car with the daughter when she refused to go in. Ryan trusted the last therapist they had and said he could begin to see change happening when there was a gradual approach, although he also liked the intensive reunification program they attended. He noted that he observed steps forward and steps back in the course of treatment, as his daughter began to talk a little bit more. and he advised people not to expect that there would be any sudden changes.

Charlie's Story

Charlie and his wife, Ann, had been married for almost ten years and had three young children when Ann said she wanted a divorce. Charlie was surprised and shocked by this—he had felt that Ann came from a strong "family unit" and he expected her mother to tell her to get in line, but this did not happen. Charlie has given a great deal of thought to Ann's family background as it related to her decision to divorce, and in his interview he referred to a lack of attention that he felt Ann had experienced as the youngest "afterthought" in her family. (He also mentioned what he considered societal factors as possible causes; these will be discussed later.) Charlie felt that his wife's sisters had influenced her to seek divorce, and that one of them had even "bankrolled" Ann's finances.

Not long after they separated, Ann reported Charlie to child protective services for what he described as "neglect". In his interview, Charlie said that he had smacked one of the children for running into the street. There was an investigation, but it was closed—until a short time later Charlie was told that a charge of sexual assault had been added.

The new charge, Charlie said, led to a "running battle" in which he did not see the children freely for two years. On occasional supervised visitations, one of the children alluded to Charlie "putting his thumb up [my] butt". The case was sent for investigation to their state's sexual assault intervention network, which uses a multidisciplinary approach and attempts to cause the least possible secondary trauma to victims. Charlie felt that the interviews with the children, intended to be non-leading, were actually "trying to get the kids to tell". Fortunately, Charlie said, some neighbors allowed Charlie and the children to have visits at the neighbors' house, and supervised the visits. Asked whether there might have been any accidental contact that a child would have interpreted as sexual, Charlie thought something might have happened in the course of "roughhousing". However, he also felt that after a while he could see that people did not think the allegations were true, and that the system began to work for him rather than against him.

At this point, Charlie reported, Ann "went berserk". She accused Charlie's family of recording and selling footage of sexual assaults on the children. Charlie noted that although this story was "a complete fabrication", it was not possible to achieve an equally complete vindication. He felt that Ann's stories became more and more fantastic and that she was coaching the children. He also felt that she was trying to provoke him to slug her and that this was a ploy divorce lawyers suggested. (He did not slug her.) Charlie noted in the interview that he could have "destroyed her legally" but did not because he wanted Ann to be the best mother she could be. He was very distressed by the public nature of the divorce.

Charlie had never heard of parental alienation before this point in the divorce was reached, but when he came across the term he read everything about it that he could find. He felt that the issue did not arise for the first year after the separation, but that after that point Ann did not want the children to see him. He also believed that Ann's sister had brought up parental alienation with her and that her lawyer encouraged allegations in a way related to parental alienation. He felt that Ann and the oldest child had become "enmeshed", in the opinion of the guardian *ad litem*, and that this created a problem for Charlie's relationship with that child, who, according to Charlie, had some autistic-like characteristics of shyness and social withdrawal.

Charlie noted in the interview that at this time he was also still concerned about the allegations of child sexual abuse. He did not want to go to prison and recognized the danger in prison for anyone thought to be a child sexual abuser. His brother was able to lend him a considerable sum for legal representation. Charlie's lawyer knew the psychotherapist who later proved to be helpful to the family and was liked even by Ann.

The family court ordered Ann into therapy, and then the whole family to an intensive reunification program. Charlie feels that the program was not necessary for him, but that in going, he did the right thing for Ann. It was, he said, the Christian thing to do, and in addition he still loves her. Before the reunification program, Charlie feels he had done all the "heavy lifting" to try to improve Ann, but the program and their therapist were helpful. Describing the program, Charlie noted that all the kids, ranging in age from 6 to 17, bonded with each other very quickly. He also stated that some of the 8 families present had fathers who were actually alienators. He noted that in two families, the fathers (who, he emphasized, shared Charlie's ethnicity) were unforgiving and would not change their black-and-white worldview.

Charlie's children are now young adults and are on good visiting terms with him and his present wife. Although they were eventually on a 50/50 parenting plan, the children have never lived permanently in Charlie's home. One of the children is in college on another continent, which Charlie attributes to problems in the child's relationship with Ann. Charlie feels that over time the children have begun to question Ann's stability. Charlie has never discussed Ann's actions or any of the past events, including the allegations of child sexual abuse, with the now-adult children. He feels that at present Ann relies too much on one of the children for social support, and he has encouraged that child to "cut the apronstrings". At the time of the interview, Charlie said, Ann had a boyfriend planning to move in with her, and the children were not enthusiastic. Ann and one of the children recently had serious conflicts.

As it was noted earlier in this section, Charlie considers the divorce and child custody problems he experienced to be partly due to systematic social issues. He has strong feelings about the position of men in modern society and their need for different social resources than women want. He noted that in the difficult days following his separation from Ann, he was much helped by a male acupuncturist who spent time talking with him. Charlie referred to loyalty and camaraderie among men, especially as evidenced in ancient Greece, and seemed to contrast this with his sense of betrayal in marriage. He also referenced Jordan Peterson, the Canadian psychologist and social media figure who has spoken of a crisis of masculinity and criticized legislation in response to identity-related political issues. Charlie spoke of his conviction that feminism has destroyed American women, who feel they do not have to stay married, and that family courts are too lenient with women. However, he praised his mother and sisters for supporting him through the divorce and mentioned his psychotherapist's kindness and "grandmotherliness".

When asked if he could give advice to other men who found themselves in the position he experienced, Charlie had several suggestions. He advised that they should stay strong and have confidence that "the world will turn" and the situation will work out. The children, Charlie felt, would eventually figure out what was really happening. He cautioned that it would be better not to criticize the children's mother and not to "slug her or anything". Charlie noted that sometimes men feel powerless in court and just give up, and he pointed to this as happening globally, not just in North America.

Charlie referred to the feeling that "nobody cares about you" and suggested that it might be helpful to be with other men having the same experiences. He compared the situation to that of a military veteran trying to recover from war experiences and noted that "vets heal vets". But, he said, though men need that kind of contact they probably won't seek it (but perhaps they might).

Discussion

As in previous chapters, there are some questions to answer about these two interviews.

Were These Two Fathers Typical of People in Parental Alienation Cases?

As was noted in earlier chapters, the lack of foundational research on parental alienation makes it difficult or impossible to know what is typical of all families in parental alienation cases. However, it is usually assumed (correctly or incorrectly) that mothers more often are alleged to try to alienate fathers, and fathers are less often the butt of similar allegations. Charlie and Ryan were in that sense typical, as they felt that their children's mothers had made efforts to alienate the children from them.

However, it is also the case that the other fathers, as well as the mothers, interviewed for this book had negative views of parental alienation concepts and of reunification programs. Relative to those other participants, the two fathers whose narratives appear in this chapter were atypical in their positive views. But this is, of course, not evidence that the latter individuals are atypical compared to the whole population of families where parental alienation has been alleged. The apparent difference in frequency of positive and negative attitudes may have to do only with the ways in which parents came to participate in this project.

Looking through the two fathers' narratives, some notable points are relevant to the question of typicality. In Ryan's case, his wife appears to have had considerable financial advantage over Ryan, whereas in the accounts of mothers' cases it is almost invariably the husband who has financial and other resources. In Charlie's case, too, the wife seems to have had financial help from her sisters, which she needed even to start the divorce process. Charlie's case was different from those of other parents described in this book in that he was investigated by child protective services and eventually defended himself against child sexual abuse allegations; Charlie's risks were not simply of sequestration from his children, but possibly of imprisonment and being affected in multiple serious ways.

Ryan's and Charlie's experiences of reunification therapies were somewhat atypical in comparison to the experiences of other parents discussed in this book. This difference results in obvious part from the fact that these fathers wanted and sought reunification treatment, whereas the other parents regarded the treatment as intrusive and harmful to the children. Both Ryan and Charlie were appreciative of the efforts of their therapists and felt them to have been very helpful. Ryan regarded the intensive reunification program as a "turning point" in his relationship with his daughter. Although Charlie did not think the intensive program was necessary for him personally, he found it a good experience, but he did not comment on any resulting changes in his relationships with the children. Neither Ryan nor Charlie reported any anger or resentment associated with the treatment programs, nor did they report that their children were in any way harmed by them or that any adverse experiences occurred.

The outcomes of the treatment programs, as described by Ryan and by Charlie, were somewhat different from those reported by the other parents. Although reunification programs on the whole state that children need good relationships with both parents, none have published any research showing that such relationships (with both parents) have resulted from the programs. All of the parents interviewed for other chapters reported that, following reunification therapy and placement of the child with the rejected parent until age 18, their children later had minimal or no contact with the parent they had originally rejected (the event that led to the allegations of parental alienation). Ryan and Charlie, however, eventually both experienced something approaching a 50/50 parenting plan, and the now-adult children have reasonably positive relationships with both parents, although there remain some difficulties in those relationships.

It is common for beliefs about child custody, marriage, and the roles of men and of women to be associated with certain religious or political positions, and for laws and customs to reflect this fact. For example, laws in the United States, the United Kingdom, Canada, and other countries influenced by Britain employed the concept of the "tender years"—that mothers were especially qualified to care for infants and young children, and that custody decisions should be based on that assumption. Some views about marriage and children tend to be associated with a liberal political and religious position, others with a more conservative stance. Charlie and Ryan both professed somewhat conservative beliefs that were not mentioned by the other parents who were interviewed. For example, Ryan mentioned that he had not been vaccinated against COVID but depended for treatment on an antiparasitic drug; these positions had emerged during the COVID pandemic of 2020–2021 as associated with political and religious conservativism. Charlie specifically stated views on male and female gender roles that reflected strong conservative positions; he blamed feminism for a number of social problems and praised women whom he saw as supportive and "grandmotherly". It is possible that the conservative views shown by Charlie and Ryan are associated with their assessments of parental alienation concepts and of the reunification programs they experienced.

How Was Parental Alienation Identified?

In both Ryan's and Charlie's cases, children were either avoiding a father or alleging that they had been abusively treated. An evaluator was said to have decided that these behaviors were signs of parental alienation. Neither father mentioned reasons why a child might avoid him other than the actions of the child's mother. Charlie spoke of his ex-wife lying in court and showed resentment of her allegations about him, but he did not name many other possible parental alienating behaviors listed in discussions of the Five Factor Model for identification of parental alienation (Bernet, 2020) although he mentioned her "badmouthing" his family and claiming that they sold recordings of child sexual abuse. Ryan described his ex-wife's anger and capriciousness, but he did not specifically relate them to the child's reluctance to see him; interestingly, he spoke of the mother's protectiveness for the child during the marriage, whereas an alienationist viewpoint would see her as abusive rather than protective.

What Was the Timeline?

The timeline of a child's avoidance of a parent is considered to be an essential piece of information for identification of parental alienation, according to the Five Factor Model used by many alienationists. That model assumes that in cases of parental alienation, a child must have had a good relationship with the now-rejected parent before the divorce, and the relationship was only spoiled by the actions of the preferred parent following the divorce. Both Ryan and Charlie reported that their relationships with their children had been good, and Charlie even noted that there were no problems for a year after he and his wife separated. Ryan considered that his daughter's avoidance had not begun for some months after the separation. Ryan's recollections contained an item that may or may not be relevant here—that his parents brought a lawsuit to have contact with Ryan's daughter before they went to Florida for the winter. This rather unusual event would seem to indicate that the grandparents thought Ryan, or his wife, or both, were in some way interfering with their relationship with the child, and this conceivably could indicate difficulties in the relationships between the parents themselves and the child. However, nothing was mentioned by either Charlie or Ryan to suggest that they were aware before their divorces of any difficulties between themselves and their children, so on that basis the Five Factor Model would not reject the possibility of parental alienation—nor would parental alienation necessarily be identified.

Reference

Bernet, W. (2020). Introduction to parental alienation. In D. Lorandos & W. Bernet (Eds.), *Parental alienation—science and law* (pp. 5–43). Charles C. Thomas.

10 Nature, Nurture, and Avoidance of a Parent

How Child Characteristics May Affect Parental Alienation Allegations

Alienationist authors from Richard Gardner's time to the present have stressed the roles of parents in causing children to avoid one parent. Those authors emphasized the idea that one parent could "brainwash" children into negative attitudes toward the other parent, and could do so by frequently denigrating the other parent and displaying fear and hatred for that person. Perhaps surprisingly, many authors who oppose the parental alienation concept have taken a very similar perspective—except that they have pointed to abusive behavior, adverse parenting, and poor parenting skills on the part of the rejected parent, and have proposed that these are the real reasons behind a child's avoidance of a parent.

Notably, neither of these opposing groups has paid much attention to the roles of children themselves in moving toward increasing avoidance of one parent. Like many people, they have concentrated on the idea that parents make children who they are, whether by reward and punishment, instruction, imitation, attention, or inattention. When children do well, their parents feel they should be proud [of themselves], and when children do badly, it is sometimes proposed that their parents should be punished. Allegations of parental alienation are often associated with the idea that one parent has made mistakes and should be corrected in ways that amount to punishment.

Although it is certainly true that both children and adults can learn from experience, an excessive concern with nurture can blind us to the power of nature in determining personality and behavior. When children's behavior is problematic, it is a mistake to assume that their parents have done the wrong things or have failed to do the right things and that the parental lapses are the sole cause of the child problems. When children's behavior is admirable, it is a mistake to assume that their parents have done the right things and refrained from doing the wrong things, and that the parental virtues are the sole cause of the children's good conduct. It is also a mistake to assume that every child will show

DOI: 10.4324/9781003454793-10

in the same way the impact of "good parenting" or "poor parenting", whether or not the parenting is in the context of divorce.

Genetic factors play important roles in determining some aspects of personality and behavior. Problem behaviors like impulsiveness or inappropriate anger and aggression have genetic components and are not necessarily learned, but children may share genetic factors with an impulsive, antisocial parent and also learn from exposure to that person in what has been called a "double whammy" (Jaffe et al., 2003).

Because genetic factors are powerful, children show individual differences in behaviors and attitudes that remain rather consistent throughout life. These individual differences in constitutional make-up are referred to as temperament. Some temperamental factors, like positive mood quality, are liked by parents and other adults, but some children are said to have "difficult temperaments" involving negative mood quality, difficulty in adapting to change, and unpredictable rhythms of eating and sleeping. Children with difficult temperaments are often unhappy, and they can make parents unhappy too, sometimes resulting in harsh or frequent punishment.

Genetic differences are probably also responsible for differences in children's resilience—the ability to develop along predictable lines even in the face of adverse experiences. Highly resilient children will do well, or at least adequately, in the face of disruptive events like divorce, or even like some levels of abuse. Highly vulnerable children, on the contrary, are easily affected negatively by disturbing experiences and do not easily weather the impact of changes that adults create.

The issue of neurodiversity is an important one to consider with respect to characteristics children bring to divorce and to situations where parental alienation is alleged. Children described as neurodiverse comprise a varied group, ranging from those who have experienced nervous system injuries and have specific difficulties, to those affected by poorly understood problems such as autistic spectrum disorder and related issues. While different in the specific causes of their problems, these children tend to share certain characteristics like difficulty adapting to change and a high degree of sensitivity to the environment. They may be easily distracted or have difficulty shifting their attention, but as a general rule they do not readily process changes like going from one parent's house to the other's. Pressure to change, to hurry, or to do something different tends to make these children panic and resist strongly, whereas a gentle, step-by-step approach may be effective. Medications for nervous system problems can also affect their responses. The difficulties for these children may be increased if one or both of their parents share the children's problems and respond with increased distress if the children do not cooperate.

Although most children do not have serious emotional disturbances even under the stress of divorce, some do have mental conditions that can affect their behavior with one or with both parents. Conduct disorders and disruptive antisocial behavior may be more obvious when with one parent than when with the other, and may be interpreted by one parent as resistance caused by the other parent. Obsessive-compulsive disorders and anxiety disorders may make affected children appear obstinate and resistant, especially to a parent who does not manage the child's needs well.

It would seem unnecessary to point to age differences as child characteristics that affect children's responses to divorce, but unfortunately most of the existing research on the parental alienation concept has lumped together children and adolescents of all ages. For example, the often-cited case series studied by Clawar and Rivlin (1991, 2013) included children from birth to age 20 and made no distinctions among them. Nevertheless, there are many reasons for age differences to affect children's responses to divorce and their attitudes toward parents. To name just two: young children respond differently to familiar and less familiar people, and adolescents have different views of their parents' sexuality than do younger children.

This stress on constitutional factors that influence children is not intended to suggest that no individual differences are related to experience. Cultural factors can readily affect a child's expectations about a parent and the parent's expectations about a child; when these are at odds, perhaps because the child is growing up in a different culture than the one the parent experienced, the clash can lead to the child resisting contact with the parent. In addition to cultural factors, adverse experiences with a parent, whether abuse, observation of domestic violence, or simply poor parenting and social skills, can cause contact resistance.

Cultural factors and other experiences can help to determine whether or not a child welcomes contact with a parent. Alienationists (e.g. Baker, Mehta & Chong, 2013) have claimed that even physical abuse does not diminish a child's desire to be with a parent, but this statement is based on surveyed opinions of a group of mental health professionals and not on studies of children who are in foster care because of abuse or neglect. Studies of foster children give a different view. For example, Maaskant et al. (2016) found that foster children in their study had stronger attachment to the foster parents than to the biological parents and could more easily turn for help to their foster parents, whom the children regarded as more psychologically available to them than their biological parents. In a third of the cases studied by Chapman et al. (2004), foster children wanted to be adopted by their foster parents. These and other studies of foster children suggest that experiences of abuse or neglect, combined with good care by foster parents, make children less welcoming to contact with biological parents; the evidence does not support the idea that children continue to long for contact with parents who have harmed them.

Two Cases Where Child Characteristics May Have Affected Family Functioning

In the two stories that follow, both constitutional factors and experiences appear to have been at work to make children welcome or reject contact with one of their parents.

Lainie's Story

Lainie is a medical professional living on the west coast of the United States. Her two children, in their teens at the time of this story, were both neurodivergent in various ways. The children were different from each other, but they shared characteristics that made life more complicated for them and for their parents. They disliked change and were disturbed even by minor deviations from routine, like taking a different route when driving to school. They needed support to calm themselves.

The daughter had unusual difficulty with numbers and spatial directions, so there were some school issues too. Both children, but particularly the daughter, had unusual developmental trajectories. The daughter received speech and language services, occupational therapy, and physical therapy from an early age, and needed learning interventions although her learning problems were not very obvious in casual conversation (in fact, she later showed that she could write quite well). She had an individual educational plan (IEP) from second grade on, indicating that her school agreed that her special needs required accommodation and that she would have special needs into adulthood. Her brother, on the other hand, was described as "spectrum-adjacent", socially reticent, and having difficulty adapting to change, but was doing well before the allegations of parental alienation began.

Following the parents' divorce, family therapy was not progressing well. The children's father participated in transitional activities with the mother and the children, like walking the dog and having frequent dinner nights; he visited the children at Lainie's house. The father wanted a 50/50 parenting plan, but the teenage children did not want this. The daughter was especially resistant and would hit herself and her father when they were together after the court ordered more contact time than she was comfortable with. Her father told her she needed psychiatric hospitalization. When the children were ordered to be with their father and their visits with Lainie were monitored, the son became frightened when a monitor was present at a visit and would not talk.

These difficulties added to the complications when the father chose to take their case to a private judge, a retired judicial officer who could be hired to make decisions in the state where they lived. As it happened, the private judge chosen was on the board of directors of a treatment program for parental alienation, the program being one of a small number that actually had a camp-like atmosphere with outdoor activities. That judge ordered Lainie's children and Lainie herself to attend the treatment program.

Lainie described the treatment program as costing tens of thousands of dollars, including costs like airline fares and car rentals. She also noted that the program made no accommodation for the children's neurodivergence and special needs, but expected them to comply with the proceedings as if they were neurotypical; this was also their experience with other treatment programs they attended later.

Lainie noted that once at the "camp", they were told they could not leave the premises. There were cabins for the mothers, other cabins for the fathers, and tents for the children of five families who attended at the same time. Lainie recalled that there were staff members/interns who were there at all times (with one intern for each family member), slept in the cabins and stood outside the bathrooms. Lainie reported that if a child or a parent appeared to resist compliance, the interns would gather around the person, implying a physical threat, and force them to go where they were ordered. Lainie's children, she recalled, said the program was useless.

Like other reunification therapy programs, the "camp" was to be followed by a vacation period in which the children were to go with the parent they had been avoiding. This change was difficult for the neurodivergent children, especially the son, although Lainie tried to start preparing him for it several days ahead. The son began to cry when in the car with his father, who did not respond to him. Lainie recalled that she gave him a phone to play with and calm himself, although she knew that this would be interpreted as an "alienating behavior" on her part.

Returning to their home state, Lainie found that their newly appointed family therapist was a former director of the "camp". She recalled that fees of $200,000 were paid to that therapist alone as they worked on transitions. Lainie reported that she attempted to tell the therapist that the children would respond well to very small changes, but rather than taking this into account, the therapist threatened to report her to child protective services because the child was "out of parental control".

Lainie's son was forced to go to his father's house, but ran away and barricaded himself in a room at Lainie's house. This led the therapist to state that "other influences" were at work, meaning parental alienation.

Like some other cases discussed in this book, Lainie's case was derailed by the COVID pandemic. It dragged on for a year as the judge ordered the children to go to a different reunification program. Lainie was supposed to sign a contract but she felt the treatment plan was not clear. She offered a neuropsychologist's reports as the therapist's resumé showed no experience in that area. The treatment team's names kept changing and there appeared to be no background checks. The program recommended a person to live in with the father, and help with the children; the man had been an intern with the previous reunification program, and had apparently been a cult member for some earlier years. Lainie was finally sent a contract to sign and informed that if she failed to sign, the court would find her in contempt and fine her as punishment. But Lainie argued that the contract was incomplete—it should contain a list of risks and benefits of the treatment as well as Health Insurance Portability and Accountability Act information. At that point, the program director said Lainie was "contentious" and declined to work with her.

At this point, the family therapist found a third reunification program whose director was a marriage and family therapist and claimed that her method is 100% successful. Lainie was ordered not to tell the children what was happening, but to take them to their father's house, where youth transport service workers would pick them up. The transporters took the children's phones and put them into their van. Lainie was able to find out later where the children were taken.

Lainie later learned from her daughter that the program stressed videos like the often-used "Welcome Back, Pluto", which emphasizes the need to include the father as part of the family. It also employed photos and videos from earlier times as proof that the children's relationships with their father had at one time been very positive. The children were threatened with the possibility that Lainie could go to jail. Discussion about their father's behavior was shut down. The court also wanted Lainie to write a letter acknowledging that she was responsible for the children's attitudes toward their father, but she did not do this, partly because it would have been a false statement and in part because such a "confession" would have led to her being ordered to pay all the expenses of the program and further treatment.

When the children were released from the program, they went to their father's house. The son stopped talking until his father told him that if he did not talk, he would have to go back to the program; he then began to talk again. The daughter, who left and returned to her mother's house on her 18th birthday, has been writing about this experience. (In spite of her learning disabilities, she writes well.) She has recounted feeling trapped at her father's house, always under surveillance and never alone, with a nanny hired who even went into the garden with her.

Lainie's daughter now says she is "triggered" into emotional distress and experiences flashbacks of seeing the fence at the treatment venue, hearing her father's car sound, and seeing the transporters' type of van. Lainie says the girl had "terrible" obsessive-compulsive symptoms and distressing intrusive thoughts, but these are subsiding. The son, who had just turned 17 at the time of the interview, is still with his father.

When Lainie was asked what had been the impact of this experience on her own thoughts and feelings, she replied that her reactions changed in stages over the years of the conflict. At first, she was simply disbelieving—how could this possibly be happening? After a while, she said, and especially after the children were taken away, she became focused on getting them back and was to some extent dissociated, not putting energy into an emotional reaction. She also described herself as disoriented at that time. Now that her daughter is back and the son will be 18 soon, she is beginning to really feel things again. She has nightmares. Lainie has talked to her daughter about her own experience, told her how anxious she was, and they have cried together. Her sense is still that her children are experiencing severe emotional and psychological consequences of the reunification programs. Lainie has talked to her son's therapist, who says he shows selective mutism as a result of his experiences, but she feels things are better for him now that she can see him without a monitor.

Lainie has also joined a group of mothers who are fighting for legislation that would prevent families from having the experiences Lainie's family has undergone. She says it hurts to do nothing about this. She especially recalls giving her advice about how to help the children go to their father by making changes in small increments, and having this opinion interpreted as evidence of parental alienation when she was in fact trying to work toward improving the children's relationships with the father.

Marla's Story

All families are complex, but Marla's story is more complicated than most. It involves a child with highly disruptive, not to say dangerous, behavior, as well as disagreement by authorities about whether one or the other parent was causing alienation. An evaluator considered Marla's former husband to have been alienating the children from Marla, and

Marla has for years had little contact with them. Whether this situation is or is not due to the children's father's actions is far from clear, but it is possible that characteristics of one of the children have at least contributed to the lack of contact, along with other factors. When reunification therapy was ordered, one child's behavior caused the therapist to resign from the case; whether or not continued treatment would have improved the situation cannot be known, nor did Marla's interview reveal anything about her brief experience of the treatment.

In Marla's interview, she described herself as having been an intelligent and competent young woman, but one without strong interests or "passions". She had been living in a western area of the United States but when she married an ambitious man with an eye on political advancement, the couple began a journey that covered at least two countries and many states. Marla was involved in work on political issues and managed the household, which increased rapidly in size as she had three children in five years.

Marla loved having children and was fully committed to their care, saying in her interview, "what else am I going to do?". She said she practiced attachment parenting, a method that stresses engaging with the baby soon after birth, breastfeeding, "baby-wearing" with slings or similar devices, and sleeping close to the baby. As children get older, attachment parenting emphasizes nurturing and showing empathy for the child's needs rather than disciplining and enforcing rules.

Marla's oldest child was very bright but prone to frequent emotional meltdowns. Marla says she always focused on him. His grandmother could not or would not take care of him. According to Marla, the child's father tried to be involved but had a great deal of his own work to do.

The family had been vegetarians, as the father preferred, but when the oldest child was five, Marla decided to try the "GAPS diet" as a way to help the oldest child's behavioral problems. This diet is intended to treat a posited Gut and Psychology Syndrome (GAPS), which proponents consider to be a phenomenon in which bacteria and other substances "leak" through the walls of the digestive tract, possibly causing a range of psychological and behavioral problems. The diet emphasizes meats, fish, and animal fats and excludes complex carbohydrates—almost the opposite of a vegetarian diet. Marla felt that the diet greatly helped her oldest child's problems, that he "mellowed", was thriving socially, and even was relieved of leg pains he had been experiencing.

Marla had wanted to begin writing a novel and started to make some arrangements for time to write. She hired a nanny for several hours a day. The family was going to a vacation home for the summer and Marla had agreed with her husband that he would take over the children for four hours each day. She reported in her interview that during the summer she was aware of "the demise of the marriage", with her husband having "meltdowns" just when the disruptive child became calmer. Marla did not want the marriage to break up, but as the children were happy she left things as they were. On returning home in the autumn, however, Marla found that her husband was contemplating having an affair and she was very distressed.

Marla decided at this point to go back to the vacation home for a month to work and think things over. When she returned, though, her husband had changed the locks. There was also an incident where the oldest child attacked Marla and she took him to the backyard where she yelled at him and gave him a baseball bat with instructions to hit some hay bales; neighbors reported the yelling to child protective services and there was an investigation, which concluded that the report was unfounded. A mediator was brought in and suggested a 50/50 parenting plan, but there was a temporary protective order against Marla which prevented her from seeing the children for a couple of months.

Marla reported in her interview that the children's father had returned them to their former vegetarian diet. The oldest child, now 9 or 10, was especially unsettled now. He held a knife on his younger sister and grabbed and threw down a camera at a family reunion. Marla felt the children settled down better when they had more time with her, but after the father filed a motion for more control, saying that the GAPS diet was bad for the children, she had only one overnight with the disruptive oldest child—and the child used the opportunity to punch her. On another occasion, the father "weaponized" the oldest child and held him so he could punch Marla. Marla saw the children very little and said their father would drop them off, then pick them up 10 minutes later. Marla was deeply disappointed that her own family was unsupportive, objected to the GAPS diet, and tried to give the children candy without Marla knowing about it.

A child custody evaluation at this time suggested that the issues would work themselves out and there should be a gradual increase in parenting time for Marla. The evaluator thought the children's father was alienating them from Marla, according to Marla's report. However, Marla said, the father threatened that the evaluator would lose her license and she backed off. Marla said that the therapist whom they saw briefly wrote letters to the court pointing out that the father was still interfering with Marla's contact with the children.

The family court ordered office-based reunification therapy, but the therapist quit after the eldest child trashed the office. The child also threw things at the guardian *ad litem* and was expelled from school for hitting a teacher. He grabbed the steering wheel and jerked it violently while Marla was driving. Residential treatment was recommended for him. The youngest child, now about five, smeared excrement when at Marla's house and was said also to do this at his father's house. According to Marla, child protective services said this behavior was caused by stress and was Marla's fault.

Marla was worried about the oldest child's possible suicide at this point. On a visit during the reunification therapy period, he came into a room where she was lying on the floor and asked her a question—when she hesitated, he kicked her in the nose. While a child custody evaluator was at the house, the oldest child suddenly began to act out. He ran outside and threw rocks at the door, then broke Marla's car windshield. Marla recalls the evaluator agreeing that Marla had done or said nothing to provoke this outburst.

Marla says she now believes that a reunification therapy "camp" would be good for the oldest child. However, he has apparently never received any psychological treatment, at least that Marla knows about. Now in his late teens, he lives with his father and stepmother and has a separate small apartment where he is separated from the younger siblings and a young half-sibling, but joins them for meals. He has little contact with Marla and has told her nothing about his college applications or acceptance.

Marla has remarried and is a foster mother to a teenage girl whom she and her husband hope to adopt. She has given up having more than minor contact with her children and regrets that she did not have children with her new partner while she still could.

Discussion

As is the case for all the interviews in this book, it is not possible to know whether the participant's memory is accurate or not, or whether questions asked by the interviewer influenced the responses. Neither is it possible to know how typical these two cases are of all the many ways child characteristics can play out in families where parental alienation is alleged. Nevertheless, the information given by the interviewees is an important addition to our understanding, and one that has never been included in alienationists' discussion of cases where children avoid one of their divorced parents.

Constitutional Issues

Both Lainie and Marla gave examples of the effects of their children's constitutional (biological and possibly genetic) contributions to their avoidance of a parent. This issue was certainly clearest in Lainie's case.

Lainie's neurodivergent children brought to the situation serious difficulties in adapting to change. Whereas typical teenagers would have no trouble at all in dealing with driving a new route to school, and might not even notice that this was happening, Lainie's daughter was quite distressed when her father drove her a different way from their usual route. Typical teenagers easily deal with sleeping at a hotel or a grandparent's house, and like to have sleepovers with friends, but Lainie's children found going to their father's house disturbing, perhaps simply because it was a less familiar place and perhaps partly because it demanded social contact which the son, particularly, found painfully challenging.

Lainie, who was very knowledgeable about the cognitive and emotional effects of the children's conditions, offered her opinions to the father and therapists, suggesting that gradual changes with plenty of preparation and emotional support would help the children in their visits and their relationships with their father, but these suggestions were rejected. The alienationist belief system would interpret Lainie's offered plan to slow down as simply another parental alienation behavior designed to interfere with the father–child relationships. As the mother of children resisting contact with their father "without justification", she would be seen as working actively to alienate the children. The alternative to following Lainie's suggestions was to demand and force contact, a proceeding that was likely to frighten and disturb the children and harden their negative attitudes.

As the alienationist system does not consider individual child characteristics as factors in avoidance of a parent, Lainie's children's neurodivergence was never considered as a possible cause in their case, and their avoidance was attributed solely to experiences the children were having with their mother. However, considering the children's constitutional make-up allows us to see how their avoidance of their father could occur without inappropriate behavior by either parent.

Marla's case was a much more complicated one to understand, and with the information available it is still very puzzling. The behavior of the oldest child was highly disruptive from an early age, according to Marla, who also described him as very bright and of an "ethereal beauty". As he got older, he physically attacked other people, including his sister, but may have focused somewhat on Marla. (Whether he behaved similarly at his father's house was not revealed in Marla's interview, and she might well not know what he did there.) He was expelled from school for hitting a teacher and residential treatment was recommended but never implemented. He behaved impulsively and destructively even with therapists, evaluators, and court officers. This behavior by the age of 9 or 10 is indicative of a serious emotional disturbance of a constitutional type (as opposed to a disturbance created by traumatic experiences, although these cannot be ruled out in this case).

Any connection between the oldest child's condition and the children's avoidance of Marla is purely a matter of speculation, but it is possible that the boy's violent attacks on Marla served to "crystallize" negative attitudes on the part of the younger children. If the father found the boy's behavior tolerable—which seems possible, given that the recommended treatment was not sought—the younger children may have followed the oldest's lead in avoiding Marla. The youngest child was reported by Marla to have had episodes of smearing feces at an age when this is no longer just toddler play, so his condition also may have played a part, but Marla did not seem to see him as disturbed in the same sense as his older brother.

Marla's report that the oldest child changed behaviorally when given a different diet should be taken into consideration as a possible indication of constitutional issues, but without further evidence it is hard to know what to think about this aspect of the case. It is all too easy for worried parents to see what they expect to see when they find a new treatment for their child, but of course we cannot know that Marla was confused in that way. There is very little evidence that the diet Marla used has predictable psychological effects.

Experiences

In Lainie's case, it seems fairly clear that the experiences of the children during and after the parents' divorce could be enough to trigger avoidance of one parent, given the constitutional factors that were present. As is the case for many aspects of child development and behavior, single factors were probably not enough to cause the observed outcome; instead, understanding the situation requires looking at interactions between factors. Children who were neurodivergent might not have developed avoidance of their father if not subjected to certain experiences, and children who were more neurotypical might not have reacted badly to the same experiences. Both factors would be needed to create the outcome of avoidance of a parent, so only neurodivergent children subjected to particular experiences would develop avoidance.

Lainie's children initially experienced the shock and stress of the divorce, with its dramatic changes not only in the household but in the moods and attitudes of the parents. Divorce has been studied as an adverse childhood experience that affects even neurotypical children negatively (Felitti et al., 1998). It is to be expected that neurodivergent children would have an exceptionally difficult time navigating the changes caused by divorce and would respond by trying to keep their environment as stable as possible.

Lainie's children were put under sufficient pressure by the court, therapists, and their father to experience distress which might not have occurred if they were more neurotypical. According to Lainie's interview, none of her recommendations to slow and buffer the children's new experiences were implemented. If the recommendations had been accepted, the children might not have begun to avoid their father. Unfortunately, the alienationist view interpreted Lainie's suggestions as efforts to interfere with the father's parenting time.

Lainie's children's experience of reunification therapy would have been stressful for any child, as was shown in interviews in earlier chapters of this book. For neurodivergent children, such strange events would have been especially stressful and much to be avoided, if possible. Difficulties for Lainie's children began with the prohibition on any explanation that might have been given by Lainie. Lainie normally prepared the children for changes or disturbing events and acted to buffer their experiences and help them cope, but the reunification therapist forbade her to tell the children what was to happen. She had to drive them to their father's house without explanation, and once there they were immediately taken by youth transport service workers and placed in a van to be taken to the treatment venue where their father met them. This bizarre experience alone could be expected to be disturbing for any person, child or adult, neurotypical or otherwise, but would have been exceptionally frightening and distressing for Lainie's children. At the treatment venue, the children encountered more unknown people who threatened that their mother could go to jail if they did not follow directions—a situation that demanded the rapid adjustment that was so difficult for these neurodivergent children.

Following the several days of the reunification program, the children were taken to their father's house, a place relatively unfamiliar to them. Rather than spend all their time with their father, they had to cope with a hired helper who was a stranger to them. Lainie's daughter felt especially distressed by constant surveillance. She was rarely actually alone, but at the same time she did not have access to familiar people with whom she had established relationships. Contact with Lainie was prohibited for some time, of course.

The treatment and post-treatment programs could hardly have been better designed to be disruptive for neurodivergent children.

In Marla's case, the severe disruptive behavior of the oldest child seems to have been a focus both during the marriage and after the divorce, but at the same time was not addressed by seeking professional help. This behavior did not consist simply of tantrums, but involved serious attacks on others, including threatening a sibling with a knife and kicking Marla in the face. Marla was concerned about this, though her description of it in her interview did not suggest that she thinks much about it now. She was willing to go against the children's father's wishes about vegetarianism to use a diet that she still believes was beneficial for the boy's behavior. Nevertheless, as far as can be told from the interview, neither Marla nor the children's father sought help in serious situations with long-term implications—the boy's expulsion from school, a therapist's resignation, and intentional property damage, as well as physical attacks on others. One can only speculate on whether Marla and the father essentially "froze" in their decision-making because of their intense conflict, so that neither could seek help effectively, or whether the disruptive boy had the task of acting out anger and aggression for one or both parents. It is possible, also, that if the father preferred for the children to avoid Marla, it would have been easier for him to minimize their contact if the oldest boy continued to behave disruptively; it would be logical, if not necessarily correct, to entertain the idea that the child's behavior was in some way caused by contact with Marla.

The impact of the oldest boy's behavior on the younger children may be one of the keys to this family's situation. Although allegations of parental alienation often focus on parents' actions as if no siblings were present, oldest children can have serious effects on the attitudes and behavior of their younger siblings. An oldest child who is dangerous to adults as well as to other children may have a powerful influence on younger siblings, who can either be persuaded or are actually convinced that one parent is to be avoided. Marla's long, perhaps permanent, estrangement from all the children could have started with the influence of the disruptive older child. It is purely speculative but interesting to consider whether these relationship patterns could have been changed by having the younger siblings visit Marla separately from their older brother.

The experiences the younger children and Marla had with the oldest child may have had strong effects, but they are not the only relevant experiences that may have influenced the children's attitude toward Marla. In her interview, Marla described her intense involvement with the children early in their lives, using attachment parenting and feeling that being a mother was the only thing she really wanted. However, when Marla began to see the fragility of her marriage and was told that her husband was contemplating an affair, she went away for a month, leaving the still-young children and their father to deal with her absence. Although this was not necessarily a surprising or inappropriate thing for her to do under the circumstances, her action may have provided a beginning to a series of steps that increasingly separated her from the children.

Marla was surprised when she returned to find the locks had been changed, presumably indicating that her husband had taken her departure as final, and perhaps had communicated this to the children. The children had thus experienced an abrupt transition from a relationship with a deeply engaged mother to that mother's absence (and possibly the belief that she would never come back)—and the month of her voluntary absence was followed by no contact for a couple of months, by court order. It would be overreach to claim that this experience alone could have caused the children to avoid Marla, but in combination with other factors it may have been the beginning of negative attitudes that developed into avoidance. Unless their father had made a point of assuring them about the mother's continued love for them, it is hard to see how the children would have interpreted these months without their mother as anything but an indication that she had abandoned them.

This discussion of Marla's case has not touched on the role of the children's father and whether or not he acted in ways that alienated the children from Marla. Marla did not in fact know much about this, although she noted that at times he would drop the children off and return very quickly to pick them up. While that behavior would certainly interfere with Marla's parenting time, it would not necessarily in itself affect the children's attitudes toward her.

Abuse or Neglect

Evidence of abusive treatment or neglect is a factor that rules out parental alienation as an explanation of children's avoidance of a parent. An additional factor that has been suggested (but not accepted by alienationists) is the presence of adverse parenting practices that do not rise to the intensity of abuse. We need to ask, were abuse or neglect present in either Lainie's or Marla's cases? What about adverse parenting by either parent?

In the case of Lainie's family, no abuse or neglect was ever alleged, although the reunification program itself might well be considered abusive. The children's father's apparent lack of empathy and reluctance to be guided by the children's unusual needs may be characterized as adverse parenting and should be considered as a factor in the children's reluctance to be with him, but it is notable that he was advised and supported in his actions by alienationist therapists and court officials.

Marla's situation, once again, was quite complex. On the whole, the children were carefully nurtured and neither abused nor neglected. Marla's departure when she learned of her husband's possible infidelity was not intended to be harmful to the children, whom she left behind because they needed to attend school, but it might be considered by some as a form of abandonment and as an adverse type of parenting. The failure of Marla and her then-husband to seek effective treatment for their impulsive, disruptive eldest child could be classified as neglect or as adverse parenting. But none of these events seem sufficient to account for the children's avoidance of contact with Marla, and possibly neglectful actions are not by themselves enough to explain the oldest boy's physical attacks on his mother or other people.

One last comment on abuse and neglect issues in Marla's family has to do with her current status as a foster parent. Only in very unusual cases would a person with a history of child abuse or neglect be permitted to be involved with foster children, and Marla's foster parenthood is evidence that the authorities where she lives do not believe that her biological children avoid her because she has abused or neglected them.

References

Baker, A., Mehta, N., & Chong, J. (2013). Foster children caught in loyalty conflicts: Implications for mental health treatment providers. *American Journal of Family Therapy*, 41, 363–375. https://doi.org/10.1080/01926187.2012.728902.

Chapman, M., Wall, A., & Barth, R. (2004). Children's voices: The perceptions of children in foster care. *American Journal of Orthopsychiatry*, 74(3), 293–304. https://doi.org/10.1037/0002-9432.74.3.293.

Clawar, S., & Rivlin, B. (1991, 2013). *Children held hostage*. American Bar Association.

Felitti, V., Anda, R., et al. (1998). Relationship of childhood abuse and household dysfunction to many of the leading causes of death in adults. The Adverse Childhood Experiences (ACE) Study. *American Journal of Preventive Medicine*, 14, 245–258. https://doi.org/10.1016/S0749-377(98)00017-8.

Jaffe, S., Moffitt, T., Caspi, A., & Taylor, A. (2003). Life with (or without) father: The benefits of living with two biological parents depend on the father's antisocial behavior. *Child Development*, 74, 109–126. https://doi.org/10.1111/1467-8624.101-1-00524.

Maaskant, A., van Rooij, F., Bos, H., & Hermaans, J. (2016). The wellbeing of foster children and their relationship with foster parents and biological parents: A child's perspective. *Journal of Social Work Practice*, 30, 379–395. http://dx.doi.org/10.1080/02650533.2015.1092952.

11 Conclusions and Directions

Dealing with Parental Alienation Allegations

About the Narratives

This book has presented 21 narratives drawn from interviews with people who have experienced—or in some cases made—allegations of parental alienation. *Somebody has said parental alienation*, for one reason or another, and rather predictable consequences have followed. In much of the world today, when somebody says parental alienation, courts are likely to listen and to make decisions based on the statement.

Most of the narratives in the foregoing chapters tell the stories of people who remember their experiences with parental alienation allegations as fraught with distress, regret, and continued anxiety. This is especially true of the young adults who as children or teenagers went through threatened or actual reunification programs, intensive or otherwise, and who recall their fear and disbelief when the courts they had been taught to respect failed to help them. These young people did not end with the good relationships with both parents that reunification programs are advertised to produce.

Both mothers and fathers who were alleged to have alienated their children remember their experiences with horror as well as rage. When they were asked to look over the narratives for accuracy and anonymity, a number of the parents delayed reading the drafts—they said they had to get themselves ready to recall the events that had been so disturbing, the threats that they would lose contact with their children, that the children might be harmed, and that all of their resources might have to be expended to try to prevent the worst outcomes.

In two cases, fathers felt that their allegations of parental alienation against an ex-spouse had been correct, but that nonetheless the interviewees had suffered as the legal system dealt with problems of abuse accusations and of their children's intransigence. In one case, a mother believed strongly that her ex-husband had alienated their children from

DOI: 10.4324/9781003454793-11

her and was even able to report that an evaluator had agreed with this, but because of a child's disruptive behavior, therapists and caseworkers could not help, and the custody case was gradually dropped. This mother remains (after years) with minimal contact with her children and has essentially given up. These cases raise the question of whether allegations of parental alienation are helpful even in situations where children's alignment with one parent seems to be the result of the other parent's influence.

How Trustworthy Is the Narrative Evidence?

Do these narratives tell us anything about allegations of parental alienation, whether true allegations or false? Yes, they tell us something—but they do not tell us everything, by any means. Collecting individual narratives or anecdotes provides research information, but it is at a low *level of evidence*. We should not have the kind of confidence in this material that we would have in systematic, sophisticated investigations that control for some of the many biases human beings bring to research. The idea of levels of evidence, the relative trustworthiness of information found in different ways, is important in the social sciences and in medicine. A version of this concept exists in judicial proceedings, as well, and judges may or may not accept evidence that has certain sources (for example, hearsay).

The narratives provided by interviewees for this book are by no means to be relied upon as more complex research might be. No general statement about parental alienation cases should be drawn from them. They are reports given by individuals whose memories may be inaccurate or who may have reason to forget some points and remember others. Their willingness to be interviewed may have been based on their unhappiness with their experiences and outcomes, and there may be hundreds of satisfied individuals who see no reason to talk about an unimportant part of their lives. However, the narratives presented in the previous chapters are exceptions to the claims made by alienationists that reunification programs are 100% successful and they thus are at the very least "the exceptions that prove (i.e., test) the rule". If not precisely black swans, these cases are the rare birds that have been declared not to exist—but that do exist. This evidence of existence was necessary before any research with a higher level of evidence could sensibly be proposed.

One more simple issue needs to be considered when we think about the interview material in this book. Many (but not all) of the stories told here involve events during the COVID pandemic of roughly 2020 to 2022. This was a period of time when choices of health care took on political connotations, as well as one in which quarantine could interfere severely with standing or new parenting plans. Some parents accused their co-parents of interfering with parenting time, when in fact the co-parents might well have been trying to comply with public health measures. Anger as well as anxiety rose high in many families. The extent to which the pandemic exacerbated feelings and led to allegations of parental alienation is not known.

What Are the Problems with the Parental Alienation Concept?

The purpose of presenting the narratives in this book was *not* to try to argue that parental alienation does not exist. Human beings do all sorts of strange things in the course of family life, and alienating behaviors that influence children's attitudes may well be among them. Indeed, one of a parent's tasks is to teach children to stay away from dangerous things, and if one parent believes (rightly or wrongly) that the other is dangerous, teaching the children to avoid the dangerous person is the right thing to do.

The first real problem, then, is not to try to contradict the possibility of parental alienation in general, but to establish whether it does really exist in a case where *somebody has said parental alienation*. The second real problem is to decide whether it is actually harmful for children to be alienated from a parent, and the third is to decide how to intervene in cases where parental alienation exists and can be predicted to be harmful. Whether interventions are themselves potentially harmful is a fourth question that is relevant to the second and third.

Richard Warshak, one of the alienationists involved with the Family Bridges program, has pointed out the possibility of false positive identifications of parental alienation (Warshak, 2020)—cases where *somebody says parental alienation* but where a child's avoidance of a parent occurs for reasons quite different from the other parent's machinations. False positive identifications, like true identifications, may be met with the heavy artillery of the family court system, including orders for the child to have no contact with the preferred parent, attendance at intensive reunification programs, and residence (perhaps for years) with the possibly-abusive avoided parent. These heavy responses also target the preferred parent, who is alleged to have alienated the child and even to be guilty of child abuse on that ground alone.

Why Are False Positive Identifications a Problem?

False allegations of parental alienation can have horrible outcomes, ranging from child abuse to child death. At the extreme end of the outcome spectrum, there have been child deaths associated with situations where a preferred parent warned against the abusive tendencies of the other parent, the warnings were said to be attempts at alienation, the child was ordered into contact with the avoided parent—and the avoided parent killed the child. The model Kayden's Law, the California Piqui's Law, and the Utah Om's Law are all named for children killed by the parent they tried to avoid, to whom they were sent on the grounds that the preferred parent was an alienator. When courts accept false positive identifications of parental alienation as if they were valid, doors are opened for tragedy, possibly including child suicides as well as murders.

Most false positive identifications of parental alienation do not end in child deaths, of course. But they do, in many cases, lead to court orders to attend reunification therapies of various types. As was discussed earlier in this book, such treatments are essentially experimental therapies, as they have never been tested according to established rules for this kind of work. Notably, investigations of reunification therapies have generally omitted any consideration of whether the treatments can be harmful. The one study that even looked at this issue limited its measures to the time when the child was actually at the treatment venue and in the presence of an adult almost all the time. No long term measures of harm have ever been done, in spite of the fact that now-adult children interviewed for this book have reported treatment for post-traumatic stress disorder and have spoken of continuing, worsened avoidance of one parent (and sometimes of both). The harms potentially done by reunification therapies and no-contact orders can include disruption of children's education and their developing relationships with peers which prepare them for later friendships and life partnerships; these issues remain unstudied.

What about cases in which false positive identifications of parental alienation conceal real needs for treatment? One or both parents, or their children, may have emotional problems that are the actual causes of a child's wish to avoid a parent. Incorrectly pointing to parental alienating behaviors as causes of a child's avoidance, and demanding that a court order reunification therapy, are actions that can conceal either adult or child problems that would otherwise receive treatment. For example, a father, whose teenage daughters avoid him because they know that he had "groomed" their young neighbor in the past, needs treatment for his inappropriate sexual impulses and support for his attempts to make peace with the daughters. A parent whose children throw food at them needs education and coaching about effective parenting, and the children need help on appropriate expression of the anger they surely have. Children who are generally anxious may show this in apparently unfounded fear of a parent, which will not be alleviated by forced contact but instead needs to be addressed as an aspect of their anxiety. Children who are oppositional or behave disruptively need help on these issues, which may cause both avoidance of a parent and other social difficulties in school, in sports, or with peers. Falsely identifying parental alienation, and assuming that reunification therapy will be an effective treatment, are actions that are likely to exacerbate both parent and child problems.

Some Thoughts for Families Experiencing Allegations of Parental Alienation

It would be foolhardy rather than brave to offer definitive advice to people dealing with allegations of parental alienation. Families are different from each other and allegations can also be different. What people need to know and the decisions they have to make also depend on their role in the parental alienation drama—are they preferred parents, avoided parents, the children who are said to be avoiding, or participants with other roles? The events look different to each of these people, and their options are also different. Nevertheless, it is possible to draw from the interviews in this book and from other sources of information some ideas that each person might fruitfully consider as they decide how best to conduct themselves in a parental alienation crisis, or as they anticipate such a situation.

Many of the suggestions about legal issues that follow are based on extremely helpful discussions with Suzanne Chester, J.D., director emeritus of The Child's Advocate in Raleigh, North Carolina, who contributed ideas out of her lengthy experience with cases where parental alienation was alleged.

Some Thoughts for Preferred Parents Alleged to Be Alienators

You probably can't prove that you did not ever act in a way that alienated your child from the other parent. It is a good idea to ask your lawyer what allegations you can realistically fight.

Anything you do or don't do can be interpreted as a parental alienating behavior. If nothing else, you can be identified as not being a sufficiently "friendly parent" and failing to encourage your child to want contact with the other parent. A recent question on a listserv for child custody experts asked whether a preferred parent should have to punish a child who resisted contact with the other parent, suggesting that your failure to punish, or to punish severely enough, could be seen as an alienating behavior.

Texts or emails you have sent in the past may be given heavy weight in the courtroom, especially if they can be interpreted as adversarial or even simply as failing to promote a child's relationship with the other parent. This can happen whether the texts are through a service like Our Family Wizard or otherwise. For current communications, you may want to have your attorney advise you or even review texts before sending them. If your texts have been contentious, it can be helpful to show that the other parent sent similar texts.

You must have legal representation if you are entangled in parental alienation allegations. Yes, it is expensive, and yes, it can be difficult to find a lawyer who understands parental alienation concepts. However, representing yourself is very difficult if you have no legal training, and the mistakes you will probably make will harm rather than help you.

Rather than simply search for lawyers on the Internet, parents alleged to have alienated their children may want to contact local domestic violence agencies, shelters, or child advocacy organizations. These groups may be able to suggest attorneys whom they know to be both knowledgeable and sympathetic to preferred parents accused of parental alienation.

The alternatives are not just representing yourself or having a full-time lawyer at considerable expense. Some law firms are willing to provide "unbundled services" in which a parent might buy a few hours of a lawyer's time to provide guidance on dealing with the family court. (These services are sometimes referred to as "limited scope".)

If the court sees you as noncompliant and in contempt, the results for you can be disastrous. On the other hand, the interviews with parents in this book suggest that the greatest successes for preferred parents involve some degree of noncompliance with reunification therapists. Negotiation is possible. Preferred parents who have been through parental alienation allegations suggest that people should not write the "apology letter" or employ a therapist recommended by the reunification program, as each of these actions pulls preferred parents deeper into the allegations they are trying to escape.

You need to understand that this fight can take all your money and property as well as all your emotional resources. At some point these facts may force you to a decision about going on. Your child's age may make a significant difference to your decision. Your thoughts and conclusion are likely to be different if the child is going to be emancipated in six months than they would be if the child were only 12 years old. Your other responsibilities can also be factors. Do you have other children at home, or elderly parents who depend on you? The process of the parental alienation case is designed to make you give up, and there are practical considerations that may force you to do that.

Don't assume that past intimate partner violence in your case will cancel out allegations of parental alienation. A history of domestic violence may or may not be considered by the court to be a predictor of child abuse or of post-litigation abuse. Even if you have evidence of past violence, your argument that a child avoids a parent because of that history can be distorted into alienating behavior based on the idea that you have failed to be a friendly parent by permitting the child to know about past events.

Sometimes preferred parents think that a guardian *ad litem* or attorney appearing for the child will be concerned about domestic violence or child abuse, but this is not necessarily the case. Preferred parents need to identify attorneys who have experience with domestic violence or child abuse cases. One way to manage this is by consulting with local domestic violence or child advocacy groups and asking them for some recommendations for suitable lawyers.

Often preferred parents do not raise the issues of domestic violence or child abuse until they are already in litigation. If people anticipate that separation may occur, it is wise to develop records of events, for example by calling the police when there are incidents. Some attorneys advise preferred parents not to raise domestic violence issues, but on the whole this may be a mistake—although as every case is different, there are probably some where this may be the best decision.

If you believe there has been physical abuse of the child, you need to consider whether this should be brought up. Actions that many people would consider abusive (for instance, locking a child out of the house on a cold night) may also be interpreted as appropriate discipline and insistence on respect for authority. Complaints about physical abuse of children can lead to decisions that preferred parents are liars, intentional alienators, or mentally unstable persons.

If you have concerns about adverse parenting (not at the level of abuse) by the other parent, you will need evidence of this other than the child telling you about it, or it will not help your situation. If the child has told a therapist (for example, that the other parent comes into the bathroom or bedroom with them against their wishes), that person's testimony will be useful, or if you witnessed the behavior while you were still married you can testify about that.

If you believe there has been sexual abuse of the child, you need to consider carefully how to, or whether to, refer to this. Is it possible that an investigation would substantiate sexual abuse? Substantiation is not necessarily achieved unless there has been some physical injury or recording of some type. If an event could have occurred by accident, or if the child has perhaps misinterpreted some adult behavior, reporting sexual abuse may lead to the preferred parent being labeled an alienator. But, again, if the child has disclosed sexual abuse to a therapist, the therapist can testify about that.

The issue of sexual abuse (and to some extent other physical abuse) is complicated by legal context. In some parts of the United States, for example, every adult, including a child's parent, is a mandated reporter and required to tell authorities of any form of child abuse. A parent who does not report abuse may be accountable because of failure to protect the child. However, a report of child abuse that is not later substantiated may well be taken as evidence of alienation. If there is abuse, either reporting or refraining from reporting may cause repercussions for the non-abusive parent.

If you need further information about parental alienation allegations, Internet searches can be helpful, but you need to be cautious about sources of information. There is ongoing interest in the topic of parental alienation, and academic or professional conferences on this subject occur frequently. Information from those conferences is often available on the Internet. For example, a 2024 conference at the University of Manchester included several papers touching on legal and practical aspects of pursuing parenting rights in the course of divorce litigation (https://www.shera-research.com/resources/shera-research-group-and-university-of-manchester-health-and-justice-conference-11th-june-2024). Information associated with universities or major professional organizations, like the American Psychological Association or the British Psychological Society, is likely to be worth reading. Information coming from law firms or life coaches, or from mental health professionals who advertise themselves as specializing in parental alienation, is probably going to be less so.

Some Thoughts for Avoided/Rejected Parents

Think about whether the child is actually avoiding you, or what the behavior is that concerns you. Certainly, there are children who actively avoid a divorced parent, crying or screaming when they see the parent, and strongly resisting any form of contact. That sort of behavior alerts everyone to the possibility that the child has been convinced by another adult that the avoided parent is dangerous. If that kind of behavior is absent, however, you should think about whatever behavior is concerning you. Is the child not very affectionate with you? Is the child disrespectful to you, or to a stepparent, boyfriend, or girlfriend? Does the child sulk and withdraw when at your home? Or is the child trying to request changes or negotiate contact with you for their convenience or for sports participation or friend activities? If the child is not actively resisting contact, you might want to consider other ways you could improve the relationship without starting allegations of parental alienation. If you can find a good parenting coach, that person might be able to give you useful guidance—but as there is little regulation of coaching, there is no sure way of knowing who is "good".

Think about whether the child is afraid of you or angry with you. Just like adults, children and adolescents can have emotional reactions that seem unreasonable to other people. Adult anger can be frightening to children even if it is not directed toward them. Children and adolescents, like adults, can be offended and angry when they are frustrated or feel insulted or ridiculed. Children's feelings of anger or fear, though often labeled as "frivolous" by alienationists, can last a long time and be sufficient to cause avoidance of a parent. If this is the case with a child who seems to reject you, consider whether you have ever apologized or tried to either explain or make amends for your actions that were the beginning (not "the cause") of the trouble. Adults are sometimes afraid that if they apologize to children, adult authority will be compromised. This is not usually the case, and if you can model apologizing, you might make it possible for the child to apologize to you.

Think about what might be a cause for the child's avoidance, other than the preferred parent's possible alienating behaviors. Was there ever domestic violence in your home, or have there been angry confrontations since you separated from your spouse? Your child can respond to these by trying to avoid you, even though it was clear that the violence or anger was not directed at them. Have there been occasions when the child was unnecessarily uncomfortable at your house—for example, being forced into sharing space with a new stepsibling, or overhearing complaints about them from your new partner? You might find that discussing and resolving these issues is a more effective way to improve the relationship with your child than alleging parental alienation by the other parent. If you are already involved with reunification therapy, however, your therapist will probably advise you not to have such discussions.

Think about whether an avoiding child may be reacting to other people in your life rather than to you. If a child is willing to meet you somewhere away from home, but does not want to go to or sleep over at your house, he or she may have concerns about new partners or friends or their children. If you usually want the child to be with you together with new partners, the child may feel that your old parent–child relationship has been abandoned and may feel angry and lonely because of this. Similar feelings may result if you have left your child alone at your house while you go out at night to visit a boyfriend or girlfriend. Resolving these issues may more effectively improve your relationship with the child than alleging parental alienation and seeking reunification therapy.

Think about whether the child has complained to you or the preferred parent about adverse parenting on your part. Some actions that seem acceptable to adults can be problematic for children. For example, children may be embarrassed when they often arrive late at school because a parent is slow in the morning, or if they have to wear dirty clothes to school. Children may be both uncomfortable and frightened if they are sick or hurt and a parent dismisses their problems as unimportant. Lack of meal planning can make children feel they are not cared for—even though they eventually get fed. If children have complained about issues like these, the avoided parent might want to think about the possibility that avoidance is a response to adverse parenting rather than to alienating behaviors by the other parent.

Some Thoughts for Lawyers in Cases Where Parental Alienation Is Alleged

Parents and children in situations where parental alienation is alleged are likely to find themselves confused and even frantic as they try to decide what they should do. In many cases, lawyers who have not previously encountered alienationist claims are almost as confused as their clients. Although all cases are different, there are some general ideas that may help lawyers do a good job of dealing with claims about parental alienation. (As mentioned earlier, Suzanne Chester, J.D., a highly experienced attorney in North Carolina (USA) has been a great help in formulating these thoughts.)

Lawyers need to be thoroughly aware of changing laws in their countries or in individual states of the United States. Developed countries have laws governing child custody and parenting plans following divorce, but most do not presently have laws that either support or oppose the use of alienationist concepts in making custody decisions. Brazil, however, has over the last ten years or so struggled with criminalization and decriminalization of alienating behaviors, so parents who were said to be alienators might or might not actually experience criminal penalties as well as losing contact with their children. (At the time of this writing, a repeal of the relevant law is being discussed.) Malta has not gone that far, but has begun to give educational credit for studies of parental alienation, which suggests that some legislation might be contemplated and supported by academics.

Some relevant legislation has looked at a parent's history of abuse or violence as a factor in their rights to contact with their children. The British legislation Jade's Law takes away parental rights and responsibilities from parents who have killed the co-parent of their children. In the United States, some states have similar legislation and some do not.

In the United States, legislation by states relevant to child custody decisions has been encouraged by a piece of federal legislation in 2023. The reauthorization of the Violence Against Women Act included a model law, Kayden's Law. States that enact similar laws gain some federal funding, and several have passed such laws at the time of this writing.

Kayden's Law, among other things, prohibits sending children in custody cases to reunification therapies that have inadequate scientific support (see Chapter 3 of this book for a discussion of the available scientific evidence for reunification programs). Kayden's Law stresses the inappropriateness of limiting contact between children and their preferred parents. Piqui's Law in California and Kayden's Law in Pennsylvania (the Federal law is named after a Pennsylvania child) are examples of laws meeting the requirements of the federal legislation.

The state laws modeled on the federal Kayden's Law example are, tragically, named after children who were killed by their fathers after being forced into contact in spite of the mothers' objections and concerns about abuse. As only a small minority of parental alienation cases end in this dreadful way, this book has emphasized the majority of cases with their painful but not fatal consequences. Nevertheless, it would be wise for lawyers as well as involved parents to keep in mind the possible irreversible harm that can be done by erroneous decisions about children.

Questioning parental alienation testimony about scientific support can be an important step for lawyers. Attorneys who work with family issues are not necessarily experts at challenging scientific testimony, but should know that there are real weaknesses in the work presented as scientific support for alienationism. These weaknesses range from claims about the instinctual nature of children's need for both parents to predictions of disastrous outcomes for children in parental alienation cases to statements that reunification programs are safe and effective. It is quite possible to challenge such claims, and important to do so as they provide major arguments for alienationist judicial decisions. However, attorneys need to realize the need for preparation for such challenges; earlier chapters in this book as well as other publications can help them prepare.

Both judges and lawyers can seek less biased information about therapies by consulting two Internet sources that specialize in examining the scientific support for psychosocial treatments. One of these is the

California Evidence Based Clearinghouse for Child Welfare (cebc4cw.org), which assesses therapies in terms of the strength of the evidence supporting them. The other, Effective Child Therapies (effectivechildtherapies.org), is a service of a division of the American Psychological Association that provides criteria for strong evidentiary support and lists psychosocial treatments for children and adolescents that meet those standards. At the time of this writing, no reunification therapy is listed by either of these Internet sources.

Reunification treatments can be addressed as fraudulent. At the time of this writing, there is one case in which a reunification therapist is being sued for fraud because of claims made about the evidence for and effectiveness of the reunification program. (Another similar case was dropped after the death of the preferred parent.) If a reunification program were presented as an experimental treatment, the program could not be considered fraudulent; there are many psychosocial treatments that are transparent about the moderate evidence for their effectiveness and cannot be called fraudulent. Programs that claim to have 90% to 100% success rates, and that make those claims on the basis of weak evidence, are open to accusations of fraud, especially in cases where demonstrable harm was done by the program.

Some Thoughts for Children and Adolescents Who Are Ordered to Treatment for Parental Alienation

Preteens and teenagers who find themselves the subjects of parental alienation allegations usually have no idea what is going on. They may never have heard of parental alienation or met anyone who has experienced related events. Their preferred parents may be prohibited from telling the children what is happening in court or what court-ordered reunification therapies will entail. The children's ignorance leads to shocked surprise when events like transportation to a treatment venue occur, and makes the frightening circumstances of intensive reunification therapy that much more disturbing. Even the "lite" office-based reunification therapy has elements that make many children both frightened and angry.

Here are some thoughts that might help allegedly alienated children get through their treatment with less discomfort:

Fake it until you make it. The advice of most young adults who went through reunification treatment is not to resist. There is little or nothing you can do once you are ordered into a program, and serious efforts like running away may well have serious negative consequences. There is no shame in pretending and keeping your opinion to yourself, however bad this feels to you. When your phone, ID, and money are taken away from you, you need to realize that you are in no way in charge and will do best to just wait it out.

If you are taken to a treatment venue by youth transport service workers, you will have special reason to "fake it". There is no point trying to resist or argue with these people. They will tell you that they will take you down or handcuff you, and that is true. They will probably not answer questions or tell you where you are going. They will probably insist on going to the bathroom with you. If they have a court order, they have a legal right to do these things. This is appalling, of course, but trying to resist will only make things worse for you.

Remember that you may find yourself ordered into reunification treatment even though you did not actually avoid one of your parents. You may have been less affectionate than was wanted, or you may have tried to negotiate some point. Alienationists nowadays sometimes talk about "early intervention" and suggest that treatment is needed for behavior that they think might be followed by avoidance. Arguing that you did not avoid a parent is likely to be interpreted as resistance—and further evidence that you are alienated and need treatment.

You are likely to be called a liar, unless everything you say is positive about the avoided parent and negative about your preferred parent. One of the supposed symptoms of parental alienation is referred to as "borrowed scenarios". These are statements about each parent (or other things) that are said to be outside the child's experience and "must have" been taught to them by the preferred parent. Presenting "borrowed scenarios"—for example, if you talked about why you do not want contact with one parent—is considered both lying and a symptom of parental alienation. It is extremely uncomfortable to be told to your face that you are a liar, but it may help you tolerate the situation if you recognize that this is going to happen and it is not really a statement about your integrity. You should not expect your explanation to be given any value, though.

In reunification therapy, you are likely to see adults behaving badly. In the course of your life, you have probably learned from adults that some kinds of behavior are not acceptable. You learned not to make fun of other people, not to insult them, not to threaten them, and not to grab them physically to make them do what you want. On your trip to reunification treatment and in the treatment itself, you are likely to see adults doing some or all of these things. This is likely to make you feel disgusted with or contemptuous of them, but it will be best for you if you keep this to yourself.

What Research Is Needed?

Until extensive research is done, it will not be possible to assess the positive or negative effects of reunification therapies. It is important to realize that research on the outcomes of psychosocial treatments is never a matter of a single study. As an example, readers can look at the United States government Internet publication on Programs and Services Reviewed, posted by the Title IV-E Prevention Services Clearinghouse (preventionservices.acf.hhs.gov). This publication categorizes treatments as "well-supported" or otherwise, but most saliently it indicates how many studies were considered and whether their results were favorable to use of a treatment, or unfavorable, or indicative that no effect of the treatment was demonstrated. For example, for one "well-supported" treatment, 17 favorable studies were listed, no unfavorable studies, and one study that reported no effect of the treatment. For another treatment, classified as "promising", there were three favorable studies, no unfavorable studies, and one reporting no effect. Similar information about reunification programs is needed before such treatments can even be said to be "promising". Claims based on one or two studies are not sufficient.

Foundational Studies

As mentioned before in this book, foundational studies are missing for basic information about parental alienation cases. Records have not been kept about numbers of divorce cases in which parental alienation has been alleged. Ages and genders of affected children are not known, nor are other child characteristics, or characteristics of either preferred or avoided parents. Without this baseline information, researchers are missing guidance toward research questions that could reveal cause and effect relationships in parental alienation cases. These kinds of information are critical both to establishing valid methods of identifying parental alienation cases and to assessment of reunification programs of all types.

Connections with Domestic Violence and Child Abuse

The literature on alienationism shows connections between parental alienation cases in court and allegations of domestic violence or of child abuse (or both) by one or both parties. Anecdotally, it appears that allegations of parental alienation against one parent may be used as strategies to counter claims that the other parent has been violent or abusive. Allegations of child sexual abuse, for example, may carry great weight in conflicts where allegations and counter-allegations are made.

Systematic research needs to examine the timing of parental alienation allegations and allegations of violence or abuse. If one type of allegation regularly antedated the other—for example, *somebody says parental alienation* only after abuse has been alleged—it might become apparent that claims about parental alienation are influenced by events during litigation as well as by actual family dynamics. The practical value of this information would be applicable in cases where lawyers must decide whether or not to advise a preferred parent to refer to past violence or abuse by the avoided parent.

Adverse Parenting

Adverse parenting by the avoided parent is an almost untouched research area. Systematic research is badly needed to see whether problematic behavior by one parent is the major cause of children's rejection and avoidance. Alienationists using the Five Factor Model appear to see substantiated abuse or neglect as the only legitimate reasons for a child's avoidance of one parent. Other rationales for avoidance are classed as "frivolous" or as "borrowed scenarios" provided by the preferred parent. Yet interviews with young adults who have been through parental alienation cases indicate that parental behaviors that cannot be defined as abuse can seriously damage children's attitudes toward one parent and lead to avoidance. This is especially the case when a child repeatedly asks the parent to stop a behavior and is repeatedly refused.

A number of examples of annoying or distressing parental behavior appeared in earlier chapters of this book. A parent who withholds ordinary life comforts like food the child likes or sufficient hot water will not be considered abusive by authorities, but those actions can make the child wish to avoid that parent. A parent who ignores a child's modesty and wish for privacy by going uninvited into bedrooms and bathrooms can make that child wish to avoid all contact. "Joking" parental behavior like chasing or tickling, which may have been delightful for a younger child, can make adolescents avoid and reject. All of these actions are even more likely to cause avoidance if the child has asked for them to stop, and been refused. That objection to such parental behavior is not "frivolous" becomes obvious when one imagines the behavior as directed toward an adult spouse. Many adults would leave a marriage where that kind of intrusive and unresponsive behavior was frequent. Yet alienationists have never systematically explored adverse parental behaviors that may be salient to parental alienation cases.

A final point about these unexamined, problematic parental behaviors has to do with the possible ongoing effects on children's attitudes of past parental behavior. A history of domestic violence or child abuse would be expected to make a child wary of a parent's anger or impulsiveness and prone to avoid that parent. But other unwanted behaviors can have similar effects even though a child was not directly involved. For example, in one case a father of preteen children was revealed to be courting and "grooming" a mid-teen neighbor and the marriage broke up in the ensuing scandal. As his children reached their middle teens, they were suspicious of all affectionate contact with their father, believed that he was sexually attracted to them, and did their best to avoid him. Again, there has never been, but needs to be, systematic research examining the association between past parental behavior and the readiness of children to avoid that parent.

Can Existing Evidence-Based Psychotherapies Help in Parental Alienation Cases?

Some alienationists have stated that conventional psychotherapies exacerbate rather than help parental alienation cases. There is little or no evidence that this is true, however, or indeed that anyone has tried systematically to use existing treatments for children or parents involved in parental alienation cases. A reason for this may be that the goal of reunification programs appears to be to persuade children to have extensive contact with a parent they would prefer to avoid, while the goal of conventional psychotherapies is to improve a client's satisfaction with life and ability to function in the world. A second problem with the alienationist goal is that it focuses exclusively on changing the child and the preferred parent, omitting consideration of mental health or behavioral problems of the avoided parent—problems that may be causing the child's avoidance and may even have been a cause of the divorce.

As long as alienationists stress parental alienating behaviors as the primary cause of children's avoidance of one parent, they are not likely to think of children's psychological issues that may need treatment and that may also be the beginning of a cascade of events that culminate in avoidance of a parent. For example, antisocial behavior, depression, and irritability can all have negative effects on social relationships, and can affect parent–child relationships as well as relationships with peers. As Hupp, Macphee, and Pelham (2018) have pointed out, there is a science of psychotherapy with youth and there exist evidence-based psychosocial treatments for a range of emotional problems experienced by children and adolescents. Only systematic investigation can tell whether evidence-based treatments for children's emotional troubles can be useful in parental alienation cases. This investigation has not occurred, as far as published work on this topic shows.

What Is the Most Important Missing Piece in Parental Alienation Research?

None of the foundational research just described can be accomplished until one task is done: to establish a reliable, valid method for identifying parental alienation. Such a method would tell the difference between children who avoid a parent because the other parent has persuaded them to do so, and children who avoid a parent because of other factors like abuse, violent behavior, or adverse parenting practices. No such method exists at this time; Chapter 2 of this book discussed the many weaknesses of the Five Factor Model that is claimed to identify parental alienation accurately. Thus, when we deal with cases where parental alienation is alleged, we need to realize that the criterion for identifying these cases may be only that, once again, *somebody said parental alienation*.

References

Hupp, S., Macphee, F., & Pelham, W. (2018). The science of psychotherapy with youth. In S. Hupp (Ed.), *Child and adolescent psychotherapy*. Cambridge University Press.

Warshak, R. (2020). When evaluators get it wrong: False positive IDs and parental alienation. *Psychology, Public Policy, and Law*, 26, 54–68. https://doi.org/10.1037/law0000216.

Index

Kolibri 360 GmbH
Ferdinand-Jühlke-Straße 7
99095 Erfurt, Deutschland
produktsicherheit@kolibri360.de